CATHERINE THE GREAT

Also by Marc Raeff

M. M. SPERANSKY: STATESMAN OF IMPERIAL RUSSIA

SIBERIA AND THE REFORMS OF 1822

ORIGINS OF THE RUSSIAN INTELLIGENTSIA: THE
EIGHTEENTH-CENTURY NOBILITY

IMPERIAL RUSSIA, 1682–1825: THE COMING OF AGE
OF MODERN RUSSIA

Catherine the Great
A PROFILE

Edited by Marc Raeff

WORLD PROFILES

General Editor: Aïda DiPace Donald

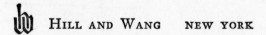 HILL AND WANG   NEW YORK

Contents

v

Contents

v

Introduction

THE PERSONAL LIFE of Sophie Frederike Augusta von Anhalt-Zerbst who became Catherine II, Empress of Russia, is a glittering erotic tale, while her rule proved to be of profound and lasting significance for both European politics and Russian society. Naturally enough, the former has attracted writers more than the latter; the bibliography alone of popular and more or less inventive accounts of Catherine's love life would fit a volume. Unfortunately, too, most authors of these accounts have been tempted into adding their own spices to an already well-seasoned dish, and the results are quite unpalatable fare either as literature or as history. Whatever can be found out with certainty about Catherine's personal life—and she was remarkably discreet and tactful about it—has been told and retold in practically all European languages.[1] Because it would be superfluous, I have not chosen to draw on these easily accessible works for the present profile.

The accomplishments of Catherine II as a ruler, however, have not been well illuminated in Western historiography. This is due in part to the fact that the personal role of a ruler is difficult to isolate during a long period of gradual social, economic, and institutional transformations. Another obstacle to knowing Catherine is that Russian history is still deficient in modern, perceptive, informed studies of her major legislative acts and of their social and economic impact. Whenever such topics are dealt with at all in the monographic literature, their treatment ranges widely beyond the limits of Catherine's reign. For these reasons the selections presented in this volume only highlight the major social, political, and cultural aspects of Russia in the second half of the eighteenth century, and then only as they relate to Catherine. The Empress is on center stage, but that stage is so vast that, perforce, to keep Catherine in focus, the profile is necessarily narrow.

The writings here collected stress most particularly Catherine's intellectual development and accomplishments and her influence on contemporary Russian cultural and social life because it is in this domain that the Empress' personal impact can best be identified and described. Indeed, Catherine's activities in these fields set the stage for the first serious conflict between educated society and the imperial establishment, a struggle that became a dominant

---

1. The classic early representative of the genre was K. Waliszewski, *The Romance of an Empress,* first published in French in 1893 and in English, in two volumes, in 1894–1895. Among the better and more recent works of popular biography are: G. P. Gooch, *Catherine the Great and Other Studies* (1954); Z. Oldenbourg, *Catherine the Great* (1965); K. Anthony, *Catherine the Great.* All these authors rely heavily on Catherine's own memoirs, *Memoirs of Catherine the Great,* edited by D. Maroger, translated by M. Budberg (1961).

theme in Russia's political and cultural history of the nineteenth century.[2]

I have made an effort to give as catholic a selection as possible within the space allowed and the literature available. With the exception of detailed analyses of the nature and background of well-known and seminal legislative acts (e.g., the Charters to the Nobility and the Towns of 1785, the Statute on Provinces of 1775), I have tried to offer a glimpse of all significant facets of Catherine's public activities[3]: connections with West European intellectual leaders, contributions to Russian literature, efforts at molding public opinion and education, ambiguous relations with educated society and "progressive" thinkers, and the style and achievements of her diplomacy, imperial expansion, social legislation, and ecclesiastical policy. In the Postscript, Catherine's rule is placed in the perspective of Russian historiography and assayed in the institutional development of her country.

The contributors in this volume are representative of both Soviet and non-Soviet (pre-1917 and Western) history. I have made an effort to present items that heretofore have not been available in English. I hope thereby to acquaint the reader with another historiographical manner as well as with facts and conclusions that have not been adequately reflected in Western writing on Russian history.

The dates given in the Russian articles are those of the Julian Calendar and the transliteration used is that of the Library of

2. This justifies the inclusion of the article by Allen McConnell which deals with Catherine II only in the context of the persecution of A. Radishchev which marked the opening shot in the battle between educated élite and establishment in Russia.

3. The famous *Instruction* (*Nakaz*) to the Commission on Codification of 1767 was published repeatedly; the first English translation by Michel Tatischeff appeared in London in 1768. The most recent English edition is by W. F. Reddaway, *Documents of Catherine the Great* (Cambridge, 1931). The Fall 1970 issue of the *Canadian Slavic Studies* illustrates the most recent English and American scholarship on the institutional reforms of Catherine II.

Congress, simplified. The original footnotes of translated articles
have been omitted since they refer in most cases to Russian sources
and documents. Unless otherwise specified, the explanatory notes
are by the editor.

Chronology

Apr. 21, 1729   Sophie Frederike Augusta von Anhalt-Zerbst is born in Stettin, where her father is Prussian governor.

Jan. 10, 1744   Leaves Zerbst with her mother for Russia.

Feb. 3, 1744   Arrives in St. Petersburg and on February 9 is presented to Empress Elizabeth and Grand Duke Peter in Moscow.

June 28, 1744   Converts to Greek Orthodoxy.

Aug. 21, 1745   Marries Grand Duke Peter of Holstein, heir to the Russian throne.

Sept. 20, 1754   Birth of Catherine's son, Grand Duke Paul, future Emperor.

Dec. 25, 1761   Death of Empress Elizabeth, accession of Grand Duke Peter under the name of Peter III.

June 28, 1762   Coup d'état against Peter III, who is forced to
                 abdicate. Catherine proclaimed Empress and sole
                 ruler.

July 6, 1762   Sudden death of ex-Emperor Peter III (probably
                 murdered by the Orlov brothers assigned to guard
                 him at the summer palace of Ropsha near St.
                 Petersburg).

1766   Elections ordered for the Commission on Codifica-
                 tion.

July 1767–   Commission on Codification meets first in Moscow
Nov. 1768   and then in St. Petersburg

1768–1774   First war with Turkey ends with the Treaty of
                 Kuchuk-Kainardji.

1772   First partition of Poland.

1773–1774   Peasant uprising under the leadership of Emelian
                 Pugachev engulfs all of eastern Russia and threat-
                 ens the central provinces.

Nov. 7, 1775   Statute on Provinces, reforming the local adminis-
                 tration.

Dec. 12, 1777   Birth of grandson Alexander, later to become Em-
                 peror Alexander I.

Apr. 8, 1782   General Police Regulation (*Ustav blagochiniia*)
                 for town and country.

Apr. 21, 1785   Charter to the Nobility and Charter to the Towns
                 granting corporate status and some degree of self-
                 administration to the provincial nobility and the
                 upper merchantry.

1783   Annexation of the Crimea.

1787–1792   Second war against Turkey, ending in the Treaty
                 of Jassy.

1788–1790   War against Sweden ended by the Peace of Werre-
            loe.

1793   Second partition of Poland.

1795   Third partition of Poland.

June 25, 1796   Birth of grandson Nicholas, the future Emperor
                Nicholas I.

Nov. 6, 1796   Death of Catherine II. Paul I becomes Emperor.

PART ONE

The Individual

ALEKSANDR A. KIZEVETTER

Portrait of an Enlightened Autocrat

WHEN PETER THE GREAT set about transforming Russian state institutions, modeling them after their West European counterparts, he improved the external techniques of the administrative apparatus and also made some changes in the social organization of the estates. However, neither his administrative nor his social reform altered the basic principles upon which the Russian political order of that time rested. Though Russia had been provided with Swedish-type government institutions and dressed in German camisoles instead of semi-Asiatic

Aleksandr A. Kizevetter, "Ekaterina II," in *Istoricheskie Siluety—Liudi i sobytiia* (Berlin: Parabola, 1931), pp. 7–28. Translated by Mary Mackler.

3

kaftans, it remained a polity enserved from top to bottom, an autocratic monarchy in which all strata of the population without exception were required to perform service and pay dues to the ruler.

After Peter's death, the very foundations of the state system began to change profoundly, and Russia gradually turned into an [aristocratic] *Ständestaat,* i.e., a monarchy based on social estates. The nobility was no longer required to give service but became a privileged class of owners of land and souls,[1] free from obligations, whereas the townspeople remained in fiscal dependence, and the bondage of the peasants on the landed estates was intensified and extended so that it came very close to being actual slavery.

At the time of Catherine's accession to the throne the metamorphosis had been completed. Peter III's Manifesto on the Freedom of the Nobility[2] had been the final preparatory step. It fell to Catherine's lot to give final legal form to the newly developed system of state and social relationships and to establish new institutions which would be in keeping with the nature of the *Ständestaat.* Catherine and her assistants, one might say, had to *gather the crop* from a field that had been plowed, sown, and cultivated by their predecessors. This was an important task; failure to complete it would have nullified all previous efforts and achievements. It was also a gratifying task, for harvesters, if they do their work well, invariably eclipse the plowmen and sowers: the joy of anticipation dims before the happiness in achieving the final goal. The brilliant success of Catherine's efforts and the halo that surrounds her name are due primarily to the fact that the basic task of the period happened to suit the distinctive features of her personality. Catherine was neither above nor below the task, but pre-

1. Souls—male peasants (exclusive of children and the old) who were subject to the capitation, hence male serfs. They alone were included in the official census and provided the basis for the assessment of a noble's wealth.

2. The Manifesto of February 18, 1762, freed the nobility from compulsory service obligations to which they had been astrained by Peter the Great.

cisely at its level. By nature, she was not a plower or a sower, whose task it is to create the conditions for the success of the future crop, but a harvester, who has to keep from spoiling the conditions others have created and to use those conditions to the best advantage.

There was no lack of complicated and dangerous obstacles in Catherine's path, but she surmounted them all, and not so much by direct resistance as by great flexibility and resourcefulness. To challenge inimical elements in open battle and meet them in frontal attack, one must be a genius. But one need not be a genius to advance toward one's goal along the path of least resistance, not overthrowing one's enemies but taming them, not outstripping the surroundings, but keeping in step with them; for this it is sufficient to have talent. One need not be a Peter; to be a Catherine is enough.

Catherine embarked on her political career amidst seemingly insuperable obstacles and perils. She was born and raised in the family of a petty German princeling who was so poor he had to enter the service of the Prussian king to make a living and was lucky enough to be appointed governor of Stettin. Her father's house was small and uncomfortable and run very parsimoniously. When little Ficke (Sophia)—the future Catherine—went with her mother to visit with more well-to-do relatives, she felt like a beggar, being received and fed out of charity.

Then her life changed as if by magic. From distant St. Petersburg came an unexpected invitation to proceed to the glittering court of the Russian Empress Elizabeth where she was to become the wife of the heir to the Russian throne. The matter had been arranged by Frederick II, who soon expected considerable advantages to accrue to Prussia from this match.

The future Empress of Russia set out on the journey to St. Petersburg with luggage so scant it would have been considered shabby even for a second-rate provincial actress. Some lingerie and three or four dresses were all the dowry she had received from her parents. An uncle had added a length of fabric, embroidered with silver thread, and this was the most splendid article in the young traveler's wardrobe. It was "a wandering and poor princess" indeed who arrived in St. Petersburg, a fifteen-year-old girl in an alien land, to face a suspicious empress and a fiancé who declared the moment he saw her that he had no liking for her. Catherine entered a broad stage, teeming with intrigues and set with dangerous traps for which she had to watch out at every step. Her situation was further complicated by her mother's behavior. Immediately upon their arrival in St. Petersburg the latter began hurriedly and clumsily, with an irresponsibility equal only to her stupidity, to carry out the Prussian king's secret instructions, aimed at deposing Chancellor Bestuzhev at all cost.[3] The lady conducted this delicate matter so awkwardly and with so many flagrant blunders that at one point her daughter's marriage was very nearly called off, and mother and daughter were a hairbreadth away from having to return to Stettin in disgrace. The mother did not escape that disgrace. The daughter, however, not only stayed on, but succeeded in overcoming all the difficulties of her situation, married the heir to the Russian crown, won Elizabeth's trust, safely weathered many storms, and upon Elizabeth's death, promptly swept her foolish husband from her path and held undivided possession of the Russian throne for thirty-four years despite the fact that even in the circles closest to her there were some who believed that she had usurped the rights of her son Paul.

Catherine ruled in such a manner that those thirty-four years have gone down as "the age of Catherine," although in her statesmanship she followed people and circumstances rather than led them; and she herself has gone down in the minds of admirers as a truly "Russian empress," although to the end of her life she distorted the Russian language mercilessly, speaking it with a German accent and rebelling against the rules of grammar in her numerous Russian writings.

3. Aleksei P. Bestuzhev-Riumin, 1693–1766, chancellor 1744–1758, pursued a pro-Austrian policy and fell from grace as a result of the "reversal of alliances" of 1756.

What, then, was the source of Catherine's success? In this writer's view, it lay in her extraordinary personality, with its rare combination of two ordinarily mutually exclusive traits—impassioned desires and calculating self-control in the selection of ways and means to gain those desires.

II

That Catherine had a passionate nature is beyond any doubt. Her passion showed in the burning gaze of her eyes. The British envoy Williams, who knew Catherine when she was a young crown princess, compared the look in her eyes to that of a small wild animal and said that it was so piercing and full of desire that it was difficult to endure. A superficial observer might have taken this untamable energy for the manifestation of genius, but he would have been very much mistaken.

An insatiable thirst for sensual pleasures and inexhaustible vanity were the main components of Catherine's passionate nature. She had love affairs without end from the time she was a young girl and into old age. By the most reliable calculations, she had twenty-one lovers in the course of forty-four years. That is an average of one every two years. Between 1752 and 1758, while Elizabeth was still alive, her lovers were Saltykov and Poniatovskii. At that time she was twenty-three to twenty-seven years of age. Then came her eleven-year cohabitation with Grigorii Orlov (1761–1772), when she was in her thirties. Between the ages of forty and fifty (1772–1780), she had at least nine favorites—Vasil'chikov, Potemkin, Zavadovskii, Zorich, Korsakov, Stakhiev, Strakhov, Levashov, and Rantsov. Between the ages of fifty and sixty, she had at least five—Vysotskii, Mordvinov, Lanskoi, Yermolov, and Mamonov. I say *at least,* because there were three—Stoianov, Miloradovich, and Miklashevskii—the dates of whose liaisons with Catherine cannot be determined. And finally, in the last decade of her life, from 1786 to 1796, Platon Zubov reigned supreme in her aged heart.

This is an astonishing collection, not only in numbers, but also in diversity. It leads us to believe that sensuality played a larger part than true feeling in her epic of love, though it would be wrong to attribute Catherine's behavior to physiological sensuality alone. Her love for Poniatovskii was a genuine passion. Orlov's unfaithfulness after eleven years as her lover caused her real pain; she admitted that she would have gone on loving him forever had his faithlessness not repelled her. After Lanskoi's death she went into paroxysms of grief, lost her appetite, could not sleep, wept for days on end, and would not see anyone. She finally got over it with the help of the many-volumed work of the French philologist Coeur de Gebelin, from which she got the idea of compiling a comparative dictionary of all languages. She surrounded herself with dictionaries, used up a ton of writing paper, and, although she did not enrich philology significantly, she was cured of the serious after-effects of her passion.

Such episodes would not have occurred if her love affairs had arisen from primitive sensuality alone. On the other hand, unrestrained sensuality is the only explanation for the succession of lovers, their rapid turnover, and her lack of taste in choosing them. It was a motley collection indeed. The refined, pampered Poniatovskii was followed by the rather coarse, very Russian Grigorii Orlov; the talented but ugly Potemkin was succeeded after a while by the untalented, emptyheaded but handsome Platon Zubov, Catherine's favorite during the sunset of her life. An orgy of sensuality is the only possible description for the period between 1776 and 1789, when she changed lovers practically every year, the men being chosen for this role, as if for paid positions, with the approval of Potemkin, who, after losing his place in Catherine's heart, became a sort of manager of a mobile male harem for her. Obviously, Catherine's passions were not of a high order and arose not so much from deep emotions as from a rebellion of the flesh, which neither age nor the affairs of state could tame.

Nor was Catherine's passion in the field of politics that of a creative genius either. She was incapable of challenging destiny in order to satisfy her ambitions. She always preferred to make a deal with circumstances and she usually made her way to success by employing the techniques of a skillful actress on the stage of life.

At the very beginning of her political career she employed those techniques brilliantly. When she arrived at the court of Elizabeth as a fifteen-year-old girl, she resolved to melt the ice in the Empress' heart and to separate herself very clearly from her fiancé in the eyes of public opinion. With extraordinary perspicacity she chose the right weapon for her purposes—outstanding zeal in the practice of the Russian Orthodox religion. When she fell ill, she summoned a priest and captured Elizabeth's heart by the piety of her confession. At church services, she always prayed fervently, touching her head to the ground earnestly, while her fiancé embarrassed everybody with childish pranks.

Not long after her arrival at court she emerged victorious from a very dangerous situation, acting the part of injured innocence very skillfully after being caught practically red-handed in a political intrigue that bordered on treason. The British envoy Williams, who had come to Russia for the express purpose of disrupting the Austro-Russian alliance, drew Catherine into his intrigues with the help of Bestuzhev. Catherine had gone very far along that slippery path: she had accepted quite a large sum of money from Williams and, with Bestuzhev as a go-between, had carried on a compromising correspondence. Williams' intrigues were discovered. Bestuzhev fell, a victim of the exposure. A yawning abyss opened up before Catherine's very feet. But it took Catherine only two interviews with Elizabeth to emerge unsullied. Catherine's handling of Elizabeth revealed a profound knowledge of the human heart and great skill in influencing it for her own benefit. Elizabeth had sent for Catherine with the intention of acting the part of a stern and punitive judge. Catherine entered and threw herself at the Empress' feet, imploring to be allowed to go home to Germany immediately. In a few minutes she had already taken the posture of one who had been insulted by unmerited suspicion and Elizabeth was weeping and kissing her.

Catherine never lost this ability to play on people's heartstrings and it was her principal tool of government. She let those around her feel her power, but at the right time and in the right measure she could adopt a tone of trustfulness and relaxed humor with anyone she happened to be talking to, or even suddenly flash a ray of royal favor upon him.

III

But in the "craft of ruling" Catherine attached even greater importance to *advertisement,* and she was infinitely skillful at this. She was equally adept at self-promotion and at using others to advance her. She was in her element in this field, and every step she took, every movement she made, was perfect.

One need only read her numerous manifestos and edicts of the first months of her reign. They repeated nearly every day the completely unsubstantiated claim that Catherine had seized the throne from her husband in fulfillment of the unanimous desire of all her subjects. When and how was this will of the people manifested? Naturally, no mention was made of this in the manifestos and edicts.

In point of fact, the claim could not even be made that there was silent agreement of all groups of the population to the coup, for there was no lack of expressions of discontent in the early years of Catherine's reign and several plots were uncovered. This, however, only increased the need to publicize the popularity of the coup. And so Catherine sang her own praises in every key and on every pretext, claiming to be the people's choice. She was not afraid of repeating this too often. She knew that an idea oft repeated becomes familiar, a cliché, and that nothing takes stronger root in the minds of the masses than a cliché.

Catherine's first manifesto, proclaiming Peter III's dethronement and her own accession (the manifesto was written by Teplov[4]),

4. Grigorii N. Teplov, 1717–1779, Catherine's state secretary, president of the Academy of Sciences, most active in the economic administration of the empire.

stated that the rule of Peter III threatened the Orthodox faith in Russia, would besmirch the country's glory by conclusion of peace with Prussia, which had just been defeated by victorious Russian arms, and would destroy the domestic order of the state. For this reason, the manifesto continued, to avert all such dangers, Catherine had ascended the throne "with God's help and *seeing that this was the desire of all her loyal subjects.*" The latter theme became the obligatory refrain of every more or less important official act.

On July 5, 1762, a week after the first manifesto was issued, Catherine signed an edict lowering the price of salt by 10 kopecks a *pud*. The edict stated that the Empress had done this because she wished to ease the condition of her subjects, having ascended the Russian throne "at the unanimous wish of the loyal and true sons of Russia." A day after that, a manifesto was issued setting the coronation for September 1762. From the very first sentence and throughout, the manifesto repeated over and over again that the Empress had been compelled to accept the throne by her piety, love of her Russian fatherland, and "the strong wish of all Our loyal subjects to see Us on the throne."

In an edict, issued in her name eleven days later, on the need to put a stop to extortion by usury, Catherine presented the same idea more broadly. While exhorting her subjects to refrain from extortion, she took the opportunity to explain in detail her motives for taking the throne. "It was not the wish to win the lofty title of Russian Empress or to gain riches . . . it was not the desire for power or any other kind of self-interest that compelled us to act as We did with God's guidance in carrying out our righteous plan and to accept this burden of government, but our sincere love of the fatherland and *the visible desire of the whole people.*" An edict, inviting runaways from Russia and deserters to return to the fatherland without fear of punishment, issued the next day, began with the words: "Inasmuch as We ascended the all-Russian throne in accordance with the unanimous and sincere desire and *at the persistent request of Our subjects* and loving sons of Our

fatherland . . ." Here we have not only a desire, but a persistent
request, of subjects, though no one could have told when and in
what form this total will of the people had been expressed. This
was long the leitmotif of the official manifestos and edicts that
came from Catherine's pen.

Two years later a manifesto was issued, stating that Mirovich,
who had tried to rescue Anna Leopoldovna's son Ivan Antonovich[5] from a cell in a fortress and to proclaim him emperor once
again, would be brought to trial. While Catherine had seized the
throne by a violent palace coup, Ivan Antonovich, who had been
designated by Anna as her successor, had become the emperor for
a short time in complete accordance with Peter the Great's law,
under the terms of which the reigning monarch himself designated
his successor. These circumstances did not prevent Catherine from
making two patently untrue statements in a single sentence in the
introduction to the manifesto: "In ascending the throne *according*
to the desire of all subjects, We wished to alleviate the situation of
Prince Ioann, son of Anton of Braunschweig and Anna of Meck-
lenburg, who had been *illegally* placed on the throne for a short
time." Thus, while she presented her own seizure of the throne
as enthronement at the request of the whole people, she at the
same time proclaimed the undoubtedly legal emperor, Ivan Antonovich, a usurper.

Of course, the frequency, uniformity, and excessive zeal in asserting undoubted and indubitable rights, manifested in the constant repetition of the above ideas in Catherine's proclamations,
could only have given rise to doubts in a subtle observer's mind as
to the validity of the claims. However, Catherine knew very well
that advertisement is not intended for subtle observers; it is intended for the masses, the mob, who are easily hypnotized by a

5. Ivan VI Antonovich, nephew of Empress Anna; as a baby he became
emperor for a few months (1740–1741) under the regency of his mother
Anna Leopoldovna of Brunswick. He was overthrown by Elizabeth and
spent his life in prison. During Captain Mirovich's attempt at rescuing him
from Shlisselburg Fortress, 1764, he was killed by the officers guarding
him.

vigorous, bold, and unsophisticated approach. She knew what she was doing when she kept repeating the lie tirelessly. As a result of those repetitions, the lie turned into an officially confirmed platitude in the minds of the masses, a familiar cliché, no longer requiring proof.

Self-advertisement, however, is only the lowest form of the art of publicity. The highest form is the ability to put praise of one's self into the mouths of others. We shall now see how skillfully Catherine did this.

IV

In weaving the verbal wreath of her political glory, Catherine did not restrict her audience to the loyal sons of the fatherland. She considered it necessary to influence western Europe, too. She greatly valued her reputation as a liberal and enlightened monarch and was herself most energetic in spreading that reputation in Europe. In some cases, the official statements she addressed to high state institutions concerning government actions were in fact intended chiefly for European consumption. For example, once she had decided in favor of secularization, she prepared a long speech for the Synod, pointing out in it that it was very wrong for enlightened church dignitaries to own slaves. Clearly, the aim of the speech was to stress the liberal nature of the reform. Obviously, such arguments were not likely to convince members of the Synod. Besides, there was no need for Catherine to try to persuade or make requests when a mere expression of her will was sufficient. Apparently, the speech was meant for foreign ears, to which she wished to present her secularization policy in a liberal light. It was no accident that the speech was printed in French at the time and distributed abroad in pamphlet form.

However, monologues in which Catherine was her own advocate were not enough to influence West European public opinion. To these monologues it was necessary to add a chorus of assiduous and admiring adulators from the outside. Of course,

Catherine had no difficulty in obtaining all the foreign hired pens she wanted to write laudatory pamphlets, and she did not neglect services of that kind. But she achieved much more. The best-known luminaries of West European philosophical thought, headed by Voltaire himself, placed their literary talents and prestigious names at her feet and sang praises to the "northern Minerva" or "Semiramis" in all keys, neither skimping on the flattery nor hesitating to use the most exaggerated hyperboles. No remuneration would have been enough to pay for so powerful a mouthpiece in spreading Catherine's fame far and wide; but none was necessary, as the "philosophers" of that age, succumbing to the flattery of a crowned head, were satisfied with gifts so trifling as to come nowhere near the value of their paeans.

To assert that Catherine carried on a literary flirtation with the philosophical celebrities of Europe for practical reasons alone would be in poor taste indeed. There is no doubt that she was a sincere admirer of Voltaire's writings and that it flattered her vanity to consider herself his disciple. And if she sometimes permitted herself to wax ironic about philosophers who had little understanding of the practical matters of politics, this was in self-defense when the "philosophers" turned from panegyrics to critical exhortations. This happened to Diderot, when in conversation with Catherine during a visit to St. Petersburg, he spoke freely, pointed out the shortcomings in her system of government, and gave her to understand that there were spots on the sun of her reign, too. Catherine shrugged such occurrences away with ironic remarks about the difference in the situation of a philosopher, whose thoughts floated somewhere above the clouds, and a ruler, who must "write laws on human skin."

Passing disagreements of this kind did not detract in the least from Catherine's being flattered by her association with the leaders of Europe's intellectual movement. . . . Practical calculations, however, did play an important role in her contacts with her renowned correspondents. When ominous clouds loomed on her brilliant horizon and she wished to camouflage her anxiety and fears concerning the possibility of dangerous upheavals inside the country, she wrote Voltaire a few carefree lines, knowing that "all Europe" would soon hear that Catherine was gay and contented and that the rumors of dangers threatening her were unfounded.

As one reads Catherine's letters, it is not difficult to notice that she is gayest and most entertaining with the pen precisely when times are the most troubled. Take the merry jokes she made about "Marquis Pugachev," [6] at a time when she was so frightened by the successes of the Pugachev movement that she sent Suvorov[7] himself to quell the rebellion. Or her poking fun at the Turkish sultan at a time when a simultaneous struggle on two fronts— against Turkey and against Sweden—confronted her with great perils and she was even thinking of evacuating St. Petersburg, where the sound of guns from the Swedish flotilla could be heard.

Her correspondence served not only to camouflage her moods but also to touch up facts she did not want revealed as they really were. At the height of a crop failure and famine she wrote Voltaire a self-satisfied description of the well-being of the well-fed Russian peasants. After the cruel reprisals she took against Bishop Arsenii Matsevich, who had protested against secularization, she wrote to Voltaire: "I forgave him and merely demoted him to the rank of simple monk." [8] It was, of course, neither necessary nor possible to demote a monk to monkhood, and Voltaire, naturally, never guessed that demotion to monkhood meant that Arsenii had been

6. Emelian Pugachev, leader of the most serious peasant revolt (late summer 1773–early fall 1774) which Catherine had to put down by means of a regular military campaign.

7. Aleksandr V. Suvorov, 1729–1800, most famous and distinguished Russian military commander, best known for his brilliant successes against the Turks and his daring retreat over the Alps.

8. In 1764 Catherine II took over the lands and peasants owned by the Church and put them under the administration of the College of Economy (see "Church Affairs," p. 290). Bishop Arsenii Matsevich was the only bishop to protest the action energetically; he was imprisoned under very harsh conditions.

exiled to a remote monastery in the far north and from there, after a supposed pardon, transferred to the stone trap of the Revel [Talinn] fortress, where he spent the rest of his days. Such information was obviously not intended for Voltaire alone, but for European public opinion, over which the patriarch of Fernay reigned autocratically. In some instances, Catherine asked Voltaire outright to do something she required for publicity. For example, in the same case of Arsenii Matsevich, she sent Voltaire a special note, requesting him to publish it in Europe and authorizing him to say that he had received the pertinent information from a reliable source.

The ostentatious aspects of the ruler's art were always in the forefront of Catherine's concerns. Never for a moment did she cease to think of what people were saying about her, what impression she was making. She was so afraid of unfavorable opinion that she often became overanxious, as when she turned down the suggestion that the shrine of Dmitrii of Rostov[9] be sealed up in preparation for the removal of Dmitrii's remains because she was afraid that "the common people might think that the remains were being concealed from me." In every matter, big or small, her first concern was for a respectable appearance; the substance of the matter was secondary, for it is the appearance that gives rise to rumors and affects the opinions and mood of the mob. In connection with the proposal made in 1768 to establish granaries in the villages of the recently secularized estates, Catherine wrote: "It is necessary that it appear to the peasants that granaries will be opened and that they will live better under the care of the Empress than under the management of the Church." It was not important that the welfare of the peasants really be improved; what was important was that the beneficence of the Empress' actions be impressed on their minds.

9. Dmitrii Savvich Tuptalo, 1651–1709, bishop of Rostov, author and theologian, active as educator. He supported Peter the Great's Church settlement and was canonized in the middle of the eighteenth century.

V

Catherine's deliberate self-advertisement of her achievements, successes, and virtues gradually led her to believe that nothing but good could emanate from her, that everybody around her and under her wing was bound to prosper and bloom with happiness and contentment. Truly great and strong spirits are sometimes willing to evoke a general murmur against themselves in order to achieve aims which they consider good and necessary. The desire to eliminate all that harms their cause impels them constantly to look for blemishes in their own actions. Not so Catherine. She wanted above all that no one complain around her. For persistent endeavors to achieve general well-being, she tended to substitute the conviction that well-being had already been achieved, that the world at the head of which *she* stood was the best of all possible worlds and that only malicious and dishonest people refused to recognize this.

This is what constituted the natural egotistic optimism of her temperament. Catherine saw everything that emanated from her through the rose-tinted glasses of that optimism. She would never have been capable of admitting publicly that any order of hers had "not been properly considered," as Peter the Great was wont to do. She suffered from none of the attacks of doubt, none of the disillusionment with results achieved that are so familiar to truly creative natures. Errors and failures had no place in her record.

It is common knowledge that the commission of deputies she established for the purpose of drafting a code[10] functioned poorly. Yet she said: "My assembly of deputies was successful because I

10. In 1766 Catherine ordered the election of deputies (from among all free classes) who met in 1767 in Moscow to draft a new code of laws (the last code dated from 1649). To guide the work of this "Great Commission" Catherine wrote an *Instruction* (*Nakaz*) setting forth her basic principles of social, political, and economic organization. The commission was adjourned *sine die* in 1768 after the outbreak of the war with Turkey.

said to them: 'These are my principles; now state your grievances; say where the shoe pinches you. We will try to remedy it. I have no particular system. All I want is the general good.' "

Catherine's notes about her first steps in government and her first decisions in the Senate present telling examples of her self-confidence. If one is to believe them, the young Empress instantly, as if by instinct, solved the most difficult problems of governmental practice that had baffled senators, grown gray in the service of the state.

In June 1763, the Senate, in Catherine's presence, discussed the problems involved in undertaking a new census. The senators spoke of the difficulties, the arguments certain to arise, the runaways and deceptions to be expected, and the complex machinery that would have to be set up to carry out the work. But in Catherine's view it could be done very simply: "Let each village report the number of souls in it to the office of the district chief," she said. "Let that office report to the province [*gubernia*], and the provinces to the Senate."

It is hardly likely that the elderly senators required this explanation of the normal administrative procedures through channels. They pointed out that under this system of collecting data many souls would be concealed. Catherine unhesitatingly came up with a solution: "Issue a pardon to all who have formerly concealed [souls] and order the villages to enter all the formerly concealed [souls] into the present reports." In her *Notes* she added to this: "And to this day that is how a census is taken and *there are no omitted souls and nothing is heard about* there being any such." Catherine believed this, for this was the way she wanted it to be.

This egotistic optimism, which contained as much deliberate calculation as involuntary inclination to self-satisfaction and peace of mind, enabled Catherine to find consolatory aspects even in unquestionable national disasters. Of course, Catherine was too intelligent not to perceive the dark sides of the reality that surrounded her. But she shrugged them off with a sophism or a quip, which she tried to pass off as serious reasoning. "I am being robbed, just as others are," she wrote to Mme. Bielke in 1775, "but this is a good sign, for it proves that there is something to steal."

Rarely, very rarely, did clouds of depression or faintheartedness cross her mood, but she quickly swept them away, leaving the horizon of her inner life clear again in the azure of calm self-satisfaction. If anyone ventured to criticize her rule openly, she gave him up as a shallow person, undeserving of serious attention. After Raynal remarked that Catherine did not succeed in many things, Catherine began to speak of him as a mediocre writer. When Turgot and other French economists subjected her *Instruction* [*Nakaz*] to a critical analysis and then trustfully sent that analysis to her, she called them fools and sectarians, harmful to the state.

Catherine's indestructible confidence in the invariable success of her enterprises gave her the resolution to act in the most diverse fields without being the least embarrassed by a lack of proper training. Her *Instruction* to the commission of deputies was a political treatise, setting forth the general principles of her political philosophy with the help of quotations from Montesquieu's *Esprit des lois,* which she doctored to suit her purposes. She drew up extensive statutes and regulations, liberally seasoned with showy platitudes, but sadly lacking in juridical method and precise basic definitions. As long as she lived, she never let the pen out of her hand. She was a prolific playwright and an indefatigable feuilletonist. She undertook an exposition of the ancient chronicles and the compilation of a comparative dictionary of languages, and many, many more scholarly enterprises. All this indicates some ability. Some of her work was naively dilettantist (her philological research); some was helplessly primitive (her imitation of Shakespeare's historical plays); some was sharp and garish (a comedy she wrote about Russian life and the feuilletons in *This and That*). It was all just good enough for the literary level generally accepted at the time. This all-encompassing dilettantism was the expression of a cheerful nature, avid for impressions, but aimed precisely at absorbing available impressions to the fullest rather than at challenging reality for the sake of original, creative ideas.

These traits of Catherine's personality proved to be highly suitable to the political task at hand—the task of giving shape to and consolidating trends which had reached full development in Russia by the time she took power. . . . Having completed the organization of an eighteenth-century Russian *Ständestaat,* Catherine managed to give to it all the cultural polish and brilliance that could be attained at that period. As a matter of fact, it is not too much to say that her success was due as much to her weaknesses and shortcomings as to her positive qualities and talents.

VASILII A. BIL'BASSOV

The Intellectual Formation of Catherine II

ALONE OF ALL THE SOVEREIGNS who occupied the throne of the Russian Empire, Catherine II earned the unanimously high opinion of both contemporaries and posterity. Peter the Great was often cursed during his life, and some condemn him even today; Catherine II ascended the throne to the triumphal cries of all Russia, was acclaimed throughout her entire thirty-five-year reign, and is praised to our day; she continues to stimulate the historian's sympathetic interest. Opinions of Peter I may differ, but they are unanimous on Catherine II. Her contemporaries called

Vasilii A. Bil'bassov, *Istoricheskie monografii* (St. Petersburg, 1901), IV, 241–272. Translated by Robert Drumm.

her "great" and she is still considered so, and it is doubtful that this appellation ever will be disputed seriously. She has full right to it by both her good and bad qualities.

Catherine II was undoubtedly the first to characterize herself as "great" in her own writings and even more through her actions. In 1766, shortly after ascending the throne, she wrote to Count Gyllenborg that "the desire to accomplish 'great deeds'" had developed in her "more than twenty years ago," and if one believes her *Memoirs,* specifically in 1744, in the first days after her arrival in Russia.

Catherine II represented the exact opposite of Peter III. They had only one common trait, which was purely external: both were brought to Russia at fourteen, Peter from Kiel and Catherine from Zerbst. There was one other similarity, but it was precisely the thing that led them to opposite extremes. They both inherited the blood of their fathers, not of their mothers. Peter inherited nothing from his mother, a Russian grand duchess, and much from his father, a genuine Holsteiner. Catherine II had none of the characteristics of her mother, a Holstein princess, but a great many of her father's, who had Brandenburg blood in his veins. There was nothing Russian about Peter and little of the Holsteiner in Catherine.

Peter III went to Petersburg a Holstein soldier and remained one the rest of his life. Poorly educated and brought up, he was never capable of understanding his position as the heir to the Russian throne, let alone as the emperor of Russia. Although he was brought from Holstein for the express purpose of being made the Russian ruler, he scorned Russian ways. Having scarcely become emperor, for example, he directed Archbishop Dmitri of Novgorod to take all the icons except "Christ and the Virgin" out of the churches, and commanded all the "priests to cut their beards" and wear "the same clothing as foreign pastors." He was so coarse and perverse that at his first meeting with his fiancée he admitted to her that he was in love with the lady-in-waiting

Lopukhin and "wished to marry her," but that he was ready to marry Catherine "since my aunt wishes it."

It was quite different in Catherine's case. Though born a German Lutheran, she defended Orthodoxy and pursued purely Russian interests in politics; though originally a petty German princess, she later widely extended the boundaries of the Russian Empire and continued Peter I's internal policy with regard to the spread of European education in the semi-Asiatic society of Russia. She wrote laws, created industries, developed trade, organized the army, and educated the people. Bypassing her own homeland, she embraced the French philosophes, "robbed" Montesquieu, corresponded with Voltaire, and invited Diderot to St. Petersburg so that she could meet the famous Encyclopedist personally.

"My mind is of a philosophic nature," Catherine wrote as a grand duchess. Count Gyllenborg recognized this tendency in her when she was still a child. While visiting Catherine's parents in Hamburg he reproached her mother for the fact that she concerned herself with her daughter "little or not at all," and then added that this "child is very mature for her age" and that she had "a very philosophical mind." Several years later in Russia the same Count Gyllenborg called her "a philosopher at fifteen," and advised her to turn to serious reading. During her lifetime she read Plato, Cicero, Tacitus, Montesquieu, and many philosophical treatises. She took Voltaire as her special model: "In my youth I wanted to follow the spirit and writings of Voltaire in everything." In the course of her life she "read, reread and studied everything that came from Voltaire's pen." In 1778, on receiving the news of Voltaire's death, Catherine wrote to Grimm: "Voltaire is my teacher (*c'est mon maître*). He, or more accurately, his works, shaped my mind, my intellect. I have said to you many times, I think, that I am his pupil (*je suis son écolière*): when I was younger I loved to please him; my actions satisfied me only when they were worth reporting to Voltaire, and I immediately told him about them. He was so accustomed to this that he scolded me (*il me grondait*) when I forgot to tell him the latest news and he heard it from someone else. My conscientiousness in this respect weakened in the latter years as a result of the rapid course of events."

Neither her philosophical mind nor the reading of ancient writers nor her correspondence with Voltaire overshadowed the woman in Catherine II. Even the dry and methodical Englishman Deemsdale, who came to Petersburg in 1768 to vaccinate the imperial family against smallpox, described Catherine as follows: "The Russian Empress Catherine the Second is of above-average height; she has much grace and grandeur, so that even if one could forget her high rank one would admit her to be one of the most pleasing members of her sex. To her natural charms one must add the greatest politeness, sweetness and good humor, and withall such reasonableness that it is manifest at every step, so that one cannot but be amazed at it." Catherine knew of her "natural charms" and used them. She was able to enjoy herself, was always ready to dance, and loved finery. She told with satisfaction of a compliment paid her by the Marquis de la Chétardie on a coiffure *à la Moïse,* and recalled her white dress, *juste-au-corps,* which captivated everyone at the ball. "I had an attractive appearance and I was attentive in conversation. Anyone who spoke with me a quarter of an hour felt like an old acquaintance." She felt restricted by conventional proprieties and did not like to suppress her feelings in this respect. She did not like royal visits, "because they are usually boring, dull (*insipides*) people, and I have to stand at attention in their presence." During a meeting with the Swedish King Gustav III she wrote to Grimm: "Here I am again in the role of a simpleton at court. My usual shyness and bashfulness are again being displayed in all their brilliance. Pray for me." At a meeting in Mogilev with Joseph II she felt very shy at first. Even famous personages (*les personnages renommés*) bothered her because she was forced to listen, and she really loved to chatter (*jaser comme quartre*) herself.

Catherine also had masculine character traits, which existed side by side with and sometimes predominated over her purely feminine characteristics. As a child, during the trip from Zerbst to Moscow she wrote to her father from Libau that she became sick on the road, which she admitted was her own fault, since "I drank all the beer that I could find." As a grand duchess, hearing the advice given her husband that "all the wounded must be shot," she whispered to her neighbor, "I would begin by blowing that counselor's brains out." In her *Memoirs* she wrote: "I was a true and noble knight, with a more masculine than feminine spirit; everyone found that I had the allure of a quite amiable woman together with a man's character." In a letter to Madame Bielke, a friend of her mother's, Catherine admitted that she could "converse well only with men." She noted with outrage that men "could not imagine that a consistent pattern of action could be the product of a feminine intellect."

In February 1778, Catherine still loved to dance and have a good time in spite of her forty-nine years, and scheduled eleven masquerades in the course of two weeks, "not counting the dinners and banquets to which I was invited." Writing to Grimm, in Paris, about this she jokingly added, "Fearing death I ordered my epitaph yesterday. I told them to hurry since I wanted to have the satisfaction of correcting it. While waiting I began to compose my own epitaph for amusement." This humorous epitaph is preserved in the State Archive. Here is how Catherine described herself in it: "Here lies Catherine the Second, born in Stettin April 21 [May 2], 1729. She went to Russia in 1744 to marry Peter the Third. At fourteen she made a three-point resolution: to please her husband, Empress Elizabeth, and the nation. She did not miss a chance to be successful in this. Eighteen years of boredom and solitude gave her the opportunity to read a lot. Having become empress she endeavored to give her subjects happiness, liberty, and prosperity. She forgave everyone willingly and hated no one. She was tolerant, loved life, and was jovial by nature, with a republican spirit and a good heart, and had many friends. Work was easy for her and she liked society and art."

Through the efforts of the Russian Historical Society, which has already published several volumes of the "Papers of Empress Catherine II," we can gain a rather good idea of Catherine's personality as it comes through in her correspondence, and can check the image she sketched in her epitaph against her own words.

Catherine II wrote readily and a lot, and not merely to pass the time or to amuse herself. One can scarcely trust her remark: *"le lire et l'écrire devient amusement, quand on y est accoutumé."* In Sybel's words, Catherine's pen served her well. She wrote well enough to jot a few trusting, casual lines to a friend or to write the witty letters to Voltaire and the Encyclopedists which were praised throughout Europe. She could arrange a playlet for her own court theatre or draft the state plans which established her name as a legislator. Catherine was too intelligent to be completely frank in her letters to Voltaire, d'Alembert, and the other "personages" of her time who had great influence on public opinion. She was ambitious and had suffered a lot in her life; she understood people well and never failed to be cautious in her dealings with them, especially in writing. Just as in conversation she could remain silent when she saw that others attempted to draw her out, in writing she was all the more able to turn to subjects that would result in people saying about her what she needed and wanted. There is no doubt that of all her writings her letters are the best material from which to get an idea of her true self. But the letters differ greatly in character and significance. Her letters to d'Alembert, assuring him that there is more liberty (*plus de liberté*) in Russia than in France, and to Voltaire, categorically informing him that Russia enjoys complete tolerance, must be distinguished from those to Grimm in which she comments on serious matters together with an almost day-by-day description of all sorts of petty details—from news about her grandson Grand Duke Alexander Pavlovich's nightshirt to the health of Monsieur Thomas, her lapdog. Catherine read, reread and studied Voltaire's works, and in the same manner she wrote and rewrote her letters to him, reflecting on every word. Her letters to Grimm, on the other hand, were rough copies without a preconceived purpose, or at least without any ulterior motive. In Catherine's letters to Voltaire she suggests material for the compilation of a work entitled *Siècle de Catherine II*, as a *pendant* to his *Siècle de Louis XIV*. Her letters to Grimm express a need to speak out, to share her joy and her grief, and sometimes simply to chat with an intelligent man, rarely forgetting that this particular intelligent man decreed the view of many courts on works of art and literature through his *Correspondance littéraire*.

The correspondence published by the Russian Historical Society is far from complete. Among other things there is not one letter from Catherine to Diderot in it. This correspondence was not intended to be printed. "I fear publication like fire. Do not give a copy to a living soul." This refrain is repeated constantly in Catherine's letters, but it would be a mistake to take this refrain literally. Catherine accepted any approbation in print, wherever it came from. She generously rewarded such praise, and never expressed serious dissatisfaction at the publication of her letters, but wanted the letters to serve only as material for the laudatory articles to which she paid close attention. *"Le gazetier de Cologne en fera du bruit"* was the magic argument which would always make her more conciliatory.

The people who knew Catherine as a girl or as a child could never explain for themselves how the modest Sophie-Dorothea-Frederike could have grown into the "extremely renowned" Catherine II. "In front of my own eyes she was born, grew, and was brought up," said the Baroness von Printzen, lady-in-waiting at the tiny court of Anhalt-Zerbst. "I witnessed her school studies and successes, and I myself helped her to pack before her departure for Russia. I enjoyed her trust to the point that I thought I knew her better than anyone else, but I never would have guessed that she would become as famous as she did. I noticed only that as a girl she had a serious, calculating, and cold mind; but only through error, whimsy, or flippancy could she have been called outstanding or brilliant. In a word, I got the impression of quite an ordinary person." This is the way she appeared in her parents' home, where Mademoiselle Cardel taught her not to spare the use of the word *monsieur* in conversation, from which the jaws would not fall apart, and the *"ehrwürdige pasteur"* Wagner taught the "subjects" and German orthography, Loran taught French calligraphy, and Rellig taught music. The girl grew up alone, without friends. One of the rare distractions was the appearance of an old aunt who was forever carried away by Luther's *Table Talk*. The child's upbringing and education were so neglected that Count Gyllenborg, a friend of the family, considered it fair to reproach Sophie-Dorothea-Frederike's mother for this.

It is clear, however, from Catherine's letters that the seeds of the changes that occurred later were planted in the modest surroundings of this minuscule court. "What is there for you to do in Stettin?" Catherine asked Grimm in a letter dated June 29, 1776. "If you are still so eager to visit Stettin you may as well know that I was born in the Greifenheim house (*in Greifenheims Hause auf dem Marien Kirchhof*), and that I lived and was brought up in the left corner of the castle, occupying the three vaulted rooms on the upper floor. There Mademoiselle Cardel taught me the proper moral precepts (*m'endoctrinait*) and Herr Wagner taught me my lessons." The child's "philosophical mind" first developed in these vaulted rooms of the Greifenheim house. Wagner and Cardel were two complete opposites, each of whom had a certain influence on the impressionable girl, and both gave rise to comparisons which perhaps led to her first doubts. Wagner was a Lutheran and Cardel a Calvinist; he did not understand any French and she not a word of German. Wagner was a dull pedant who knew only his *"ennuyeuses Prüfungen,"* but Cardel "knew almost everything without having studied anything, just like her pupil"; Wagner was "stupid" and Cardel was an "intelligent girl" who "knew on her fingers all the comedies and tragedies" and gave her pupil a taste for Molière's comedies. Not without reason Cardel called the girl an *"esprit gauche"* [*perverse mind*]—Sophie-Dorothea-Frederike understood all of Cardel's admonitions in her own way and did everything differently from others. Her old aunt read Luther's *Tischreden* to her with great praise for their author, from which the girl obtained an aversion both to the *Tischreden* and to their author. Cardel did not of course read Voltaire's *Lettres philosophiques* with her student, but the philosophical skepticism of the century penetrated into the Greifenheim house not only through Molière. Of all Wagner's "boring" admonitions the girl remembered only the precept that "examples mean nothing—everything depends on the *nature* of man," that is, precisely the premise that Helvétius, Diderot, and Holbach later took as their gospel. "As a girl," Catherine wrote, "I told myself that to be *something* (*quelque chose*) in this world one needs the qualities which this *something* (*quelque chose*) demands. Let us look seriously at our little inner self—do we have these qualities or not? If we do not, we will develop them. Is this nothing or Lutheranism? [*Y a-t-il du rien ou du luthérien à cela?*][1] Certainly not Lutheranism. Martin Luther was a boor (*rustre*)—he did not teach anybody anything." If we dismiss the word "boor" and the attacks on Lutheranism generally as an expression of later developments and political considerations, we see that "philosophical turn of mind" which was noted in this *"esprit gauche"* even by Count Gyllenborg, and which required only an outside influence to turn this tendency in a more serious direction.

Her trip to Russia was the needed influence. In less than a month the Zerbst princess was taken from Zerbst to Moscow. This was more than a trip from one city to another; it was a move to a completely different world, where people felt, thought, dressed, and ate differently. Jules Verne's fantastic voyage could not produce on us as strong an impression as Russian society of the middle of the 18th century must have made on the fourteen-year-old princess, even though *"toute faite,"* as Frederick II put it in a letter to Empress Elizabeth. The gold and brocade, luxury and indulgence blinded and captivated her before she could see that it was not gold and indulgence but gilt and depravity. This was a morass in which it was not easy to get one's bearings, difficult to feel

1. A pun on the French *"du rien"* (of nothing) and *"du luthérien"* (of something Lutheran).

comfortable, and even more difficult to live. The morass was more moral than political or economic. Intrigues, machinations, gossip, and scandal were the premises of human relations; actions and deeds were valued by the extent of their success; moral feeling was replaced by external decorum; hypocrisy and servility were substituted for religiosity and service to a cause. There could be no thought of love and sincere affection when mothers urged their daughters to have lovers if only to get a grandson. Ignorance was the rule among all strata of society and had even reached the steps of the throne; a bishop officially admitted to the Synod that he was "weak in the head." There was no discipline anywhere— a bishop struck a governor (*voevoda*) in the face; a governor's assistant tortured a priest to death; members of the colleges and chancelleries avoided their service, which resulted in massive red tape; and no one paid any attention to the Senate's reprimands. For years no collections were made or accounts kept of the taxes on individuals; the armies were robbed by their military leaders and ships rotted in the harbors; agriculture was burdened with irregular requisitions. The soldiers plundered, mutinied, and stole, and the police were powerless to stop them; industry suffered from a lack of workers, who had all turned to embezzlement and easy money. No one anywhere felt a sense of duty or was conscious of its value. Petr Fedorovich, Sophie-Dorothea-Frederike's fiancé, later her husband, spent whole days with his servants playing with dolls, or with Holstein soldiers drinking, not letting the pipe out of his mouth. He set up a kennel next to his bedroom and carried on in the bedroom itself with masked servants and chambermaids. He unashamedly told his bride about his amorous experiences and did not hide his relations with court ladies from his wife. This was a case of arrested development, a depraved child—he loved to eavesdrop, to spy, to beat his dogs with sticks for hours, and to hang mice in his room for days on end.

This was the milieu in which Catherine was to live. Soon after her arrival at the Russian court she already felt alone, without a guide or a friend. It was a difficult situation. Catherine was saved by her cold, calculating Brandenburg mind.

The Zerbst princess who arrived in Russia was not really a "naïve child." In this respect Catherine was the opposite of Peter III; until his death he remained a child, but she discarded swaddling clothes rather early. Shortly after her arrival in Moscow she understood the seriousness of her position and became ill. For several days she was "between life and death," and lay in bed more than a month. Her youth and strong nature helped her to bear the ailment, and the moral crisis passed. She got out of bed with the firm resolve to be friendly to everyone, not to interfere in anything, not to push herself forward, to obey the Empress without question and respect the Grand Prince deeply, and to make every effort to deserve the respect of everyone in her new homeland. This resolution was made quite consciously and carried out with a surprising steadfastness, especially for a woman. The princess was not restrained either by her father's admonitions, his "Pro memoria," or by the promises she gave him, and she changed from Lutheranism to Orthodoxy just as easily as several years later she was able to banter about the rites of the Greek church, scoff at Protestantism, and smile during a Catholic mass in Mogilev or while greeting the Jesuits in Polotsk.

Where is the reason for such a change? Where can one find the clue to her resolve to tie her fate to a world so completely alien and unattractive?

Catherine herself gave a rather categorical answer a hundred years ago, which is continually repeated today: while she realized that the present was difficult and foresaw a bitter future, she decided to endure it and suffer everything because she was "not indifferent to the Russian crown." To which crown? Empress Elizabeth was in the prime of life at thirty-six and Grand Duke Petr Fedorovich was a youth only a year older than Catherine herself. What crown could Grand Duchess Ekaterina Alekseevna dream of in 1744? Here, evidently, the later facts are recalled to justify the preceding decisions. It seems unnecessary to repeat Catherine's words about the crown, which had no significance at the time, when nearer and more natural motives exist. Catherine brought them from her homeland; they sustained her during the trip from Zerbst to Moscow; they helped her to understand the Orthodox teachings of the [Ipatsk] archimandrite, and they motivated her toward a change which influenced her whole life.

Catherine had been reared in the rather modest circumstances of a minuscule court, in the midst of barren seaside surroundings. Her mind and imagination had been constantly filled with stories of the mighty power famed for its great victories, known for its countless riches and its dazzling, luxurious life. Russian troops had been in Pomerania not long before; in nearby Denmark the Russian tsar had led his troops to victory in water up to his waist; and everywhere there seemed to loom the grandiose figure of Peter [the Great] commanding the fleets of four states. Holstein ships sailed the Oder with Catherine's countrymen going to seek their fortune in Russia. In Stettin and Zerbst, Braunschweig and Berlin she heard stories of the bravery of the Russian soldiers, about the riches of Russian magnates and the grandeur of Russia, and these stories sank deeply into the soul of a child with an ambitious, strongly agitated imagination, which pictured alluring, fascinating perspectives. When these tempting images later took on a more conscious significance, and when the difference between Zerbst and Russia became real, she received an invitation to go to Russia and become a Russian grand duchess.

She saw this trip as the fulfillment of her childhood dreams or perhaps her youthful fantasies, and went willingly. On the way she was like a soldier, meeting danger with equanimity, and slept soundly while they unloaded the broken sledge after it had struck the corner of a building at full gallop. On the road and in Moscow everything attested to riches and luxury: "everything was adorned with gold lace and inlaid with gold, and it was magnificent"; everything was dazzling—the star on the order of St. Catherine and the choker; the diamond earrings, valued at 60,000 rubles; the diamond cuff-links and diamond necklaces worth 150,000 rubles. And honor and respect? "We live like queens. When we ride out we have such a marvelous equipage." The splendid suite, the crowd of courtiers, the brilliant ceremonial *baise-main* [*kissing the hand*] —to throw all this away for the sake of the "creed" and return again to the miserly surroundings of a "minor" court? If Paris was worth a mass, then Russia was all the more worth the "creed," and Catherine *"d'une voix nette et claire et d'une prononciation, qui a étonné tout le monde, en récita tous les articles sans broncher d'une syllabe."* In the first days, months, or even years of Catherine's stay in Russia she could not even have had thoughts of "the Russian crown"—even after her marriage, August 21, 1745. The "Russian crown" as the reason for Catherine's decision or as the cause of her actions only appears significantly later when she had thought out the plan of her *Memoirs* and felt the need to give her actions a motive of a higher order, of state importance.

In the eighteen years from her arrival in Russia until she gained the throne Catherine had to read the "Veruiu" [credo] many times. She had to be extremely careful not to arouse the suspicions of the Empress, the chancellor, or the mass of spies who followed her every step. She was forbidden to correspond with her mother and she was forced to accept the help of foreign musicians at court to outwit the vigilant informers around her. In the midst of the court turmoil she was completely alone; the Empress did not trust her, her husband did not love her, and those close to the court who wished to remain in the Empress' good graces avoided Catherine. Even the domestics, to get in good with their mistress, scorned her. She kept her resolve to maintain the position she had taken, seeing, observing, attempting to understand everything, saying nothing and keeping to herself; outwardly she remained gracious and polite, attentive and obliging to everyone. Little by little her behavior was rewarded. In 1755 the British ambassador Williams wrote to his court that "as soon as Catherine arrived she made every effort to be liked by the Russians. She achieved her goal and enjoys great love and respect here. She has a very winning manner."

The time remaining from the duties required by court etiquette Catherine spent in riding, reading, and talking with ladies-in-waiting. Taking the advice of a friend of the family to "nourish her soul with serious reading," she gradually went from novels such as *Tristan le blanc* and the various *Vies* of Brantôme to more serious works such as the *Vie de Henry IV* by Périfixe or Barry's *Histoire d'Allemagne;* she read Plutarch and Cicero, labored over Montesquieu, devoured the *Lettres de Mme de Sévigné* with delight, and first became acquainted with the works of Voltaire in 1746. She also read Bayle's *Dictionnaire historique et critique,* Plato's *Politics,* and Baronius' *Secular and Ecclesiastical History.* She read a great deal, selecting the books from catalogues which the Academy sent to her.

If life developed Catherine's character, then reading formed her intellect, disciplining it in a general philosophical direction. When Count Gyllenborg saw Catherine in 1745 he called her "a philosopher at fifteen"; in 1750 she told her mother in a letter that "I am a philosopher as much as I can be, and I will not give in to my passions," and a year later, in 1751, Diderot began to publish his *Encyclopédie,* which was Catherine's constant companion until she died. Reading the philosophes of her century, especially the Encyclopedists, Catherine achieved a political maturity that she never could have obtained by practice or experience. She proved this not so much by gaining the throne itself as by the actions preparing the overthrow of June 28, 1762. Practical considerations and everyday experience changed her political views and convictions to a significant extent, and not in a direction that would have pleased her teachers, the philosophes. As a grand duchess she read philosophical and political works for her own development, to enlighten her mind; later as Empress she involved herself directly with the philosophes, intending to use their influence on public opinion to serve her own purposes.

A history of Catherine's relations with the philosophes of her time has yet to be compiled; even the material needed for such a work has not been assembled and published. A future historian probably will note two clearly expressed peculiarities of this involvement: first, that the philosophical premises which Catherine praised so highly were not applied in practice, but that nevertheless she achieved the most practical goals from these contacts; and second, that the less Catherine followed the admonitions of philosophy the more she expressed her devotion to the philosophes.

Of all the contemporary philosophes Catherine felt most strongly about two of them: she hated Rousseau and was fascinated by Montesquieu. The reasons why Catherine hated Rousseau are not clear from her papers. Perhaps she did not like his idealism or his rhetoric, but it is also possible that her astute mind saw where the equality that Rousseau preached might lead, and foresaw the possibility of an enactment of the famous night of August 4, 1789.[2] Though Rousseau was not concerned with the question of property and, it seems, did not share the views which Morelly expressed in his *Code de la Nature,* Catherine nevertheless considered the principle of equality which Rousseau advanced to be so harmful that soon after ascending the throne she issued the following edict on September 6, 1763: "It has become known that books are being sold in the Academy of Sciences which are against the law and good morals, and which have been banned in the whole world, such as, for example, *Emile* by Rousseau . . . It is urged that the Academy of Sciences keep watch in the most careful fashion that such disorders do not happen again in its bookshop." In referring to the late Rousseau Catherine added *"de douteuse mémoire,"* but when it was advantageous she cited Rousseau's words to defend her own opinion. To a letter written May 12, 1791, she added a long excerpt from Rousseau's works in which one reads that *"les lois de liberté sont plus austères que n'est dur le joug des tyrans."*

Catherine studied Montesquieu's works especially carefully: "For two years my main activity has consisted of copying and evaluating Montesquieu's principles. I try to understand him, and I strongly criticize one day what I found very good the day before."

2. On the night of August 4–5, 1789, the French National Assembly voted the abolition of all feudal rights, dues, and privileges.

She needed Montesquieu's principles in compiling her *Instruction to the Commission for Drafting a New Code of Laws*. The draft involved general principles of public law and required juridical definitions and the expression of political tendencies, and Catherine took these from Montesquieu, sometimes altering and interpreting his "principles" so much that at times it is difficult to recognize the original from which they were taken. In 1765 she wrote to d'Alembert: "You can see from the *Instruction* how I have robbed President Montesquieu for the benefit of my empire without naming him; I hope that if from the other world he saw me working he would forgive this plagiarism for the sake of the benefits to twenty million people which will follow from it. He loved mankind too much to be insulted by this; his book serves as a prayer book for me." A year later, in 1766, Catherine informed Voltaire that she had included in her *Instruction* a selection from *Esprit des lois* referring to sorcery. For Catherine there was no higher praise than to recognize a work as worthy of Montesquieu's pen. But Catherine never corresponded with either Montesquieu or Rousseau. Montesquieu died in 1755, when Catherine could not have corresponded with anyone, and Rousseau was insufferable to her.

Having just become Empress, Catherine entered into direct relations with the philosophes, and above all with Diderot: "Within ten days after I ascended the throne," July 6, 1762, Catherine suggested that Diderot come to St. Petersburg to finish his *Encyclopedia,* as he had had many difficulties in publishing it in Paris. The *Encyclopedia* produced a great impression on the practical Catherine. She read it and kept it constantly within reach, never parting with it; she would choose subjects for theatrical plays from it, check the sense of a word, or verify particular expressions. Catherine gained her impression of Diderot from his *Encyclopedia* and grew to like him because of it; she used the first available opportunity to attract attention by buying Diderot's library and giving it to him to use for life, inviting him to be the librarian for a specified annual salary. This was a practical-minded step on her part and it completely achieved its purpose: Diderot's friends, Voltaire, d'Alembert, and Grimm, praised Catherine throughout Europe. Tempted by the success of her first move, she made a second two years later by paying Diderot his salary for fifty years in advance. This second venture was also a complete success. These first steps were followed by others. She lavished favors on Voltaire's protégés to please him and received praise from him which established her reputation in Europe as an enlightened and virtuous woman and an exemplary monarch who could bring her country happiness. One can only be amazed at the intelligence and tact with which Catherine established and maintained her ties with the philosophes. In her correspondence with Voltaire and d'Alembert, with Diderot and Grimm, and in her opinion of Metastasio, Beccaria, Euler, and Haller one can see a freethinker and a humanist; by contrast, a monarch such as Frederick II would take second place or be pushed into the background. At the same time she was a completely practical person, who had elevated personal interest to a philosophical principle. Catherine would have stopped at nothing, including a lie or deception to achieve her premeditated goal. For example she assured Voltaire that "there is not a peasant in Russia who could not eat a chicken if it suited him, and for some time they would rather have turkeys than chickens." In a letter in 1771 she wrote to this same Voltaire: "As far as notes on confession are concerned we don't know even their titles." But what's this? In that same year, perhaps on that very same day she signed "an imperial reprimand" to the governor of Tobol'sk, Chicherin, for negligence in compiling "confessional lists." [3] Catherine presented herself in relation to the philosophes so intelligently and cleverly that they appeared voluntarily as her resolute defenders in all her undertakings. She knew whom she was dealing with so well that all the "princes of philosophy" were behind Catherine even in

3. Under the terms of the Church legislation of Peter the Great, parish priests had to keep a record of the compulsory yearly confession and communion of their parishioners. These lists were then transmitted to the civil authorities, providing them with a means of checking on Old Believers and other heretics who refused to take communion from the officially appointed priests.

the Polish question. They called the Polish confederates "riffraff" and saw Catherine as almost an apostle of tolerance and a pioneer of civilization with regard to Poland! At the same time that the foreign philosophes not only justified her intervention in Polish affairs, but also considered the partition of Poland to be an act of political wisdom,[4] the Russian dignitary and ambassador, Count Semen Romanovich Vorontsov, wrote from London to his brother in St. Petersburg, Count Aleksandr Romanovich, president of the College of Commerce: "Everything that you and Messrs. Bezborodko and Markov wrote to me to justify the new partition of Poland does not convince me or change my opinion that this is a transaction of unjustifiable perfidy. The affair of itself represents an all too clear injustice, but the perfidious means of carrying it out make it even more disgusting. If it already had been decided to do this injustice then one should say directly that Poland is being ravished to obtain revenge for the fact that it wanted to conclude an offensive alliance with the Turks against us. But instead of that they speak of friendship and promulgate a manifesto with the statement that they seek only the good of Poland, that they want to guarantee the wholeness of its possessions and the use of its former government with which it flourished with such brilliance over so many centuries! Can you imagine that any court will have any trust in us after this?" From Catherine's letters it is evident that the philosophes prompted her to the partitions. Thus she wrote in 1789: "you attempt in vain to destroy the Polish nation—it works in this direction itself; at least, it did away with the Permanent Council, the only higher institution which supervised the execution of the law. But don't be alarmed: the dreadful insignificance of the nation leads it from one extreme to the other, and the time is coming when it will realize its own stupidity and will repent. In truth I must say that you are a great politician—in two pages you survey all Europe, but since you do this only from a

4. Many philosophes felt that the partition of Poland was justified by the anarchical political system and the socio-economic backwardness of the Commonwealth.

desire to tell me that I must do only that which is to my advantage, I am very grateful to you and assure you that I shall not fail to take your advice."

Reading Catherine's letters to and about Voltaire it is not difficult to convince oneself that she put him on a par with Montesquieu and above all the other philosophes of the period. She called Voltaire her teacher and took him as a model; in answer to the news of Voltaire's death she ordered one hundred copies of his works: "Give me a hundred copies of my teacher's works so that I may put them everywhere. I want them to serve as a model, to be studied and learned by heart, to nourish souls; they will produce citizens, geniuses, heroes, and authors; they will call forth a hundred thousand talents who without them would be lost in the gloom of ignorance." What a tirade! Actually, it would be a great mistake to see in these lines anything except a tirade. When the publication of the complete collected works of Voltaire was announced, Catherine wrote to Grimm: "But listen, who has the strength to read fifty-two volumes of Voltaire's works? When the publication comes out buy two copies at my expense for Vanière, send them to him in my name and tell him to note in one of the copies what is just and what is unjust, and send me that copy." Upon receiving the set already reviewed by Vanière she did not even open it. Moreover in 1767, during Voltaire's life, in sending the counts of Oldenburg to travel abroad, Catherine forbade them to visit Lausanne or Geneva "so as not to be near Voltaire."

In her correspondence with the philosophes Catherine was intelligent, shrewd, and practical to a high degree. She exploited them as far as possible, took from them everything that they could give, and used their knowledge and influence on public opinion, but she was not subject to their influence and acted independently, like a true philosopher. Having obtained the trust and the "deserved" praise of the famous "princes of philosophy," Catherine carried on a correspondence with them, asked them questions, and invited scholars, technicians, and artists to Russia at their suggestion. Catherine was occupied with a whole series of legislative tasks, was concerned about establishing educational institutions, encouraged industry, created new markets for trade, built new means of communication, and completed grandiose buildings. On the matter of all these works she wanted to hear the opinion of the philosophes and wished to obtain their approval. Catherine was not satisfied with correspondence and constantly wished to have one of the "princes of philosophy" near her, above all, of course, Montesquieu, for a direct, live exchange of thoughts. Soon after ascending the throne she invited d'Alembert to come to St. Petersburg and invited him quite persistently. "Come with all your friends; I promise you and them also all the satisfactions and conveniences which depend on me, and perhaps you will find more freedom and calm here than where you are."

D'Alembert did not come. Then, on Diderot's recommendation Catherine invited Mercier de la Rivière, the author of *De l'ordre naturel et essentiel des sociétés policées.* "I strongly urge you," she wrote to Count Panin, "to write to Shtakelberg, and if he is no longer in France, then to Golitsyn, so that he will begin discussions with Monsieur de la Rivière about the latter's trip to Russia. Having been in service in Martinique a long time, he has expressed very sensible ideas in his treatise. He will be useful to us." De la Rivière came to St. Petersburg and Catherine tried to fulfill all his wishes, but he soon lost all importance for her. He arrived in September 1767. In November, Catherine already was saying that "the author of the *ordre essentiel* spouts nonsense," and in January 1768, she wrote to Panin: "Ivan Fedorovich Glebov says that de la Rivière has become somewhat less arrogant. He is only a babbler and thinks a lot of himself, but he is like a doctor." [5] Four years later in September 1773, Grimm arrived in St. Petersburg in the retinue of the Landgräfin of Hesse-Darmstadt and brought Catherine the good news that Diderot had already left Paris at the end of May and should soon arrive in St. Petersburg.

5. Catherine II had a deep distrust of medicine and a strong dislike for all doctors.

IVAN K. LUPPOL

The Empress and
the Philosophe

> *L'oeil du philosophe et l'oeil du souverain voient bien diverse-*
> *ment.*
> DIDEROT

THE HISTORIAN-AND-BIOGRAPHER is in a comparatively favorable situation with regard to literary sources and
original materials describing the circumstances of Diderot's acquaintance with Catherine, his trip to St. Petersburg and stay there,
and, generally, his relationship with the Russian Empress—a relationship between a philosopher and an empress who liked to talk
philosophy. The scholar has at his disposal Diderot's own letters
from St. Petersburg, Catherine's letters, and letters from persons
who were in contact with both of them (Voltaire, Grimm, Dash-

---

Ivan K. Luppol, "Didro i Ekaterina II," in *Deni Didro—Ocherki zhizni
i mirovozreniia* (Moscow, 1960), pp. 91–115. Translated by Mary Mackler.

kova), reminiscences by witnesses to their relationship and, finally, monographs about the events concerned.

Nevertheless, though 150 years have gone by since that time, it is still impossible to be certain that additional materials will not turn up somewhere in archives touching directly or indirectly on this curious chapter in the lives of two individuals who have gone down in history so differently. Thus, as late as 1899, the *Mélanges philosophiques, historiques, etc.,* which Diderot had written between October 5 and December 3, 1773, during his stay in St. Petersburg, were published by Tourneux.[1] In these notes, Diderot attempted to sum up his conversations with Catherine, without trying to give them any particular unity or order. Before his departure he presented them to her, hoping that they would give her food for thought and, perhaps, influence her domestic policy. Catherine never told anyone about them. They remained in oblivion in the private library of the Russian tsars until the end of the nineteenth century. Systematized slightly by Tourneux, they fill 400 pages in his book and supply answers to a number of long-standing questions, such as: Was Diderot so charmed by the "soul of Brutus in the body of Cleopatra" that he retreated from his theoretical positions? Did he admire Catherine's policies and actions as Empress, or did he stick to his own views in his tête-à-têtes with his patroness?

Diderot's comments on Catherine's *Instruction to the Commission for Drafting a New Code of Laws* were first published in full even later, in 1920.[2] Only an excerpt from them had appeared previously in the appendix to Tourneux's book. These comments reaffirm the stand Diderot undoubtedly took in St. Petersburg and constitute a finale, as it were, to the private conversations between the philosopher and the Empress. Yet prior to their publication all that was known about them was the extremely unfavorable re-

1. Maurice Tourneux, *Diderot et Catherine II* (Paris, 1899) and recently the first complete edition, Diderot, *Mémoires pour Catherine II,* ed. P. Vernière (Paris: Garnier, 1966).

2. Most recent scholarly edition, "Observations sur le Nakaz," in Diderot, *Oeuvres politiques,* ed. P. Vernière (Paris: Garnier, 1963), pp. 331–458.

marks made by Catherine when she read them (after Diderot's death) and Diderot's own references to them in letters he wrote to Catherine on September 13, 1774, from The Hague and October 17 of the same year from Paris.

As for the literature describing and interpreting the subject of this article, with very few exceptions it shares the bias of all that has been written about Diderot and reveals a strong antipathy toward Diderot, who is presented as having managed to extract major financial advantages from Catherine's favor and as having made the long trip to the "northern Semiramis" for the sake of those advantages. . . . This tradition goes back to Diderot's contemporaries, the enemies of the Encyclopedists (who included our Fonvizin[3] at one time), who sometimes added to the inevitable contention that Diderot never advocated atheism for the masses and that he himself was probably not an atheist the statement that Diderot's "loyal" attitude to Catherine by definition excludes any possible historical truth in it. It must be admitted that the situation is far better with regard to source materials than with regard to their interpretations. We shall now proceed to examine the facts on the basis of the source materials.

II

On June 28, 1762, with the support of the Guard, the Senate, and the Synod, which were, actually, the representatives of the land-owning nobility who constituted the economically dominant class in Russia at that time, Catherine did away with Peter III and became Empress of Russia. A few days later, on July 6, she issued an invitation to Diderot to publish the *Encyclopédie,* banned in Paris, in St. Petersburg, or in Riga. Her offer was duly communicated to the Russian envoy in France, Prince D. A. Golitsyn, who was on friendly terms with some of the Encyclopedists, and to Voltaire

3. Denis I. Fonvizin, 1743–1792, most prominent and successful Russian dramatist of his time. His comedies *The Brigadier* and *The Minor* are still in the regular repertoire of the Soviet theater.

in a letter from I. I. Shuvalov (Catherine was not yet personally corresponding with Voltaire at the time). On August 20, the same Shuvalov wrote in a similar vein directly to Diderot. Outwardly, this was undoubtedly a very pretty gesture, made "for Europe." Here was the young Empress, just acceded to the throne after her husband's death from "a sudden attack of hemorrhoidal colic," offering freethinkers, persecuted in their homeland, an opportunity to continue their work of enlightenment in a country which their persecutors considered barbaric. The French authorities condemn the *Pensées philosophiques* to be burned; they fling the author of the *Lettre sur les aveugles* into the dungeon of Vincennes; they stop the publication of the *Encyclopédie* twice, whereas the Russian Empress holds out a helping hand to the author and editor of the *Encyclopédie*.

To gain a true understanding of this step it is necessary to dwell at least briefly on the preceding years of Catherine's life.

While this *"esprit naturellement philosophique,"* as Catherine referred to herself, may not have really been philosophic "by nature," that spirit did indeed receive early nourishment in Catherine's own home. The tiny court of Anhalt-Zerbst started preparing Sophie Auguste Frederike from childhood for a summons abroad, which was the usual destiny of "royal princesses." All it could give her to add to her looks was an education, and among the accessories of an education, which included the French language, music, needlework, and Luther's *Tischreden,* philosophy was not the least in importance. The seventeenth century had already had Elizabeth of the Palatinate and Christina of Sweden— the former's correspondence with Descartes and the latter's desire to have her own court philosopher were known. The same century had witnessed Sophie Charlotte's[4] correspondence with Leibniz and Toland. If the names of those three women are known today because of their personal relationships with the above thinkers,

4. Sophie Charlotte, 1668–1705, electress of Brandenburg, Queen in Prussia. She entertained lively contact and active correspondence with leading intellectuals of her time, principally with Leibniz.

there were dozens like them in the seventeenth century from aristocratic families and hundreds in the eighteenth century from aristocratic and bourgeois homes who have been forgotten and who are known to have existed only through memoirs and Molière's *Les Femmes savantes*. Is it any wonder that the fourteen-year-old Sophie Augusta had already heard a great deal about the *nature* of man and the *affects* of the soul (we have definite indications that she had heard of these) and, perhaps, of *substance, attributes, modi, monads,* etc., too?

True, she was brought to Russia at the age of fourteen, and it was already in that country, on the advice of persons who were close to her family, that she "fed her soul with serious reading." She read Plutarch, Cicero, Plato, Voltaire, Montesquieu, Bayle and, from 1751, at the age of twenty-two, the *Encyclopédie*. She especially liked Voltaire and Montesquieu, whose *Esprit des lois* she copied assiduously and tried to evaluate critically. . . . It is difficult to say how much better she did in her analysis and serious study of the philosophies of other thinkers. However, it cannot be denied that Catherine was quite well read.

Following in the footsteps of her philosophically inclined fellow countrywomen, Elizabeth and Sophie Charlotte, Catherine started a correspondence with d'Alembert by a letter of November 13, 1762. It is of interest that she mentions Christina of Sweden in that letter.

Later she enters into correspondence with Voltaire, Diderot, and Grimm. Voltaire was then already a recognized genius, an outstanding member of the *république des lettres,* a freethinker, and, what was most important, a writer listened to by the bourgeois-intellectual and liberal-aristocratic circles of society, and not only in France. Possibly, the young Empress, who could talk philosophy when the occasion arose, was even more flattered to write to and receive letters from such a man than was the "friend of King Frederick," who assailed the Heavenly King of the Catholics but never encroached on the kings of the earth. It is true that the friend of the Prussian king did not have a particularly good relationship with his own king, but the Empress of the land of barbarians must have found it pleasant to appear to French educated circles as the patroness of a thinker who was not altogether trusted in his own country.

Neither should it be forgotten that by protecting the French philosophers, Catherine was revenging herself on the French government for its policies in Poland and Turkey.[5] "All her unpleasantness came to her from Versailles, and all her consolations—from Paris. There are two Frances, one is her enemy, the other her ally. Her correspondence with philosophers often bears the mark of rancor against the ministry [of Choiseul]."

After she became Empress, Catherine retained the same sincere and trustful tone in her letters. She carried on a witty, sophisticated causerie as an equal with equals, now entering into serious discussions, thereby emphasizing her respect for her correspondents' superior judgment, now reporting with her authority as Empress that there were more freedoms in Russia than in France, that Russia had complete religious freedom, and that the peasants in that prosperous land ate chicken whenever they wished and had lately begun to prefer turkey for dinner. The truth of the matter was that the serfs never even dreamed of chicken, the "Old Believers" had no idea that they lived in a country of religious tolerance, and native "enlighteners" were treated even worse than in France. But this was all hidden from Catherine's correspondents and from the great majority of foreigners who, when they visited Russia, saw nothing but St. Petersburg. As a matter of fact, it was hidden from the "Semiramis du Nord" herself.

The sincere, simple tone of Catherine's letters was no more than a *façon de parler*. Even an Establishment historian was compelled to admit in his book that "Catherine II was too intelligent to be sincere in her letters to Voltaire, d'Alembert and all the 'celebrities

5. Throughout most of the eighteenth century France was the staunch ally of Turkey and Sweden and tried to act as the protector of Poland (Marie Leszczynska, wife of Louis XV, was the daughter of Stanislas, king of Poland and later duke of Lorraine).

of the age,' who had a great deal of influence on public opinion." [6]
To a frank statement like the above, which always painted her in
attractive colors, Catherine would often add that she feared the
press as she feared fire and that she forbade anyone to copy her
letters or to show them to anyone. It is not difficult to guess that
it was these very words that were intended for public consumption. Voltaire had written a *Siècle de Louis XIV*; why shouldn't he
write a *Siècle de Catherine II*?, and the future heroine of it went
about furnishing Voltaire with the necessary materials. Her patronage of writers who were persecuted in France and her private
correspondence with some of them were merely the means by
which she hoped to achieve these aims.

Did Catherine succeed in her enterprise? Strange as it may seem
at first glance, this question cannot be answered without reserva-
tions. There are several aspects of it to be considered.

It should be kept in mind that the French philosophes, even the
most celebrated ones, were not a homogeneous group. First, there
was Rousseau, whose ideas of equality Catherine did not even pre-
tend to share, openly labeling them pernicious. She banned the
sale of *Emile* in Russia, made no attempt to flatter the republican,
did not protect him or offer him her patronage when he was persecuted, did not seek praise or admiration from him, and did not
receive them.

Her attitude to Voltaire and to the materialist nucleus of the
Encyclopédie was different. . . . Catherine proved herself a friend
and protector of Voltaire when he took refuge in Fernay, of
d'Alembert when he was deprived of his pension, and of Diderot,
when he was refused admission to the Academy. She translated
Marmontel's *Belisarius* when it was condemned by the Sorbonne.
She subscribed to the *Encyclopédie* when its publication was
banned in France.

Voltaire replied to Shuvalov's letter: "I received your letter as I

6. Reference here is to Bil'bassov's study "Empress Catherine II and
Diderot," from which we have drawn "The Intellectual Formation of
Catherine II," p. 21.

was sitting at table and we permitted ourselves to drink to the health of Her Imperial Majesty and to wish her long years and happiness, which she richly deserves. . . . We were all moved to admiration and, while maintaining our respect for Her Majesty, permitted ourselves to link your name with hers, as in former days the name of Maecenas was linked with the name of Augustus." On the same day, September 25, 1762, Voltaire wrote to Diderot: "What do you say of the Russian Empress? Isn't her proposal the worst slap in the face to such gentlemen as Omer? [7] What a time we live in! France persecutes philosophers, while the Scythians protect them." Coming from Voltaire, these statements are comprehensible and consistent. An enemy of radical reform, a deist and an idealist, Voltaire feared revolution and was prepared to reconcile himself to the existing social and political system, demanding only freedom of conscience and speech.

Regarding the materialists, Diderot among them, the problem was more complex and cannot be dismissed as simply as Ducros seems to think when he writes: "Not only 'light,' but also encouragement and *pensions* came to the philosophers from the North." This writer would put it differently: There came not only pensions, which were not that large (fur coats for Voltaire and the members of the Academy), but also encouragement and concrete offers of assistance in completing the "big work," frequently the philosophe's life work. The Empress' secret aim could be kept in the dark, concealed from the philosophes' eyes, and only the bare fact of assistance from afar in matters that were being hampered in France was illumined by a bright light.

One must understand the style of the era of "enlightened absolutism" and the bourgeois nature of the philosophes, which permitted a republican, such as Rousseau, to have "respectful and tremulous thoughts" before the forthcoming presentation to "such a great monarch" as Louis XV, or to admit: "When I later adopted the role of anti-despot and proud republican in Paris, I, neverthe-

7. Omer Joly de Fleury, 1715–1810, *avocat général* and *président au Parlement de Paris,* censor.

less, against my will, felt a secret attraction for the government against which I was trying to rebel."

The written and oral advice that the "Enlighteners" gave to sovereigns invariably aimed at bringing about the end of feudal society and at replacing it with a bourgeois society. Diderot himself can serve as an illustration of this. How "enlightened despots" reacted to advice of this kind is another matter. Catherine can serve as an illustration of that.

The gap between the theory and the practice of sovereigns did not go unnoticed by the philosophes. It is therefore necessary to point out that the Enlighteners too managed to separate theory from practice and adopted a twofold approach to rulers: to the sovereign, monarch, despot, on the one hand, and to the individual and philosophe, on the other. This describes Diderot's attitude toward Catherine. The former was his enemy; the latter was his friend. He recognized certain achievements and merits in the former, to whom he kept giving advice, futilely, of course. He admired the latter nearsightedly, dazzled by the brilliance of the light emanating from the former.

In the negotiations with I. I. Betsky, at Catherine's instructions, about a second edition of the *Encyclopédie,* Betsky demanded new and less outspoken versions of the articles on religion and forms of government. Diderot, who was now dealing with the Russian government as his publisher, had to wriggle out of the situation, which he did in the following manner: "As for the article on governments, it would be very stupid to say anything derogatory about the government of the country where one is planning to spend the rest of one's life. After all, I am a good Frenchman and not a rebel. The nature of the publication requires and presupposes only general articles, for example, on *monarchy, oligarchy, aristocracy, democracy,* etc., in which one can preach whatever one wishes without offending or compromising anyone. As for the section on religion, that is purely historical."

Though Diderot praised Catherine highly upon his return to Paris in 1774, he also wrote the comments to her *Instruction,* in

which he expressed the view that a monarchy is powerless to set
up a government based on law. This confirms our judgment that
he drew a dividing line between Catherine as a person and Catherine, the despotic Empress. Of course, "general articles" about
monarchy and oligarchy could also have practical significance. It is
in the light of these considerations that the relations between Catherine and Diderot and the other Encyclopedists should be examined.

III

In the latter part of 1762, Catherine proposed to Diderot, as editor
of the then banned *Encyclopédie,* that he finish printing the edition
in Russia. Prince Golitsyn conducted the negotiations with Diderot,
and Voltaire wrote a letter. Though Voltaire fulfilled Shuvalov's
request, he was nevertheless a little anxious about the fate of the
Encyclopédie in Russia, as is evidenced by the following excerpt
from a letter he wrote to d'Argenteuil: "The slap in the face that
the Scythians have given to stupid and idle people has afforded me
a great deal of pleasure, which you will share with me. However,
I am very much afraid that Ivan [VI] may push our patroness off
the throne, and, after all, the young man, who was brought up by
monks, is hardly likely to be a philosophe." [8] Obviously, Voltaire
was well acquainted with Russia's history of palace coups.

By September 29, Diderot replied to Voltaire that there was no
need to go either to St. Petersburg or to Berlin—as Frederick had
suggested two years earlier—to complete the *Encyclopédie* for the
simple reason that it was continuing to be printed in Paris, but
that even if that were not the case, he could not have accepted

8. Voltaire is alluding to Ivan VI Antonovich, the baby emperor who
was overthrown by Elizabeth (see note 5 to "Portrait of an Enlightened
Autocrat," p. 12). He is wrong in believing that young Ivan was brought
up by monks since the latter spent all his conscious life in solitary confinement. Voltaire is probably thinking of Tsarevich Alexis, the son of Peter
the Great, who was indeed under strong clerical influence and who also
perished in prison.

Catherine's offer. He did not reply to Catherine personally. Their correspondence began much later.

Three years later, Catherine made another gesture of good will to Diderot. Diderot's daughter, Mme. Vandeul, reports in her memoirs that in 1763 her father made up his mind to sell his library so that he could in this undoubtedly painful way furnish her with a dowry or at least with some sort of financial security for the future. He had been negotiating with the notary Lépeaux d'Auteuil about the sale when Grimm intervened and through the same Golitsyn arranged for Catherine to purchase the library for 15,000 francs, or, as Diderot wrote in a letter to Sophie Vollan on July 21, 1765, for 16,000 livres. There is only one error in Mme. Vandeul's story: the incident took place in 1765, not 1763. . . .

Catherine's purchase of Diderot's library was not in itself an "act of charity," even if one were to assume that the library was not worth as much as she paid for it, and all it could do was to confirm what the French reading public already knew—that the Russian Empress loved and appreciated books. To evoke a new outburst of admiration and gratitude, Catherine would have to really benefit the man whom the French government and the fanatical clergy considered undesirable, and do so for all to see. So she not only paid Diderot the 15,000 francs, but left the library in his possession for his lifetime and granted him a salary of 1,000 francs a year as its custodian. This evoked grateful letters from Voltaire and d'Alembert, to which Catherine replied hypocritically: "I never thought the acquisition of a library would bring me the kind of praise you are showering on me for having bought Diderot's books. You will agree, however . . . that it would have been cruel and unfair to part a scholar from his books."

Diderot realized that the 1,000 francs a year that Catherine had promised him was a pension, but he saw nothing reprehensible in accepting it, nor was it reprehensible according to eighteenth-century standards. He did, however, consider it necessary to inquire about the reactions of the French court, which was very suspicious of Catherine's actions in this instance. In 1894 Ducros published a

hitherto unpublished letter from Diderot to Florentin, Louis XV's
minister of the court (the addressee's name was established by
Tourneux), in which Diderot explained that it was the need to
provide for his daughter that had caused him to make the sad decision to sell his library and described the circumstances of Catherine's purchase of the books. The letter closes with the following:
"I do not know whether the hundred pistoles should be termed a
pension or just a simple salary, and I do not know whether a subject may accept anything from a foreign government without first
obtaining permission to do so from his king. I make bold to ask
you, Monseigneur, to obtain such permission for one who is in
great need of the kind of charity that has been offered him. I remain, etc., Diderot, April 27, 1765." There is a note in the margin
of the letter, reading: "Reply that the King has condescended to
grant permission." No doubt, it was not with a light heart that the
King "condescended" to permit this support to a friend of Voltaire's. Only a month prior to this, on March 19, the Parliament
had condemned Voltaire's *Philosophical Dictionary* to be burned
along with Jean-Jacques Rousseau's *Letter from the Mountain*.
But, surely, Diderot had not written his letter with a light heart
either.

This was not the end of the matter of the purchase of the library. Catherine's biggest "coup" was yet to come. Diderot's daughter reports that payment of the promised salary was deliberately
withheld for a year and a half. Diderot did not bring this to anyone's attention. One day, Golitsyn, meeting Diderot, asked him
whether he was receiving the money punctually. Diderot told him
the truth, but added that he considered himself fortunate as it was,
even without the money, as Catherine had "condescended" to buy
his "little shop" and leave him the tools. Nevertheless, Golitsyn
said he would see about the oversight and soon afterward, on October 30, 1766, Diderot received 50,000 francs as salary for fifty
years in advance. This was Catherine's first and largest gift to
Diderot. It would prove to the "republic of letters" that the Russian

Empress was capable not only of a purchase, but also of an "unselfish act of charity."

It is highly improbable that Catherine had paid the 15,000 francs in the spring of 1765 and had then forgotten about it. In her letters she referred to the purchase of the books for a long time afterward. On June 29 (July 9), 1766, for example, she returned to the subject in a letter to Voltaire: "To help someone out of one's own superfluity does not mean anything. But to stand up for mankind and to defend persecuted innocence is a supreme merit." These lines are a good example of the technique mentioned at the beginning of this article: Catherine implied that her deeds were as nothing compared to the deeds of that "advocate of mankind," Voltaire. Written a year after the purchase, they prove indirectly that the forgetfulness to pay the salary was deliberate.

Naturally, the gift itself and the form in which it was made evoked a fresh outburst of praise from the Encyclopedists. "Accept my gratitude, Madam," d'Alembert wrote her, "and the gratitude of all writers and philosophes and respected people for the good deed which your Imperial Majesty has bestowed on Diderot." In this way, for the high society in Paris, St. Petersburg, and Berlin, the third quarter of the eighteenth century ended with the sensational affair of Catherine's purchase of Diderot's library. The library, together with copies of the philosopher's manuscripts, which his brother—the canon—tried hard but unsuccessfully to obtain so he could burn them, were delivered to St. Petersburg only at the end of 1785, after their owner's death.

The purchase of the library marked the beginning of a closer relationship between Diderot and Catherine. Diderot, who was not only a philosopher, but also a connoisseur and critic of art, recommended his sculptor friend Falconet to Catherine as the artist best qualified to execute the monument planned to Peter I. At the end of 1765 Falconet had already moved to St. Petersburg. In 1767, also on Diderot's recommendation, the physiocrat Mercier de la Rivière, one of the "economists," traveled to St. Petersburg. The theoretical differences between the philosophes headed by Diderot and the school of economists (Quesnay, Gourney, and de la Rivière) only arose in 1770, probably after the former's doctrine took shape in the *Système de la Nature,* which opposed both God and tyrants. In the period referred to now, Diderot had a very high opinion of de la Rivière as an economist. "He knows the true secret, the eternal and axiomatic secret, of how to achieve the well-being and happiness of the peoples," he wrote to Falconet in St. Petersburg. This panacea, as one can easily guess, was the physiocrats' principle of *laisser faire, laisser passer.* On his arrival in St. Petersburg, de la Rivière apparently began assiduously to offer advice for turning the feudal society into a bourgeois society. This did not please Russian noble landowners nor, therefore, Catherine, who after her first and last meeting with him declared that the "author of *Natural Order* is talking nonsense." Rivière's ideas concerning independent farmers (*entrepreneurs de culture*) and personally free workers (*propriétaire de sa personne et main d'oeuvre*) could not possibly appeal to them. Dissatisfied, de la Rivière soon left Russia.

Hence, Diderot's first political recommendation was a fiasco and he thereafter limited his advice for the time being to the arts. On his recommendation, Catherine, who did not understand much about art, but who wished to be a patroness in that field, purchased a number of paintings by Murillo, Van Loo, and others. She bought Baron Thiers' entire well-known gallery with works by Raphael, Van Dyck, Rembrandt, and Poussin in it, thereby laying the foundation for the Hermitage.

IV

. . . At the beginning of her reign, Catherine had invited d'Alembert to come to St. Petersburg with all his friends, but the invitation had not been accepted. Voltaire, with whom she corresponded more than with the others, was now old and feeble and never left Fernay. Of all the philosophes, Diderot was the only one

Catherine could still expect to see. Diderot himself had spoken several times of his intention to make Catherine's acquaintance. Catherine had invited him as far back as 1767, but at that time he could not leave Paris as the entire burden of the *Encyclopédie* had been on his shoulders since 1757. Finally, in 1772, the last volume of engravings came off the press. His daughter was married. He could now fulfill his wish.

He was a little fearful of undertaking so distant and at that time so unusual a journey in his declining years. He had never been outside France before, and the longest trips he had ever taken were to Langres and to the Bourbon spa. Aware of the possible surprises such a journey might have in store, he drew up a literary will before he set out, instructing Naigeon to publish his works in case of his death. He finally set out for Russia in May 1773 by way of Holland. He stopped over in The Hague to visit with his Paris acquaintance, Prince Golitsyn, who after his recall from Paris had been appointed ambassador to Holland, where he was then engaged, among other things, in publishing the late Helvétius' *De l'homme*. Diderot left The Hague in the company of Naryshkin on August 17 (August 21 according to other reports) of the same year and went straight to St. Petersburg, not stopping in Berlin as had been his intention. He was ill twice en route. He reached his destination on September 28.

Unwilling to burden strangers with his presence, Diderot went to the home of his old friend Falconet, but the sculptor received him coldly and refused to offer him hospitality on the pretext that the bed intended for him was already occupied by his son, who had arrived recently. Diderot then asked Naryshkin if he could stay with him and that is where he lived during his entire sojourn in St. Petersburg.

On the basis of available materials about the meetings and conversations between Diderot and Catherine, of their letters, of accounts by contemporaries, memoirs, and some of Diderot's later works, and, finally, Diderot's St. Petersburg manuscript, published by Tourneux, it is now possible to dismiss the several ridiculous anecdotes that have been current and to obtain a true picture of Diderot's life and impressions in St. Petersburg.

We shall dispense with long excerpts about meetings with Catherine from Diderot's letters to Princess Dashkov, Catherine's former friend, whom he knew from Paris, to his family, and to Sophie Vollan. These letters are all extremely effusive and indicate that Catherine had charmed him, chiefly, by the simplicity of her treatment of the "envoy plenipotentiary of the Encyclopedist republic," a kind of treatment to which he was not accustomed in France. Knowing the sort of person Diderot was, the sincerity of his letters cannot be doubted. The philosophe had expected to meet with the Russian sovereign two or three times at official audiences, instead of which, "quite the contrary, the doors of the sovereign's office are open to me every day from three to five o'clock, and sometimes until six. I enter, I am asked to sit down, and I talk with the kind of freedom that you permit me. And when I take my departure I am compelled to confess to myself that in the so-called land of free men I had the soul of a slave, and in the so-called land of barbarians, I have found in myself the soul of a free man." "The soul of Brutus with the charms of Cleopatra" was how Diderot referred to Catherine in several letters.

Catherine was not nearly as enthusiastic. She wrote to Voltaire of Diderot: "He is an extraordinary brain. One does not encounter such every day." She was attentive to him. She willingly conversed with him, but, what is of most interest to us, she did not attach much importance to what he said. As far as their respective situations permitted, Denis Diderot and Catherine conversed in a friendly manner. But the materialist and atheist, one of the leaders of the eighteenth century French Enlightenment and the Empress of Great, White, and Little Russia had nothing in common and did not share a language.

Did Diderot really believe that he had found a free land in northeastern Europe? After all, he had no firsthand knowledge of Russia himself. He was still only trying to learn about the country and he asked Catherine numerous questions. Actually, Catherine did not know Russia so well that she could give the philosopher precise replies. But she was certainly well informed about the general social and political system and it is obvious, therefore, that there was deliberate falsehood in her replies to Diderot, just as there was in her letters to Voltaire describing the elegant tastes of the enserved peasants. Diderot asked her: "What are the terms established between the master and the slave with regard to the cultivation of the soil?" To which she replied: "There are no terms between the landowners and their subjects (*sujets*); but every master with common sense takes care of his cow and does not demand too much of it so as to be sure he can milk it at will, without *exhausting* it. When there is no provision in law for something, the law of nature takes over immediately, and this does not make matters worse because they are at least arranged naturally, in keeping with the *nature of the matter*."

Diderot asked: "Does not the slavery of those who till the soil affect the cultivation of the land? Does not the fact that the peasants may not own property have negative consequences?" Catherine replied placidly: "I do not know whether there is any country in the world where the tiller loves his land and hearth more than he does in our Russia."

Diderot submitted approximately ninety written questions concerning the national economy of Russia to Catherine. These questions show the lines along which he was thinking. They touched on the most varied aspects of the country's economy and life: size of the population, its distribution among the estates (the clergy, nobility, *"les odnodvortsi"* or the freemen, and the peasants), the number of monks and nuns, the situation of the Jews, etc. They touched on questions of land ownership and cultivation, production and trade in grain, wine, vodka, butter, hemp, flax, tobacco, timber, tar, resin, large-horned cattle, horses, etc. Catherine replied. The following will give the reader an idea of the kind of replies she made and their profundity. Asked whether there were veterinary schools in Russia, Catherine replied: "God save us from them."

Her replies were general and reveal an ignorance of her own laws. Sometimes she would reply in an apologetic tone to a brief, terse question of Diderot's. Often she did not answer the question but told him to ask Münnich.[9] Diderot did not let the matter drop but submitted an additional thirty questions on diverse subjects to Münnich. Among other things, he inquired about the location of soap-making factories, whether there was any glass manufacture, the size of the national debt, whether there were banks and joint stock companies, etc. These were questions not only of a curious traveler, but of the editor of the *Encyclopédie,* a public figure from a country that was on the eve of industrial capitalism.

However, it is not these questions nor the replies to them that are of interest to us. What we would like to know is whether Diderot, impressed by the "charms of Cleopatra and the soul of Brutus," really believed that all was well in this newly discovered "free land." Did he agree, if only in words, with the political convictions of his patroness? Or did he openly advocate his views and suggest reform, if not revolutionary, projects? And if he did, what was Catherine's reaction to his proposals?

The most interesting and comprehensive material on this is to be found not in Diderot's letters to Catherine from The Hague and Paris, or in his plan for public education in Russia, a comprehensive but actually very special work, but in the *Mélanges philosophiques* . . . Diderot wrote *Mélanges philosophiques* intermittently over two months in Naryshkin's St. Petersburg house, fresh from his meetings with Catherine, and they undoubtedly reflected the topics of his conversations with her. The work touches on political, economic, pedagogical and ethical questions, on art, the theater, etc. It does not touch upon metaphysical questions at all. Finally, it was not intended for publication, or even for a small number of readers, but only for Catherine's own "reflection."

It is of interest not only because of the form in which it is pre-

9. Count Ernst Münnich (Minikh), 1707–1788, son of the famous Field Marshal Burchard Münnich, was president of the College of Commerce from 1774 until his death.

sented—not systematic, but fragmentary, a light and playful cascade of witticisms, yet dealing with the same kind of serious and profound ideas that characterized Diderot's writing in general—but also because this was the form Diderot chose for presentation of his ideas to the Empress. While by no means humbling himself before the "powerful and enlightened sovereign," he acted as if he were not attaching much importance to his comments, as if he considered them merely "dreams" and was not trying to impose them on her, stressing that he was well aware that *"l'oeil du philosophe et l'oeil du souverain voient bien diversement."* He respected, as it were, Catherine's superiority. Anticipating, he pointed out that his ideas were really close to those of the Empress. In his epigraph he seemed to foresee Catherine's future judgment of him. Actually, though, he was sugar-coating the bitter pill.

In the present context only those of Diderot's comments which reflect his conversations with Catherine on political and ecclesiastical-political themes are pertinent. And of these, the present article will deal only with those bearing directly on Catherine, leaving the examination of Diderot's political views as a whole to a special essay.

The French Enlighteners, Diderot included, seemed to proclaim for all to hear: In France the king is a despot, but in Prussia the king is a philosopher, a Solomon, and Russia has a wise Semiramis. Yet Diderot said to this very Semiramis: "All arbitrary government is bad, and I make no exception for arbitrary government by a kind-hearted, firm, just, and enlightened ruler. By governing according to his own taste, a despot, even if he is the best of persons, is committing an evil." It is not difficult to recognize Catherine in this despot who is "the best of persons." But Catherine, of course, does not want despotism. She has convoked a commission to draft a new code of laws. She has written her celebrated *Instruction* to that commission. True, the commission was disbanded several years before, but there were rumors that the Empress had not given up the idea of a code of laws. This provided Diderot with a pretext for writing the following in the first chapter of his *Comments* to the *Instruction:* "The Empress of Russia is surely a despot. What is her intention? To preserve despotism, to hand it down through her heirs, or to renounce it? If she intends to preserve it, then let her issue her code of laws any way she wishes. She has no need of the consent of the nation. However, if she intends to renounce it, let that renunciation be formalized, let her search together with the nation for the best means of preventing despotism from rising again and let the very first chapter proclaim the inevitable death of anyone who ever in the future should attempt to gain the kind of arbitrary authority now being overthrown. This is the first step of an *Instruction,* proposed to the peoples by so [sincere] a sovereign as Catherine II, by one so opposed to tyranny as she is."

What is the first thing a philosopher-king must do? Convoke a legislative body, of course. "Comprised of subjects, it will always better understand the public, that is, its own, interests than will the sovereign." Inasmuch as the sovereign is created for the nation, and not the nation for the sovereign, it will not be an inconvenience if that body with clearly defined responsibilities becomes very strong, especially since "sovereigns are more liable to capricious behavior than are educated peoples." What Diderot had in mind by "clearly defined responsibilities" of the legislative body is obvious from the fact that in his *Comments* he proposes that such a body determine the country's form of government. The same question is raised in *Mélanges,* not as sharply, perhaps, but more subtly. "Perhaps I shall not be departing very much from Her Imperial Majesty's way of thinking in advocating that the choice of the successor to the crown be made from among the children, but on the condition that the choice is not made by the father. It seems to me that the united nation, making a choice through a body of its representatives, would be less likely to err in the matter than the father." In speaking of the "closeness" of his views to Catherine's, Diderot may have had in mind Catherine's attitude toward the heir, Paul. Nevertheless, his conclusion could not but have startled her.

Diderot discussed religion in the same respectful but firm and persistent tone: "Out of respect for Your Majesty I shall not say anything about God. You wish to persuade yourself that there is a sort of likeness of you up there in the sky who watches what you are doing and, seeing that you are so kind and noble, so majestic and humane, smiles on you, content with a sight that the earth does not often present. Nevertheless, I venture to point out the dangers of the religious ethic." Then Diderot goes on to set forth his own antireligious substantiation of ethics.

From the few excerpts above, it is evident what Catherine had to listen to from her guest and why she said that in some areas Diderot was a sage, but that in others he was not even ten years old.

The language and substance of the letters Diderot wrote to Catherine after his departure from Russia were the same as in the St. Petersburg conversations. Congratulating Catherine on the peace of Kuchuk-Kainardji,[10] he wrote: "The blood of thousands of the enemy cannot compensate for a single drop of Russian blood. Continuous victories undoubtedly create a brilliant reign, but do they make these reigns happy? Thanks to the progress of reason, the virtues of the Alexanders and the Caesars no longer evoke our admiration. It has been discovered that it is much nicer and pleasanter to create people than to kill them." A year later he wrote to her: "Now that you have given your enemies proof of your might, utilize the remainder of your reign to give proofs of your goodness to your subjects and to all rulers, all present and future, an example of the great art of Kingship." The reason why Diderot insistently repeated this a year later was that he had not seen Russia take a single step forward in the course of that year.

We shall not discuss the reforms in public education for free universal schooling, vocational training, etc., that Diderot proposed to Catherine in his "plan." Outwardly at least they had Catherine's sympathy. The ideas on religion and the Church which he ex-

10. Treaty of Kuchuk-Kainardji, concluded July 10 (21), 1774, ended the Russo-Turkish war begun in 1768. By its terms Russia secured the northern shore of the Black Sea, the right to navigate on that sea and through the Straits, and a protectorate over the Christian populations of the Ottoman Empire.

pressed not in general articles in the *Encyclopédie,* but directly to her, a ruler, are much more surprising. In the same "plan on public education," referring to the faculty of theology he wrote: "A clergyman, whether he is a good or a bad man, is nevertheless an unreliable subject, a creature who is suspended between heaven and earth, like the little figures the physicist now lowers, now raises at will, depending on the quantity of air in them." He expressed himself even more sharply in his *Comments* to the *Instruction:* "Philosophers have said many bad things about clergymen, clergymen have said many bad things about philosophers. But philosophers have never killed a single clergyman, while clergymen have killed many philosophers." In the same work he expressed dissatisfaction because "Catherine and Montesquieu both open their work with the name of God instead of starting with the need for laws, the foundation for the happiness of the people."

Catherine had the tact to refrain from turning away from Diderot while he was alive, either because she was afraid of forfeiting the flattering reputation of patroness of Enlightenment or because she well knew that feudal Russia was still very remote from the consequences of anything Diderot or his colleagues might advocate. Diderot's plans and projects merely went into one ear and out the other. But when Diderot's library and manuscripts were forwarded to St. Petersburg and she read his *Comments,* she wrote to Grimm in annoyance: "In the catalogue of Diderot's library I found a notebook entitled *Comments on the Instruction of Her Imperial Majesty to the Deputies for Drafting Laws.* It is unadulterated nonsense. It shows absolute ignorance of the circumstances and is devoid of common sense and caution. Had my *Instruction* been to Diderot's liking, it would have turned Russia upside down."

And this was Catherine's true view of Diderot. She valued him as a means for gaining publicity in Europe, and he, willy-nilly, contributed to that publicity. Nor was he the only one of his contemporaries to play that role. Without realizing it, they created a legend about a "philosophe on the throne." But in 1787, when the true philosophe, in the eighteenth-century meaning of the word, was no longer among the living, and when nearly all the Encyclopedists had gone to their graves and the only ones left were Holbach, the completely tamed Grimm, and the irreconcilable Naigeon, Catherine said to Count Ségur: "I talked with him [Diderot] often and for long periods, but more out of curiosity than with any benefit. If I had listened to him, everything would have been turned upside down in my empire: I would have had to destroy everything—the laws, the administration, finances, and diplomacy—and to replace it all with fantastic theories." Contrary to the legend, Diderot's ideas, the ideas of the bourgeosie at the moment of its glorious birth and revolutionary dawn, were alien to the Empress of what was in fact a feudal state.

But, we repeat, it was only after Diderot's death that Catherine revealed her true feelings about him. Diderot, philosophe and guest, was treated well. When he decided to return home, he was given 3,000 rubles to cover the cost of his trip and expenses on the return journey, a miniature portrait, a carriage, and an escort. A few tears were shed at the pain of parting.

The ideological affinity with Catherine which Diderot may have still hoped for in the 1770's and which did not develop in St. Petersburg now evaporated altogether. However, Catherine continued to give the aging and ill philosophe financial assistance. In 1779, at Grimm's request, she sent him another 8,000 francs and, finally, only a few days before his death, she had a more convenient apartment rented for him.

GRIGORII A. GUKOVSKII

The Empress as Writer

CATHERINE WAS AN ACTIVE WRITER for about a quarter of a century, and an extremely prolific one, too, more prolific than Frederick II, whom she regarded as her competitor as "philosopher on the throne" and writer-monarch. In that competition she undoubtedly had the advantage, both because, unlike Frederick, she did her writing herself, in the main without substantial outside help, and because she wrote mostly in the language of her subjects, whereas the Prussian king, a native-born

Grigorii A. Gukovskii, "Ekaterina II," in *Literatura XVIII veka, Istoriia russkoi literatury*, edited by G. A. Gukovskii and V. A. Desnitskii (Moscow–Leningrad: Akademiia Nauk SSSR, Institut literatury Pushkinskii Dom, 1947), IV, part 2, 364–380. Translated by Mary Mackler.

German, had nothing but contempt for German culture and the German language, and wrote in French. In her lifetime Catherine covered literally reams of paper with her writing. As a matter of fact, she referred to her writing mania herself, not without a touch of boastful coquetry.

Apropos of this, mention must be made of the huge number of official documents and papers, as well as private letters, which came from Catherine's pen. Catherine wrote laws, very lengthy ones at that, entire volumes of legislation. She wrote the rescripts to the nobles, generals, and clergy herself. In her own hand she wrote innumerable letters to members of her staff, to friends, lovers, and many, many others. Most of the letters she wrote to Russians, she wrote in the Russian language. To her acquaintances and correspondents abroad, she wrote in French and sometimes, though rarely, in German. Of these languages, she knew German best, of course. Though she lived in Russia for over fifty years and spoke and wrote in Russian all that time, she never learned to express herself in the language correctly. Not only was she basically illiterate in the Russian language (she misspelled the simplest words), but she never learned to decline Russian names or to follow the rules of grammatical agreement, and she confused the genders of nouns. Yet she undertook with a great deal of self-assurance to discuss the Russian language and did not even hesitate to correct the style of Russian writers, such as, for example, Vasilii Petrov. This should not, however, be attributed entirely to her infatuation with her own power. Actually, Catherine had a taste and a lively feeling for the spoken language. She knew Russian colloquial speech very well. She remembered and used correctly a multitude of Russian proverbs, sayings, idioms, and characteristic local words and expressions. Consequently, her Russian was a strange mixture of top-heavy, incorrect constructions and forms, on the one hand, and lively, colorful colloquialisms, on the other.

It goes without saying that the most glaring errors of grammar and spelling were corrected before publication (as were the rescripts and other official documents she composed) by her secretaries, who helped her in her literary work generally. Among Catherine's editors and aides were I. P. Yelagin and G. V. Kozitskii, at first, then A. V. Khrapovitskii, all three of whom were distinguished Russian writers. Her French texts were corrected by her courtier Count A. P. Shuvalov, whose own poetry, which he wrote in French, was highly appreciated even in Paris. However, none of this assistance ever took the place of the work of the author herself. It never went beyond correction of manuscripts (and the corrections were exclusively of grammar), selection of materials for her quasi-scholarly works, and excerpts from other people's poetry for inclusion in her operas.

Extremely varied in genre, Catherine's writings were uniform in their ideological direction and clearly expressed political tendency. They included articles and feuilletons for magazines that were published more or less under her direct tutelage. She also wrote for outside magazines, as, for example, an article and a letter to N. I. Novikov's *Zhivopisets* [*Painter*], a magazine that was hostile to her. She wrote a voluminous quasi-scholarly opus on the history of Russia. She wrote stories for children and pedagogical essays, intended for use in the education of her grandsons, Alexander and Constantine, but which, naturally, had a broader aim in view and were addressed to the general reader. She wrote a large number of comedies, historical dramas, comic operas, and other dramatic works. Dramaturgy constitutes a very important part of Catherine's literary heritage, both in quantity and in the significance she herself attached to it. A total of twenty-five completed or nearly completed stage plays and excerpts from seven other plays have come down to us. In addition we know that she wrote several plays, which have not survived. Catherine did not write poetry—was unable to write it—but she had a passion for writing prose.

In all of the above genres, Catherine wrote in Russian. Of her writings in French, the best known, both in western Europe and in Russia, are her letters to the *philosophes*, above all, to Voltaire, then to Diderot and Grimm, and to others. Catherine's letters were

not merely private correspondence, but constitute a body of literature of a sort. They were sketches and feuilletons, presented in the
form of private letters. They expressed opinions on current political
events and cultural developments; they gave autobiographical
sketches and descriptions of Russian life, primarily at court. They
contained lively chatter about this and that, witticisms, tableaux,
and so forth. Catherine's correspondence with Voltaire has been
published many times since the death of the correspondents, both
in the original French and in Russian translation.

Catherine also wrote and published several polemical works in
French, among them a long work, entitled *Antidote,* and a pamphlet, called *The Secret of the Anti-Absurd Society. Antidote* is a
lengthy polemical exposé of the French astronomer Abbé Chappe
d'Auteroche's book *Journey to Siberia* (1768), which contained
cutting, unjust attacks on Russia, Russian society, and the Russian
people, as well as just criticism of serfdom and Russia's despotic
form of government. By refuting him, Catherine was defending
both the Russian people and herself. In her book she combined
abundant and interesting information about Russian life, customs,
geography, economy, and culture with blatantly false claims that
Russia was very well off under her monarch's scepter and enjoyed all kinds of freedom. *Antidote* was published anonymously
in 1770 (and again in 1771–1772).

*The Secret of the Anti-Absurd Society, Discovered by an Out-
sider* is a satire on freemasonry and Masonic organizations and
parodies Masonic rituals, emblems, and doctrine. It appeared in
1780 not only in French but also in German and Russian. The
Russian translation from the French original was done by A. V.
Khrapovitskii and published under the false date of 1759.

Finally, Catherine's unfinished memoirs, as well as numerous
reminiscences, were also written in French. Her memoirs cover
the period up to her accession to the throne, are written in a lively
style, and show real powers of observation. They are probably the
most interesting thing she ever wrote. The memoirs were not
intended for publication, at least not during her lifetime or soon

after her death, and Catherine is more natural and truthful in them than in her other works.

Actually, Catherine II's French writings do not belong to the history of Russian literature. As a matter of fact her Russian writings would not be at all noteworthy if their author had not been the Empress. Catherine's passion for writing was not accompanied by the requisite talent. There can be no two opinions about that. Not only was she not gifted, she did not even have great ability. Extensive practice enabled her, in the end, to write a tolerable playlet, no more. Her work rarely meets the standard even of the average literary output of the time.

Nevertheless, Catherine's writings are not devoid of interest, both for the history of Russian literature and the history of Russian society. They are interesting precisely because they were written by the Empress, because they express the real and official literary policy of the government, because they constitute a body of literature that gives expression, so to speak, to royal directives of a general ideological as well as of a special literary nature. This is why Catherine's contemporaries found her work so significant and relevant and why the reading and theater-going public and the literati of the 1760's through the 1790's showed such a great interest in it. Supporters of the government hung upon the Empress' every word, interpreting everything she wrote as instructions and guidelines. The progressive elements of society, those opposed to the government, read everything she wrote very carefully, studying the enemy, as it were, and sharpening their weapons for attack. But everybody was interested in everything the Empress wrote and published. It should be pointed out that although all of Catherine's writings for the press and for the stage were anonymous, her contemporaries knew very well who their author was. Generally speaking, though the custom of publishing anonymously was very widespread in the eighteenth century, this did not in the least prevent the public from being informed as to who the authors of the anonymous works were. Besides, except in a few instances, Catherine never tried to conceal her authorship. On the contrary, she paraded it, which only intensified the interest among the public.

As for her plays, their popularity was enhanced by the magnificent staging, the excellent music in the operas and historical dramas, and the splendid performances of the casts, who, naturally, exerted themselves to lend artistic depth to the mediocre text. The result was that Catherine herself came to believe that her plays were truly very successful. Ordinarily, she did not require much for self-delusion. She was surrounded at every step by such shameless flattery that she became firmly convinced that she was a genius in all fields. With complete equanimity and not the slightest fear of seeming boastful she wrote in her letters that her works were universally admired, praised them to the skies herself, and glibly compared herself to Molière.

Another reason for the historical and literary interest in Catherine's works is their polemical sharpness. They present a picture of the literary, and even the ideological, battles of the period, some of which were major combats indeed, politically meaningful and of state significance.

Finally, still another reason for the interest in Catherine's writings is the fact that they were so typical of the artistic styles of the period. The Empress may not have been a talented writer, but she was a careful observer and very responsive to all literary developments in the West and in Russia. She noticed and quickly grasped the latest literary trends and news and reacted to them immediately. Furthermore, she not only noticed them but tried to use them for her own ideological purposes, i.e., to adapt them to advocacy of the Russian landowner—and police-based autocracy and court culture, and to have them serve as an apologia for the existing regime. Consequently, the chief literary trends from the 1760's to the 1790's appear consecutively in Catherine's writings, albeit in a distorted, oversimplified, and internally reorganized form. In Catherine's literary works one can see the evolution of styles and artistic techniques, from classicism through early sentimentalism of various shades to the first pre-romanticist trends of the period. And, what is more, the evolution is seen through the prism of official government reaction to those literary processes. In this sense, Catherine's literary heritage is not only an expressive image of a period of eighteenth-century literary history, but also fills what would have been a gap in our knowledge had we not known the government orientation against which progressive writers of the period were struggling.

II

Catherine's first published work appeared in 1767–1768; it was the *Instruction* [*Nakaz*], an official act of state rather than a literary work. The *Instruction* was purely declaratory, not practical, but still not an individual literary expression.

During her Volga trip in 1767, Catherine organized the collective translation of Marmontel's *Belisarius*, which had just been published in France and condemned by the French authorities. Catherine's purpose was to demonstrate to all of Europe that the "Semiramis of the North" was enlightened and freedom-loving. The translators of *Belisarius* included high dignitaries, such as Count Z. G. Chernyshev, Count G. G. Orlov, S. Kozmin, A. I. Biblikov, Count V. G. Orlov, and others, and the writers, I. P. Yelagin, A. V. Naryshkin, and G. V. Kozitskii, who were close to the court and all pupils and friends of Sumarokov. Catherine personally translated the ninth chapter of the book. The translation was published in 1768; the title page read *"Belisarius*, by M. Marmontel, Member of the French Academy, translated on the Volga" and was dedicated to the Bishop of Tver, Gavril (the dedication was written by Count A. P. Shuvalov). The dedication of a disapproved book to such a dignitary was meant to demonstrate to all Europe the religious tolerance of Russia's government and the enlightened freethinking of its church in contrast to the French ecclesiastical authorities, who had attacked *Belisarius* and its author. The book appeared in successive editions.

Catherine's entry into Russian literature came a little later, precisely at the time when she felt the need to exert influence on the nation's thinking and to guide public opinion,[1] both by administrative pressure and by persuasion, persuasion being the printed word. Thus came about the publication in 1769 of a weekly magazine, called *Vsiakaia vsiachina* [*Potpourri*], under her editorship and carrying her contributions. Her technical assistant on this magazine was her secretary, the writer and philologist G. V. Kozitskii. *Vsiakaia vsiachina* was planned as a sort of literary continuation of the debates in the Commission on Codification. It had become clear to Catherine after a year and a half of the commission's work that ideas that were dangerous to her regime were firmly entrenched in the minds of her subjects. She resolved to influence public opinion—with a view to "sobering" it—through the printed word. She decided to tackle the matter herself and by her own example to direct the criticism of reality into a channel that would be acceptable to the government and at the same time to put the presumptuous freethinkers "in their place."[2]

Catherine made no secret of the official nature of her magazine. The reader was given sufficiently transparent hints of this in the materials it carried. Besides, the magazine was exceedingly boastful, and it carried very many shamelessly laudatory, servile letters to the publisher. In its declared aim *Vsiakaia vsiachina* was conceived as a satirical magazine, but Catherine had her own concept of satire. She had to wage a struggle against malcontents and, in her judgment, there were two ways to do this: by impugning the undesirable claims of the opposition, and by providing a model of "respectable" satire.

The magazine propounded respectable and moderate ethical notions and had a penchant for moralizing "in general." It avoided

1. Public opinion is used here to translate *obshchestvennoe dvizhenie*. The Russian expression actually refers to the persons—and their ideas—who acted as the intellectual élite and spearheaded the drive for the liberalization of the political and social systems of the empire. In the eighteenth and early nineteenth centuries this élite made its influence felt through informal groupings (circles, literary societies, Masonic lodges) and a select periodical press.

2. See selections: "Voices of the Land and the Autocrat," p. 113, and "The Autocrat and the Open Critic," p. 156.

political and social issues, except when defending the government
or attacking malcontents. For example, it carried a caustic attack
on freethinking women who engaged in literature and science,
clearly referring to the hostesses of the salons that served as a kind
of committees of opposition. It attacked the "old men," detractors
of present-day life, who, it contended, clung to everything obsolete
and past. It poured ridicule on the "dreamers" and "chatterboxes"
in Moscow, by whom it meant the liberals, who were concentrated
in Moscow, far from the government eye. Here are some examples
of what it carried about the projects of such people: "One project
is to turn the city of Romny into a port. Another wants to abolish
the capitation and proposes to raise an income of 70 million rubles
to take its place by sending a secret squadron of 2,000 ships to
conquer unknown islands in the Pacific, kill all the black foxes
there, and sell them to foreigners every year for silver. Another
writer, in pursuit of the good of all, wants to teach the public how
to double the number of kernels in the various grains and asks for
villages, peasants, and money so that he may carry out his useful
experiment. I inquired who had thought of these projects. I was
told: sharp-witted men. But who, precisely? It turned out that
most of them were bankrupt merchants. Who was asking for
money and villages? A young man who had squandered all his
father's estate." In this manner, Catherine (who probably wrote
that article herself) tried to discredit the opposition's social background and objectives.

At the same time *Vsiakaia vsiachina* zealously defended existing
authority. It came blithely to the defense of the office clerks, that
is, the bureaucracy, against attacks in progressive literature, and
placed all the blame for the defects in the administrative and judicial machinery on the subjects themselves. "Clerks cannot and
should not be abolished. It is not the clerks or their functions that
are harmful. . . . Is it not a fact that if there were fewer tempters
around them, there might be fewer complaints against them?"
How could the "clerks" be prevented from "harassing the people"?
"This is very easy: do not offend anyone, make your peace with

those who have offended you by mutual agreement without resorting to the clerks. Keep your word and avoid getting involved in any kind of troubles."

The magazine abhorred progressive satirists, such as Novikov,[3] whom it attacked violently, declaring that to condemn social vices was itself an even greater vice, an indication of hatred of mankind, impertinence, impudence, and the like. It did not hold with liberalism. It sternly condemned mildness in treatment of house serfs, unambiguously recommending strictness (even to the point of whippings), for it considered them all scoundrels. Extremely respectful, even servile, to the courtiers and all authorities, it also advised its readers to be submissive in all things. "It is our duty as Christians and citizens to have confidence and respect for governments, for they have been set up for our good, and not to make unfair complaints or to abuse them for deeds which, in any case, I have never known to have been committed deliberately." The conclusion was: "Kind fellow citizens, let us cease to be malicious and then we shall have no reason to complain of unjust treatment." In defending "governments," the government-sponsored magazine was at the same time refuting the criticism directed against the Empress' favorites; for example, it published a story glorifying and denying the "slander" against a certain "vizier," easily recognizable as G. G. Orlov.

When *Vsiakaia vsiachina* was not concerned with the main enemy—sedition—its satire was vague, conciliatory, and spineless, touching chiefly on the petty details of everyday life in the highest circles of society. Typical "satirical" topics were: overcrowding rooms with too much furniture, too loud voices among the women, too much drinking of coffee, tea, lemonade at costume balls, and the like.

Vsiakaia vsiachina drew a great deal of its material from foreign

3. Nikolai I. Novikov, 1744–1818, prominent publisher, satirical author, and journalist. He was a leading figure of the Masonic movement which he directed toward philanthropic and educational activities. Catherine II had him arrested and imprisoned in the Shlisselburg Fortress (1792); he was freed in 1796 by Paul I and retired to his estate near Moscow.

moralistic-satirical journalism, particularly from Addison and Steele's renowned *Spectator*, which served as a model for numerous magazines published in western Europe. A number of the articles in Catherine's magazine, purporting to describe Russian customs, turn out on closer inspection to be adaptations or translations (more or less free) from *The Spectator*. The magazine's moralism also stemmed from Addison. Its manner (and Catherine's literary manner in 1769) was based on the poetics of early Russian classicism, filtered through the government ideology. Its exposition was dry, abstract, and devoid of living, concrete colors. Its language was bureaucratic and formal. While its didacticism derived from *The Spectator*, it was not expressed in the English magazine's friendly conversational style, [which was] suffused with the sense of bourgeois virtues, but was couched in a tone of command in a doctrinaire and authoritarian style, derived from the dogma of feudal hierarchal thought.

The rebuff administered the government-sponsored magazine by Novikov and other journalists in 1769 quickly cooled Catherine's journalistic ardor, and by the end of the year she started a campaign against a number of the magazines that had been founded on her initiative or with her encouragement. Nearly all of them, including *Vsiakaia vsiachina,* ceased publication in 1769. Several articles that had been prepared for publication in *Vsiakaia vsiachina* but not yet printed appeared in 1770 in anthologies, under the title *Vsiakaia Vsiachina's Dividend*, and this marked the end of the first stage of Catherine's journalistic activities.

The year 1770 saw the publication of Catherine's *Antidote*, and in 1772 the first series of her comedies appeared in print and on the stage.

III

By the time Catherine made her entry into the field of dramaturgy, the Russian comedy had already traveled a short but creatively innovative road, which began in 1750 with Sumarokov's trenchant pamphleteering and satirical plays. Sumarokov's plays had nothing in common with the general run of drama, which portrayed the petty everyday round of life; it painted a gallery of grotesque caricatures, not held together closely by a story line. After Sumarokov's came the comedies of Kheraskov (*The Atheist,* 1761) and A. Volkov, which also showed little interest in the mores, were symbolic in form, and elaborated the techniques of Russian classicism—those of the ancient Russian theater and popular farces. At the same time, the Yelagin group became active in trying to bring the techniques of the newest comedies of morals and early sentimentalism to the Russian stage. The work of Yelagin himself and of the young Fonvizin (*Korion*), who adapted Western plays to Russian customs, developed along these lines. The same trend gave rise to the portrayal of Russian national customs on the stage. Lukin, who had close ties with Yelagin and his circle, worked in this vein. This trend's highest achievement was Fonvizin's *Brigadier,* the first play to consolidate the distinctively Russian type of comedy by realistically portraying everyday life yet closely relating to the genre tradition of Sumarokov's early plays with their very weak story line that only symbolically linked a number of grotesque scenes and caustic satirical portraits. Fonvizin's new techniques of portraying everyday life were quickly adopted by his contemporaries, including Sumarokov in his late comedies of 1768–1772.

Of the various types of comedies known to Russian literature by 1772, Catherine's plays of that year were closest to Sumarokov's early works. Their settings were symbolic, schematic, exaggerated; they had weak plots or none at all; characterization took the form of oversimplified, grotesque masquelike types. Only in one respect did Catherine utilize the experience of the Yelagin group. She learned their technique of adapting foreign plays "to our customs." Her first comedy, *Oh, the Times!* is an adaptation of Gellert's *Die Betschwester.* Catherine transferred the action to Moscow and tried to give the text local color and some of the features of contemporary Muscovite life.

In addition to this comedy, Catherine published in 1772 *Mme. Vorchalkina's Birthday*, *The Vestibule in a Noble Boyar's House*, and *Mme. Vestnikova and Her Family*. Apparently, that same year she also wrote a comedy, entitled *The Questioner*, which was incorrectly called *The Invisible Bride* when it was published in 1786 (in the collection *The Russian Theater*) and in subsequent nineteenth-century reprints. (The correct title was only restored in 1901 in the Academic edition of Catherine's works, edited by A. N. Pypin.)

Catherine's early comedies, as well as the majority of her later plays, were concerned not so much with the portrayal of characters and customs as with politics, namely, advocacy of the government's program and policy and condemnation of all who were dissatisfied with the Empress' regime. In her first comedies, Catherine directed her ridicule primarily at human shortcomings: bigotry, slander, cowardice, rudeness, even stupidity, and so forth. She wished thereby to direct contemporary satirists away from concern with acute social problems and to give them examples of peaceable moralization, intending it as a reproach to "malicious" satirists like Fonvizin and the later Sumarokov. Discarding the moral abstractions of satire for this purpose, she included a number of characters, dialogues, and scattered hints about the times that were clearly meant to support government policy.

Oh, the Times! is about ignorant old Moscow gossips, malicious, stupid, and dissatisfied with the government, who keep forecasting trouble, complain about everything under the sun, and constantly abuse the authorities for inefficiency. The bigoted Khanzhankina, for example, treats her serf-domestic very cruelly and won't permit them to get married because she is miserly and does not want to provide them with dowries. She says: "The government ought to set up an institution to dower our serfs when they get married instead of our having to do it. But to tell the truth, the state ought to see to everything. We've had enough of its not concerning itself with anything any more." Naturally, the play's ideal raisonneur, Nepustov, comes to the government's defense immediately. In another episode, Khanzhankina complains: "I don't know why the government doesn't prohibit such poor people from getting married. Nobody looks after anything now! There is nobody to do anything."

The gossip Vestnikova complains that the police are not doing their job, as a result of which "the streets are so slippery and so bad that it is impossible to drive in them," whereupon the clever servant, Mavra, explains to the audience: "We're not mentioning that the horses are not shod, the wheels have no linchpins, and the harness is of poor quality." Vestnikova generalizes: "Nobody looks after anything. Oh, what times! What will come of it all!" She spreads rumors that a flood has destroyed St. Petersburg, that people are dying of hunger there, that "there is a shortage of everything, and neither the government nor the police are thinking of anything. I know a few worse things, too. There's lots of news from there: and none of it is good. Anyhow, one shouldn't tell everything." She even hints at the expectation of serious political upheavals. Another character, the superstitious old woman Chudikhina, expresses dissatisfaction with the way girls are educated in the institute at the Smolny monastery. It is no accident that Moscow is depicted in the comedies as the center of opposition to the government and of all kinds of freethinking.

Catherine portrays her enemies as complaining old women, whereas those who defend the honor of the government are shown as intelligent, positive individuals. The subject of *Mme. Vorchalkina's Birthday* is the same, but it is presented more sharply. Vorchalkina, an old troublemaker, is in the habit of abusing and criticizing everyone and everything. Likeminded people—idlers, in Catherine's view—gather in her home. One typical member of the company is Nekopeikov, a merchant who has squandered his fortune and is now bombarding the government with ridiculous suggestions for enriching the state. He offers proposals for transportation, the fleet, rat-catching, the manufacture of ropes from rat-tails, etc. Nekopeikov, among other things, declares: "I have also discovered a way to improve the functioning of the courts and the judges," apparently agreeing with Novikov and his followers in their attacks on the clerks. He says: "What our government has come to! Everyone does as he pleases. Everyone expects to obtain judgment and punishment by means of the ancient law of muscle. It is absolutely necessary that I draft a project to avert such disorder." Other typical characters are the rude, bad-mannered noblemen Gerkulov and the vain aristocrat Spesov, who spreads stupid gossip about the government's plans. This company is critical of the actions of the police, of the opening of a home for foundlings, of taxes. Vorchalkina says, "The Treasury robs us all the time. I don't want to have anything to do with it."

In giving such an unattractive picture of all these people "who want to remake the whole world," Catherine was not only ridiculing people dissatisfied with her rule, but was also asserting that they were all fools, chatterboxes, and scoundrels, that in reality her police were good, the judicial system and the judges did not require "improvement," and that all was well in the country. Through the lips of another intelligent servant girl, Praskovia, Catherine tells the dreamer Nekopeikov: "We would be in a very sad plight indeed, and very unfortunate, too, if the general welfare depended on your brainless head, which couldn't even manage to carry on a proper trade in a market row."

This was intended for the edification of subjects who ventured to poke their noses into politics and affairs of state. The same topics surface in the plays *Mme. Vestnikova and Her Family* and *The Vestibule in a Noble Boyar's House*. The latter is a one-act play without any plot whatever, depicting a crowd of petitioners at the door of an all-powerful favorite. They have all come to him with allegedly very important matters. On closer inspection, however, it turns out that all the petitioners are parasites or knaves, who are only wasting the powerful favorite's time with their complaints and proposals. The audience sees a poor woman who has come to the capital to ask for assistance. Don't believe what you see, Catherine explains. She is hiding the fact that she owns a small village that feeds her and, besides, she drinks. The other petitioners are no better. Yet they dare to judge and to censure the government, to condemn the war with Turkey, to criticize the military leadership. The conclusion to be drawn is that the complaints that the government is not paying attention to the needs of its citizens have no basis in fact. On the contrary, Catherine finds that the complainers and the petitioners are very suspicious characters. One of the petitioners in the nobleman's vestibule is of special interest. He is a Frenchman, named Oranbar. He, too, is a project maker, and he has come from France to teach the Russian government what to do. Oranbar has a very high opinion of himself and a very low opinion of the actions of the Russian authorities. "I have brought a pocketful of good with me. There is no good without me. The whole world is stupid. I alone know everything," he says. Oranbar is easily recognizable as the French Enlightener, economist, and statesman Mercier de la Rivière, who came to Russia in 1765 at Catherine's invitation, hoping that the Empress-philosopher would give him the opportunity to carry out broad reforms in her country. Nothing came of his plans, however. Catherine saw him once and sent him home. In defending her action, Catherine had no scruples about heaping ridicule on the enlightened and learned man.

Between 1772 and 1785 there was an interval in Catherine's output of comedies. During that period she was absorbed in her "legislomania," a passion for drafting laws. But in the early 1780's she turned to writing historical, journalistic, and pedagogical works. Her major work of that period was *Notes on Russian History*, an extensive and clumsy compilation of excerpts from chronicles, of no value whatever either as scholarship or as literature. These *Notes* did not avoid politics. They glorified the autocracy as a force that always and inevitably saved the Russian state and as the only possible form of government for Russia. They were published in serial form in *Conversations for Admirers of Russian Literature,* a monthly magazine published in 1783 and 1784 by the Russian Academy under the editorship of Princess E. R. Dashkov but carefully watched over by Catherine herself. There is reason to believe that the *Notes,* which filled a sizable portion of each issue, were one of the main reasons for the establishment of the magazine in the first place.

In 1783 a series of feuilletons by Catherine, entitled "Facts and Fictions," appeared in the issues of *Conversations.* They were held together by the same characters and the same imaginary author—a wit, jester, and acute observer. "Facts and Fictions" is the least successful of all Catherine's writings and did not achieve its purpose. Though Catherine tried hard to be witty, the writing is obtuse, flat, and gloomily boring; the style is very poor, and the author's self-praise for profundity and stylistic elegance in the complete absence of both is extremely depressing.

Incidentally, "Facts and Fictions" tried to reflect the newest trend in European literature. It imitated Sterne's *Tristram Shandy,* with its casual chatter about this and that, its intimate, homey conversational tone, inconsistency in movement of themes and thoughts. But the profound ideological content of Sterne's writing was alien to Catherine, whose work did not express the cult of the free individual, but the monstrous arbitrariness of a despot, and is not concerned with the intimate life of the common man, but with court gossip. "Facts and Fictions" is a graphic illustration of the adaptation of so progressive an aesthetic phenomenon as Sterne's work to the objectives and tastes of the conservative groups that supported the serf-based autocracy.

The majority of the Empress' feuilletons reiterated the motifs of her other writings: abstract moralization and venomous attacks on malcontents and persons who thought differently from her. Catherine again castigated the satirists, such as Novikov, who, in her opinion, were angry at the whole world. She portrayed a "strange man, whose personality inclines him to be angry in circumstances that would cause other people to be filled with pity and compassion." Furthermore, she added significantly, this man should not be sought "among the living." To someone's alleged request that she "portray a tattler and bribe-taker," Catherine replied that she was "excluding everything vile and revolting from

'Facts and Fictions', everything that was not in a smiling vein."
She assailed a person who "continues to complain of the unfair-
ness of the governors [*voyevoda*] and their staffs, though they no
longer exist any more" and who is dissatisfied with other things
that have been eliminated by the concerned government. The
"mentality" of such a person is "backward," Catherine declared,
"and he does not realize how incongruous this is" because he is
obstinate in his complaining.

Through another positive character in her feuilletons, the imaginary author's grandfather, Catherine defends and praises her rule,
argues that this is a time of freedom, that "all the existing shortcomings have no significance now" because they are only the manifestation of society's rapid progress and that it is a good sign of
the "general mood" that citizens so frequently appeal to the arbitra-
tion of courts in equity that Catherine has established rather than
to ordinary courts. In fact, the courts in equity played no serious
role at all.

Actually, Catherine's world outlook was expressed not in favorable pictures, such as the above, but by her portrayal of the great
majority of people as "half-witted," frivolous, and obstinate crea-
tures. Unlike the progressive sentimentalists, who affirmed the
cult of man, Catherine had nothing but contempt for men, who,
she felt, had to be treated as children or lunatics. . . .

Earlier, before the appearance of *Conversations,* Catherine wrote
a series of pedagogical works. They included instructions for the
upbringing of her grandsons, Alexander and Constantine, based
on pedagogical theories that were progressive for those times;
Elementary Civic Education; Selected Russian Proverbs; and two
stories for children.

Elementary Civic Education was a pamphlet, containing over
200 maxims, sayings, and homilies, purporting to provide a child
with basic information on morality, life, and the world. Besides
giving the names of the months, days of the week, the seasons,
etc., it contained such gems as: "Virtue is its own reward" and
"There is nothing perfect in the world."

Selected Russian Proverbs had nothing in common with folk-lore but consisted of sayings Catherine made up herself, such as: "Ever new, rarely right," "People should not quarrel," "Money can accomplish a great deal, but truth wins out," and the like. The outward trappings of popular proverbs could not conceal the work's artificiality and bias, nor did the inclusion of a few genuine folk sayings alter the picture.

The two stories for children—"The Story of Crown Prince Fevei" and "The Story of Crown Prince Khlor"—are noteworthy if only because they were the first works written specially for children ever published in Russia. In these, too, Catherine took into account and utilized the experience of advanced literary theory of the period, but again, she used it in her own way. Written in allegorical fairy-tale form, the stories were intended for her young grandsons and therefore their moral admonitions were primarily addressed to princes. Thus Catherine took the new theory from the West that contended that a special psychological approach is needed for children and that literature for children must have its own content and style, but she not only narrowed the scope of this theory, she also gave it a specifically court character since its ideas on education and aesthetics were applicable chiefly to children of royalty. The story about Fevei describes a model offspring of the royal family, a prince endowed with all the virtues that in the role are attributed to Catherine's own grandsons. The story about Khlor tells how an ideal prince searches for a rose without thorns —i.e., virtue—with the help of Reason, Honesty, and Truth, resisting all the temptations he encounters, and how he is helped by the princess Felicia. The characters of this story have gone down in Russian literature for all time because Derzhavin used them in his celebrated "Ode to Felicia."

IV

Catherine began to write plays again in 1785. In the following four years she wrote, or began to write, about twenty plays, not counting her French playlets—"proverbs." Her writing for the theater during this period was extremely varied in genre, sources of influence, and stylistic exploration.

By 1785 the Russian comedy, as well as Russian drama in general, had long since emerged from infancy and embarked on its own distinctively Russian path. The Russian theater had produced many plays by many playwrights. Numerous ideological and artistic trends had found embodiment in a variety of theaters and dramaturgical systems. The comic opera with its more or less democratic subject matter and mood had won an honored place. Psychological analysis and "descriptions of the ways" of ordinary people in Russian society had found expression in early Russian sentimentalism. The classical division into tragedy and comedy had been replaced by a middle genre: the drama of fictionalized adventure or of mores that tended to depict everyday life with a certain measure of realism. Incisive political subject matter and serious criticism of serfdom had made their way onto the stage. All the progressive explorations of Russian dramaturgy were epitomized in the immortal *Nedorosl'* [*The Minor*], a play that opened the way to a development of the Russian national theater which led to Gogol.

Catherine assimilated the lessons of the turbulent development of Russian drama in the 1770's. She mastered the technique of dramatic construction that Russian playwrights had evolved and she responded to Western trends in the theater. But she wrote her apologist and reactionary writing in opposition to the progressive critical trend of the finest Russian dramatists of the time—Fonvizin, Kniazhnin, Nikolev, and others.

The comedy continued to interest Catherine, and even when she turned to the new dramaturgical forms she retained her earlier style and even subject matter. In 1787, for example, she started two plays, never completed, which, like her comedies of 1772, dealt with "gossips," "rumors," "fabrications," spread by persons who were dissatisfied with her rule. These plays were *The Liar* and *The Woman Is Delirious, Does the Devil Believe Her,* subtitled *Tales* (the second play is a variation of the first). Catherine also used her earlier style in three anti-Masonic comedies she wrote; she attached great political importance to them and publicized these plays energetically, not only in Russia, but abroad. The plays were entitled *The Deceiver* (1785), *Tempted* (1785), and *The Siberian Shaman* (1786), and depicted Freemasons as swindlers, deliberately linking them with international adventurers such as Cagliostro. The Freemasons are portrayed either as scoundrels who take advantage of the gullibility of wealthy fools, or wealthy fools under the influence of the mystical ravings of scoundrels. The anti-Masonic plays are malicious and aggressive. Catherine regarded Freemasonry —not without reason—as a force dangerous to her personally and to her regime; and before taking police action against it, she wanted to prepare public opinion with the help of comedies and, perhaps, win over some of the Masons, or at least frighten them.

The other comedies Catherine wrote between 1785 and 1788 were not sharply political. Most were comedies of intrigue and "harmless" jests and constituted an attempt by Catherine to bring the nonpolitical, "smiling" comedy to the Russian stage in opposition to the satirical and "engagé" dramas of a Fonvizin or a Kniazhnin. Catherine mastered the technique of linking the material by means of a plot. She based her plots on misunderstandings and errors and strove (in vain) to write lively, acute, realistic dialogue in the French manner, imitating writers like Marivaux or Beaumarchais. In these mostly domestic plays the Empress stood for good morals, partly under the influence of Western bourgeois-sentimental literature, but even more so because she wanted to uphold all traditional patriarchalism. They contained some very moderate "satire," directed against inoffensive "foibles." The sharpest satire to be found in this group of plays is in *A Family Broken Up by Intrigue and Suspicion* (1787) and is directed against gossip, but the satire is entirely of an abstract moralistic nature. Another comedy in this group was entitled *The Misunderstanding* (1788).

Catherine sought to portray psychological details, to analyze the intimate experiences of the soul which she combines with an attempt at depicting mores and everyday life on the stage. In this she revealed the influence of sentimentalist drama, not only of Marivaux and La Chaussée, but of Diderot, Mercier, and Beaumarchais. It is also obvious that she was trying to defeat Fonvizin with his own weapons. *What Kind of Jokes Are These?* (not published until 1901) and *An Unexpected Adventure* are examples of her attempts at psychological portrayal. The latter is adapted, if not actually translated "with application to our customs," from the French.

Along with psychological analysis in the sentimental vein, Catherine also began to introduce lyrical tension and external "romanticism" à la Kotzebue into her plays. One play was about a melancholy widow and her secret lover, flitting about among the trees in a red cape and broad-brimmed hat that concealed his face. The settings were of a new type, too—the wing of a house, situated in a garden or orchard, an open window with a heroine in it. *Thinking One Way and Acting Another,* a play she wrote in 1785 and containing all these elements, is an attempt to imitate Fonvizin by drawing an exaggerated picture of the life of a provincial landowner.

Needless to say, not only the absence of talent, but also inner emptiness and ideological obtuseness made her plays artistically as well as ideologically weak. They are poorly organized, poorly written, and confused. The characterization is dull and the protagonists inexpressive. Though Catherine's plays of those years are more skillfully constructed than her plays of 1772, they appear pretty wretched against the background of the improved techniques and greater depth of Russian drama in the 1780's. Russian drama was developing much more rapidly and vigorously than the Empress' literary style, try as she might to keep up with the aesthetic level of the time.

It was in the attempt to keep up with the newest artistic developments, the interest in pre-romanticism, that Catherine turned to Shakespeare and even to Calderón, who was already highly appreciated by the young writers of Europe. But whereas Herder, Radishchev, and even the young Karamzin regarded Shakespeare as a special world to be discovered and assimilated, Catherine was interested in Shakespeare, first, as a fashionable name, second, as a source of subject matter, and third, as justification for rejection of the three unities, long since done, incidentally, without reference to Shakespeare, in opera and drama in the West as well as in Russia (see Kheraskov's plays of the 1770's).

In 1786 Catherine published and produced a play which she entitled: *A Free but Slight Adaptation from Shakespeare, the Comedy: This Is the Kind of Laundry and Laundry Basket to Have.* It was an adaptation of *The Merry Wives of Windsor.* Shakespeare has disappeared from it entirely. Not only was the action transferred to St. Petersburg, but it was ironed out and smoothed over in every possible way. The play was reduced to a didactic story of retribution overtaking a conceited Don Juan—Yakov Vlasevich Polkladov, the traditional fop of eighteenth-century Russian comedy, into whom Falstaff had been transformed. Except for the masquerade scene in the fifth act with witches and sorcerers, Catherine's play was more like a comedy by Sumarokov rather than anything by Shakespeare.

In much the same way Catherine adapted *Timon of Athens.* She called it: *The Wastrel, a Comedy, a Free Adaptation from Shakespeare* (1786). (The play has not survived in its entirety, or it may not have been completed.) Catherine turned it into a didactic play, admonishing Russian nobles (its hero is a Russian nobleman, named Tratov) not to spend too much money, especially not to dispense charity too lightly. The philosophical content of Shakespeare's work has vanished from it completely. Actually, it imitated Destouches' *The Wastrel* rather than Shakespeare.

Only insignificant excerpts of a "free adaptation" by Catherine of one of Calderón's comedies have come down to us. In this instance, too, the fact that Catherine found Calderón worth adapting is of more interest and of greater historical significance than anything she may have derived from that dramatist.

Catherine invoked Shakespeare's name in connection with her "historical representations," or "chronicles of ancient Russian history." These plays did not respect the three unities and other rules of classicism, an approach that Catherine presented as her own innovation. They did not have a single theme either; they were a mixed genre, resembled faeries with music, choruses, ballet, and processions, and were intended for lavish stage productions and the sumptuousness of theater festivals at court. At the same time they had a strong political intent, glorifying the Russian autocracy.

The first chronicle—*An Imitation of Shakespeare, a Historical Spectacle Without Observance of the Usual Theatrical Rules, from the Life of Rurik* (1786)—lauded the wisdom of the ancient Russian autocrat who, according to the play, had a legitimate right to the crown because he was the grandson of Gostomysl, prince of Novgorod. The action is based on the legend of Vadim and his rebellion, a legend which subsequently inspired a number of freedom-loving works of Russian literature (by Kniazhnin, Ryleev, Pushkin, Lermontov). Catherine made Vadim a prince, too, a cousin of Rurik. According to her version, Vadim was not a republican at all, not an ideological adversary of Rurik, but merely an ambitious man who organized a conspiracy in order to usurp his cousin's power. In so doing, he took malicious advantage of the Russian people's traditional and unthinking obedience to their princes. Rurik defeats Vadim and offers him a position as his assistant. Vadim repents and is eager to atone for his guilt and prove his loyalty to his sovereign. The play's crudely reactionary message is made even more apparent by its complete absence of literary merit.

The second chronicle was entitled: *The Beginning of Oleg's Rule: An Imitation of Shakespeare Without Observance of the Usual Theatrical Rules* (1786) and is along the same ideological lines. The third play, not completed, is called *Igor* (1786) and turned out a lyrical drama. It is the story of a Bulgarian princess and her fiancé, separated by the wars and reunited through the generosity and kindness of the Russian Prince Igor.

In 1786 Catherine began work on a series of comic operas in which she tried to utilize folklore. This was a response to the pre-romantic trend that had reached Russian literature by then. In keeping with the spirit of this trend, her operas took the form of theatrical fairy tales, with fantastic and grotesque elements, and had pretensions to imagination and colorful, inventive variety. They do not contain any genuine folklore. They do contain a political message, which comes through the jesting very clearly. For example, the opera *Fevei* (1786), which is based on a fairy story Catherine wrote herself, advises Pavel Petrovich [grand Duke Paul] to obey his mother and not to try to escape from her domination or to travel abroad. In other words, this opera was a tactical move on Catherine's part in her struggle with her son. The opera *Bogatyr Boeslavich of Novgorod* (1786), referring to Vasilii Buslaevich, gives its own interpretation of the well-known epic. It depicts Vasilii, prince of Novgorod, as using force to teach the impudent people of Novgorod a lesson when they dare to disobey him and refuse to submit to him slavishly. Vasilii compels them to bow obsequiously to what is presented as the redeeming harshness of the autocracy. An opera about the ill-starred bogatyr Kosometovich, also based on a fairy tale by Catherine (1789), was a satire directed against the Swedish king Gustav III, who launched an unsuccessful war against Russia. It may also have been directed against Pavel Petrovich, who tried to join in the military operations against the Swedes but whom his mother quickly removed, fearing he would gain influence in the army.

The opera *The Brave and Bold Knight Akhrideich* (*Crown Prince Ivan*) (1786) and the comic opera *Fedul and His Children* (1790) are more "innocent." A large number of arias and choruses, many taken from poems by Trediakovsky, Lomonosov, and Sumarokov, some composed by the Empress' secretary, A. V. Khrapovitsky, and some assembled by Khrapovitsky from folk songs, were inserted into the text of Catherine's operas and historical dramas. *Fedul and His Children,* which consists entirely of poems by other poets and required hardly any work on Catherine's part, was her last work for the stage, in fact, her last literary effort altogether. Hard times had come for the monarchs of Europe. The French Revolution had shaken thrones. Catherine finally perceived the futility of her hope that her subjects would obediently follow the moral and political precepts she offered them in palace-written feuilletons, comedies, and operas. She gave up her writing, in which she was always more a monarch lecturing her subjects than a genuinely creative artist.

PART TWO

The Autocrat and Russian Educated Society

PAVEL N. MILIUKOV

Educational Reforms

ARLY IN HER REIGN Catherine, . . . fascinated by the
pedagogical ideas of Enlightenment literature, gave herself
over to a more expansive thought—radically changing the very
mission of the public school. The school up to then had only
taught; the new school had to *nurture*. To use Betsky's[1] words,

---

From Pavel N. Miliukov, *Ocherki po istorii russkoi kul'tury* (Paris:
Sovremennye Zapiski, 1931), II, Part 2, 750–765. Used by permission of the
Executor of the Estate of Professor Pavel N. Miliukov. Translated by Norman K. Sloan.
1. Ivan I. Betskoi (or Betsky), 1704–1795, president of the Academy of
Fine Arts (1763–1794), was the principal aide of Catherine II in educational matters and chief architect of the reform of the Corps of Cadets and

93

Catherine's "main intention" at that time "leaned toward not so much having sciences and the arts spread among the people as implanting gentle manners in their hearts." Thus, for the first time, school in Russia took upon itself the tasks of upbringing that up until then had belonged exclusively to the family. With this transfer of upbringing from the family to the school, a complete change of its techniques and goals was to be effected. The Old Russian family reared its members according to a definite stereotype that had evolved through the ages. At its basis lay the prescriptions of religion. Some vacillation could be noted, however, in the selection of religious principles of child-rearing in Old Rus'.[2] Religion afforded two types of child-rearing to choose from: the stern Biblical and the loving New Testament. . . . In *theory,* pre-Petrine Rus' sometimes preached the second type, but in practice it almost always abided by the first. . . . The principles of the Old Testament upbringing "do not spare the staff, maul the ribs, neither play nor laugh with children," and so forth. To replace this Old Testament pedagogical ideal there came from Catherine II a new one, not an evangelical, but a humanitarian one. In many of its effects it coincided with the New Testament ideal, but its point of departure was altogether different. Originating in the Europe of the Renaissance era, the humanitarian ideal proceeded from a respect for the rights and liberties of the individual; it eliminated from pedagogy everything that smacked of coercion or compulsion. This ideal, bowing down before nature and genuineness, limited the tasks of child-rearing to the observation and care of all the unique, original proclivities of each child. But within these limits, the new pedagogy acknowledged itself to be omnipotent. Not believing in children's inborn qualities, having little faith in heredity at all, the humanitarian ideal nevertheless did not regard a human being as a clean slate on which it was possible to write whatever

---

the establishment of the Smol'nyi Institute for Girls, the Orphanage in Moscow, and of several schools for commoners.

2. Rus' is the old and now technical term to denote the territory and political organization of medieval Russia.

one pleased; but instead it was quick to compare the child's spirit to soft clay, from which it was possible to fashion the most varied forms. The material for upbringing was recognized as already given; but in the hands of an experienced pedagogue, this material was to receive the correct shape.

The basic works of the adherents of the new child-rearing were not unknown in eighteenth-century Russia. Amos Komensky's *The Golden Door of Languages* had been used back at the beginning of the century in private boarding schools. Fonvizin, as is known, placed Fénelon's *L'éducation des filles* in the hands of Sophie. Finally, Locke's *Thoughts on Education* had become available in a Russian translation in two editions in the eighteenth century. The Empress extracted from them whole pages for her instruction (to Saltykov) on the education of her grandsons.

Following the pedagogues and philosophers of the West, Catherine dreamed of re-creating mankind through child-rearing, of creating a "new race of men." Feofan Prokopovich had pointed out the means to this end in the "Spiritual Regulation";[3] Catherine and Betsky bore a very close resemblance to him. Child-rearing was to be conducted in a closed school—such was a necessary condition for the creation of the new race of men. The children had to be isolated from all influences of surrounding society and given over wholly into the hands of the pedagogue. For this it was necessary, first of all, to place the child in an educational institution as early as possible: "No older than ten, for children of that age have not yet learned vices." Further, the child's relations with his family had to be broken off, as much as possible. Vacations at home could be permitted only for the shortest possible period, and meetings with parents in the school had to proceed in the presence of witnesses. All these techniques of Feofan were adopted by Catherine. And by the very same token, children, by her theory, were not considered wicked by nature, but their "vices" were explained

3. *Dukhovnyi reglament,* January 25, 1721, the statute which set forth the institutional organization and intellectual orientation imposed on the Church by Peter the Great.

as the consequence of bad life-experience. But, in order to remove the future generation still more fundamentally from this experience, the age for acceptance into the closed institution was lowered to four or five, and contact with the outside world, with the family, was made even more difficult. The wards were not permitted at all (or only on holidays) to have leave from school; the same situation prevailed for meetings at the school, with witnesses.

Following this design, the Empress began to reshape the existing educational institutions. Divisions for younger children of four and five were opened in the academic *gimnaziia,* just as in the noble infantry cadet corps. Parents who committed their children to the school had to take an oath that they would not demand them back. But the matter could not be confined to a reform of male institutions. Catherine's aim was to "bring about a new breed, from which the straightforward rules of upbringing could pass uninterruptedly to posterity." In other words, she wanted to create, by means of the school, a new family. Thus it was necessary to be concerned with feminine education as well. Up until then, aside from the family and a few convents, only private boarding schools, predominantly run by foreigners, had been engaged in the rearing of girls in Russia. Catherine could not leave the matter of feminine education in their hands, and she had to create Russia's first public school for women for the fulfillment of her fondest dream. Simultaneously with the formation of little children's divisions in the male schools, a closed feminine institution was set up at the Smolny Convent—at first only for the nobility, but later for middle-class girls as well. In drawing up the curriculum for the girls' school, the Empress and her aides predicated it on the belief that no distinction needed to be made with regard to general education between boys and girls. Later on, this idea, unusual for the society of that time, was abandoned; during Catherine's reign a government commission did still determine that "the intent and goal of the rearing of girls consist most of all in making [them] good homemakers, faithful wives, and caring mothers." This goal began to be pursued even more definitely when the wife of the

Emperor Paul, the Empress Maria Feodorovna, became the head of feminine education. But in those first days of the institution of the girls' school, the task of that school was put differently, and more broadly; the more expansive formulation corresponded better with the personal views of the Empress, which in this regard were unlike the tastes of her daughter-in-law. . . . The independent development of the intellect through serious reading and reflection, the working out of one's own view of life, and the preparation for an active role in life—these tasks took the forefront for Catherine. "He does not yet exist," the general plan of the Moscow child-rearing home stated, "who has lapsed so far from sane reasoning that the blessedness of the human race is imperceptible to him and he does not wish for all girls not only to be taught to read and write but also to have a mind enlightened by varied knowledge useful for civic life."

In order to put Catherine's wide-ranging enterprise into effect, too many favorable conditions were necessary, and most necessary of all were suitable educators. "If such teachers are found," Betsky surmised, regarding the reform of the noble cadet [4] corps, "then success cannot be in doubt; *if it happens, through some misfortune, that we do not acquire such people, in vain will be all the prescriptions and all the strivings* for producing good manners and success." Indeed, where such an individual was found—at the Smolny, under the directorship of Madame Lafont—at least part of the Empress' design was carried out. True, educational matters at the Smolny were relegated to the background (as Catherine's theory of pedagogy required, incidentally); the foreground was taken up by the acquisition of worldliness and ease in company. "Should some girl," the charter itself said, "make some witty remark, then, having permission, she must inform the whole class

4. Corps of Cadets, established in 1732, as an educational institution exclusively for children of the nobility. By attending the Corps, young nobles received not only a general secondary education and some smattering of military science, but also a head start on their service career, since upon graduation they were directly promoted to officer rank without having to serve as soldiers or sailors.

about it, for the original and aptly spoken *mot* will be a command
and an encouragement for the others to emulate it." As a means
for acquiring confidence in conversation, there was use of amateur
shows, concerts, and socials, to which full-fledged beaux from the
noble cadet corps were invited. Judging from the diary of one of
them, the conversations among the young people at those soirées
sometimes took a turn probably not anticipated in the charter.
Whatever the case might have been, one cannot agree with Prince
Shcherbatov's protest that the Smolny turned out "neither scholars
nor well-mannered ladies, any more than nature made them so,
and their upbringing consisted more in playing comedy than in
improving their hearts, morals, and good sense." It is probable
that the Smolny girls' ignorance of life and their impracticality,
which have become proverbial, distinguished them even then.
But we possess a whole series of reports by contemporaries showing that many of the Smolny girls brought with them into that
unknown, to them, and often quite uncouth life a high moral
complexion and lively intellectual interests. The educated woman
appeared for the first time in the Russian family, thanks to Catherine, and introduced into that last refuge of ancestral prejudices
a gush of fresh air and light.

In any case, almost all successes in rearing the "new race of
men" were confined to the Smolny. It was no problem near the
court, under the very eyes of the Empress, to achieve something.
Something was done also in the noble cadet corps, of which
Betsky was made director at the time of the establishment of the
Smolny (1765). The new director's aim was to make the cadets not
"tested officers" but "knowledgeable citizens," and contemporaries
noted that, starting with Betsky, the corps turned out men with
not a military but an encyclopedic education. According to the
remark of one unkind observer, "They played comedy well and
wrote verse, in brief, knew everything but what an officer needs to
know." And Catherine herself boasted about this directly. "They
are wrong to think," she wrote, "that my cadets are being prepared

solely for war. . . . My cadets are being made into everything they wish to be, and will choose their careers according to their own tastes and inclinations."

The situation of the small children's division at the academic *gimnaziia* corresponded least of all to the Empress' intentions. Seminary morals had taken root too strongly here among the holders of state scholarships so that some dozens of pupils transferred to the *gimnaziia* upon finishing the small children's division could not raise the moral level of the students. Besides, if we add all those "mesdames" and "mesdemoiselles" [5] who were constantly being hired into and fired from the young children's division, we will have full grounds for doubting that a new race of people could issue forth from the care of such governesses.

Catherine, fascinated by Enlightenment theories and disposed toward enthusiasm, could dream in the 1760's of creating that new race. In the 1780's, cooled by life's ordeals and disillusioned, Catherine realized that the means she had at hand were not sufficient to carry out this grandiose design. If the results attained right before her eyes, under the most meticulous supervision, were not exactly those she had envisaged, what then could be expected of the dissemination of these attempts through all of Russia? Thus, what appeared to Catherine in the 1760's to be the beginning of a great social revolution had shrunk by the 1780's down to its true size—scattered and feeble individual attempts. Naturally, the Empress little by little cooled to the idea of rearing a new race and even had to look upon the Smolny, so close to her heart, with new eyes. She had no qualms about intervening in the Smolny and removing Betsky from the directorship of the corps, the moment the commission of the 1780's had discerned the low level of instruction in both institutions. The goals of upbringing from then on ceased to be Catherine's task; for her, questions of teaching again came to the forefront. But her pedagogical infatuations had left her with a firm conviction that the school must be general-

5. I.e., foreign tutors and governesses.

educational in nature and that instruction had to pursue pedagogical, not professional, goals. She would now strive to create such a school and to spread it through all of Russia.

New faces appeared to take up the new task. The main one belonged to one Jankovic de Mirjevo, a Serb, whose name deserves to be far better known to educated Russians than it is to this day. In the second half of the eighteenth century, the Prussian school was considered the model of general-education schools. The Austrian schools (1774) were reformed according to the Prussian model under the guidance of the organizer of the Prussian schools himself, Fellbieger, whom Maria Theresa had requested from Frederick II for the purpose. The Serb Jankovic, who had studied juridical and economic sciences at Vienna University, had organized schools by the Fellbieger method in one of the districts of Hungary. At Catherine II's inquiry, Joseph II recommended Jankovic to her "as a man who has already worked at the organization of public schools, who knows the Russian language, and who professes Orthodoxy." Called to Russia, Jankovic made himself the true author of the first Russian general-education school, compared to which everything before had been only haphazard attempts. The plan he worked out (according to Fellbieger and Hehn) was adopted by the "Commission on the Establishment of Public Schools," established in 1782, and was made the basis for the "Statute of Public Schools," which the Empress ratified on August 5, 1786. According to Jankovic's plan, three types of general-education schools were to be instituted: a two-grade, a three-grade, and a four-grade. The school of the first type bore the name of *lower*; the second of *middle*; and the third, of *main*. These schools were very little concerned with the teaching of the Russian nobility's favorite subjects—foreign languages and dancing. They taught the principal general-education subjects, dividing them by grades into concentric circles, so that the program of each grade was an integrated unit. In the first grade of the lower school, reading, writing, the numbers, a brief catechism, church history, and the elements of Russian grammar were given. In the second grade there was a somewhat more detailed catechism, but without texts, along with arithmetic, the book *On the Duties of a Human Being and a Citizen,* penmanship, and drawing. The middle school comprised the same two grades but added to them a third, in which were taught the catechism with texts, explanation of the Gospels, Russian grammar with spelling exercises, general and Russian history, and a brief geography of Russia.[6] Finally, in the main public school, a fourth grade was annexed to the other three; in it, geography and history were taught in more detail [7] as well as mathematical geography, grammar with exercises in compositions of a primarily utilitarian nature (letters, invoices, catalogues, and the like), the principles of geometry, mechanics, physics, natural history, and civil architecture. The chief feature distinguishing the new school from what preceded it, however, was supposed to be not so much the curriculum as the technique for putting it into effect. Under the Austrian system, the teacher was present in the classroom not to assign lessons and hear recitations but for mastering the subjects being taught. For this, the teacher was to concern himself primarily with the entire class, not with the individual pupils. In earlier times, each pupil studied by himself: some jumped ahead and others lagged behind, so that no activity could be done in common in the classroom.[8] It was considered to be the ideal situation in the classroom when each one repeated his part of the subject aloud, and the teacher, confident that all the pupils were engaged in the work at hand, could also busy himself with his own affairs. Now this noise had to be replaced by silence and general attention to what the teacher was saying. A blackboard appeared in the class-

6. In the higher type of school, arithmetic did not end in the second grade but was carried over into the third as well. [Author's Note]

7. In the final establishment of the schools, the third type followed directly after the first type of "lower school"; hence geography and history were taught not as concentric circles but were divided outright between the third and fourth grades. [Author's Note]

8. For example, in the Ryazan arithmetic school in 1727, eleven pupils in an arithmetic class learned counting, five addition, one subtraction, three multiplication, five division, three the rule of three, one decimals, one circular geometry, and one plane trigonometry and tangents. [Author's Note]

room, and on it the teacher wrote what had to be learned so that everyone could see. Explanation and talk by the teacher were still not required in this school; at least, they did not constitute the main part of the instruction. The pupil was not yet used to studying outside of school, hence the school had to concern itself not only with explanation but with the learning of the lesson itself. Special techniques were recommended for this: the teacher read aloud from the textbook, the pupils read the same thing one after another after him, and then all in chorus; then the teacher wrote the first letters of each phrase on the board that were to be committed to memory, and had the class repeat the phrase by memory; finally, the letters were erased, and the same phrases were repeated by memory. True, in some cases Jankovic required the teacher to use his own words; where possible, he recommended resorting to visual aids; where possible, it was recommended that independent mental work be called for from the pupils in the higher grades. But the basis of teaching nonetheless remained the textbook and its mastering—literally, insofar as was possible—by the whole grade in the course of a lesson. Jankovic's school did not set itself the task of upbringing in the strictest sense, but the teacher's relations with the children were supposed to be based on new pedagogical ideas. Punishment, especially corporal, was unconditionally expelled from the school. Persuasion, admonition, warnings, threats, deprivation of pleasures, and shaming were deemed sufficient for maintaining discipline. This gradation, taken over directly from the Austrian *Methodenbuch* (as were other rules for teachers), was consistent with the essence of Catherine's instructions.

In order to put the Austrian system into operation, it was necessary first to create the proper textbooks and second to prepare teachers familiar with the new method of instruction. Both actions were insistently recommended to Catherine by all the advisers she approached on the subject of the contemplated reform. She had received the Austrian textbooks in 1780 from Joseph II himself; Jankovic was called upon to translate them and personally to guide the future teachers. By 1786, twenty-seven guidebooks and textbooks had already been prepared and printed, the majority translated or adapted from the Austrian textbooks by Jankovic himself. The contents of these textbooks corresponded to their intent —to be learned by heart. Jankovic gave the pupils in geography and history a single representative assortment of facts; for natural history, geometry, and physics (mechanics), the practical, applied aspect was moved to the forefront, and the theoretical explanations and proofs were left aside. Obviously, the school was to serve the mastering of knowledge and not the development of thinking— and herein lay its connection with earlier times.

Measures for the preparation of future teachers were undertaken no less vigorously. As many as 100 alumni of ecclesiastical seminaries and the Moscow [Theological] Academy were summoned to St. Petersburg for the purpose: a main public school was opened in St. Petersburg (1783) to train them in the method of instruction. A teachers' seminary was separated from the main training school in 1786 and continued in existence until 1801, in that interval turning out 425 teachers. The first contingent was ready by the middle of 1786; it included up to 100 alumni, of whom half were considered fit to fill teaching positions in the two upper grades and the rest in the two lower. Thus, reckoning one teacher for each of the four grades, the "Commission of Public Schools" had a supply of teachers for 26 main schools. It was ordered to open this number in time for the Empress' coronation day (September 22) in 26 provincial capitals of Russia. After the next graduation, a decree of November 3, 1788, called for the opening of "main public schools" in the remaining fourteen provinces. Of the other types designed by Jankovic, the government settled on the two-grade lower school. It was proposed to open such schools in the *uezd* (district) centers as soon as the provincial main training schools had prepared teachers for them.

Let us now see how the system of Jankovic de Mirjevo was put into practice. It must be noted first of all that the decrees on the opening of the main training schools did not create any new resources for maintaining the new educational institutions; the schools had to be supported with the funds of "Boards of Public Welfare." The boards could not refuse to make this expenditure, but they tried to do whatever was possible to cut these expenditures to the minimum. Sometimes they managed to save as much as half the estimated expenses out of teachers' salaries and to the detriment of school equipment. The material aspect of the affair was managed in one way or another. Teachers and textbooks were sent from St. Petersburg. All that remained was to find pupils, and as quickly as possible, because the main schools mandatorily had to be opened by coronation day. Since there turned out to be too few volunteers for schooling, the local authorities resorted to methods already known to us. The governor in Tambov, the poet Derzhavin, enrolled children in school by force, using the police. The vicegerent of Vyatka also signed up pupils for the public school "by the power of his authority"; in order to fill up the new school, he ordered all the old ones closed. Thus, all the local pedagogues were deprived of their earnings—the retired clerk Glukhikh, the burgher Lanskikh, the deacon Lupov, and the soldier's wife Vasilyeva—and still only 43 pupils were collected for the main school. In St. Petersburg, too, all the Russian boarding schools were closed with the establishment of the public schools, and in that way 159 extra pupils were mustered. That is probably how matters proceeded in the other provincial capitals as well. Needless to say, the nobles could not be handled in such a way; and there turned out to be very few nobles in the enrollments of the public schools. In St. Petersburg province, there were only 670 children of the nobility out of 4,136 students in 1801, or 16 percent; in Novgorod, there were only 67 nobles out of 507 students, or 13 percent. A vast majority of the pupils were the children of merchants, townsmen, and soldiers. Their parents had predestined them for continuation of their own occupations or for careers in government offices; in both cases, it sufficed for them to complete only the lower grades of the public school. The inspector Kozodavlev, sent by the "commission" in 1789, was obliged to state that the program of the "main schools" everywhere was exceeding the requirements of the population. "In all the main schools," he wrote, "I found that the number of students in the third and fourth grades was quite low and that the students in the second grade usually do not wish to continue studying in the third. This stems from the fact that the parents of the students do not see the purpose of studies taught in the higher grades. They consider that their children need only the subjects of the two lower grades, and there only reading and penmanship, while the other sciences they consider to be useless. . . . Everyone knows that only penmanship is needed to earn a place in the civil service, for which reason it is impossible to expect many to send their children to the higher grades." Indeed, a semi-learned nobleman could candidly state in an application of that time: "Russian grammar and writing I *often* can do, but the further sciences I am in no condition to learn, and having attained my majority, I no longer can have knowledge of them, and *therefore* have conceived an avid desire to serve." And an expelled seminarian wrote down with the same candor in his application: "Owing to the weakness of my health and of *certain concepts,* I was expelled from the theological school; but now, having recovered my health, I have a desire to continue state service in the office of the *gubernia* government." A further stay in school could not give this candidate for civil service any special rights over those applicants like, for example, the nobleman above, who "having studied at home to read and write Russian," were evincing a similar "avid desire" to serve, or who "having sung in the cathedral choir," wished upon "completion of the singing courses and upon the loss of melodic voice, to enter the *gubernia* administration under the sagacious guidance of the officials." These conditions explain to us why, for example, in Archangel province out of the total number in school in the years 1786–1803 (1,432), only 52 pupils received a certificate of completion for the full course.

The situation was even worse for the "lower public schools" designed for the district centers. The need for education was felt far more weakly there than in the *gubernia* cities, and the opening of the schools became dependent on the generosity of the local

city *dumas* (councils). In the earliest flush of enthusiasm, a good
number of lower schools were opened in the districts right away.
But soon the *dumas* began to find the maintenance of the schools
burdensome; not only did the opening of new schools cease to
proceed with the initial speed, but the ones opened earlier began
to close down here and there. Thus, in 1790 the residents of
Lebedianaia, Shatsk, Spassk, and Temnikovo submitted to the
gubernia authorities almost identical declarations: "There are no
children of merchants and townspeople in the schools, and we do
not intend henceforth to present our children for instruction in the
schools. For that reason, we have no desire to maintain the schools,
and we see no use in them for us." And the schools were closed.
A Kozlov merchant, the inspector of the local school, went even
further: he found that all schools in general were harmful and
that "it is useful to close them everywhere." Given this attitude
toward schools on the part of the local populace, the lower schools
were very poorly attended and often ceased to exist *de facto*. That
is how the Kozlov school, mentioned above, terminated its existence. The same happened to the school in Onega. At the Tikhvin
school, 54 of the 68 pupils dropped out immediately after the opening (1788). In the vast Yekaterinoslav territory, all efforts by the
authorities to open a lower school were smashed against passive
resistance by the nobility and the townspeople, who refused to
defray any monetary expenses for a cause from which they saw
no benefits forthcoming for themselves. Incidentally, a hostile attitude toward the new school could also be sensed in the provincial
centers. For example, in Vyatka the reasons for the small number
of pupils in the main school in 1797 were given as follows: "The
local residents, little motivated by the proposed aim of education,
are reluctant to present their children at the public school. . . .
Many would prefer that they be supplied at an early age with
knowledge of household affairs and the necessities of merchants
and townspeople, with which they themselves are conversant.
Many also . . . are presenting their children for instruction in
religious books to church officials, as they are excited when their

children are able to read the Book of Hours or the Psalter in church." On the other side of the country, in Chernigov, we encounter the exact same thing: "The school is beginning to fall hour by hour into disuse, for many impatient parents, attracted by the most negligible savings, withdrew their children and presented them at the churchmen's schools."

Thus, the old habits of family and school constituted the most important obstacle to the spread of Catherine's general-education schools and to their success in the provinces. But it must be said that these schools themselves turned out in practice to be a far cry from the way Jankovic had designed them. Having removed many obstacles to the success of his enterprise, he did not have it within his power to remove one of them, the main one: the grievous material and moral condition of the teacher in the Russian school. This condition was an inevitable consequence of the attitude of society, which we have just indicated, toward the school. Having come into the teacher's estate, for the most part not by his own will but by episcopal appointment, the eighteenth-century teacher could neither move up the social ladder nor quit except by being forced into the army for drunkenness and "bad morals." Thus, the choice of the teaching profession as a vocation and the transferral of those lacking the vocation for it to other professions were, in the vast majority of cases, out of the question. The teacher had to resign himself to his situation, from which it was impossible to escape, or seek oblivion in strong spirits. Meanwhile, for a person the least bit talented it was too difficult to be resigned to this situation. The miserly teacher's salary in most cases was not paid in full or was ordered to be delayed. An old pedagogue who had served since the very founding of the public schools said the following on the subject in 1811: "I noted in the course of twenty-five years of service that *all* teachers serving in the old conditions were always poor and had experienced great privations, but now, because of the costliness of all things, their poverty grew still more and put some of them in desperate straits. I have always grieved and now grieve in my soul, when seeing the industrious wretch." The social position of the provincial teacher was the most humiliating. He was scorned by the local rich men and the local bureaucrats, and by those who paid obeisance to rank and money, that is, by essentially everyone, not excluding even himself. The kindness of the powerful toward him was expressed in demeaning handouts; in the case of unkindness, there was the risk of being caned, with which the wife of the above-mentioned Kozlov inspector once threatened a pedagogue. Is it surprising that, given all these conditions, the people in whose breasts beat a warm heart and who had an interest in their work constituted a tiny exception?

The vast majority soon threw up their hands at it all and somehow played out their string of service. Jankovic's pedagogical techniques gave way to the old solitary memorizing; the teacher confined his duties to calling for answers, and most often even this duty he delegated to the most capable pupils. He considered himself quite exemplary if he sat in the school the whole working day, every day. Quite often not even this was achieved. In brief, teachers and pupils, to their mutual satisfaction, reduced their obligations to the minimum and entered into a tacit conspiracy to deceive the school authorities with passing marks and the local populace at annual formal ceremonies.

At the beginning of the reign of Alexander I, his mentor La Harpe summing up the results of the "public schools commission's" activity, was surprised at the contrast between its brilliant beginning and the flaccid continuation of its activity. He ascribed this flagging of energy to the personal motives guiding the commission members. "Many were talking at one time about such an immeasurable success [169 schools in 1787]," he noted; "awards were showered on him who attributed this miracle to himself . . . and also on the clients of the miracle worker. With the awards all given out, the wonders ceased. In the last two years of Catherine's reign only three schools were founded. With the accession of the Emperor Paul, the commission woke up, as it were, and suddenly founded thirteen schools, then sank back into its usual lethargy." La Harpe's insinuations no doubt had some basis; but knowing the funds with which the school's commission had to operate and the population's attitude toward its work, we find that what it did accomplish was nonetheless very much. Instead of waiting for it to continue its "wonders," thought should have been given to the fact that miracles do not happen at all. The commission came to a halt in its activity not because it had become overloaded with "awards," but because all its resources for earning awards were used up. It had become difficult simply to hold public education at the achieved level, not to mention gaining further successes. This circumstance alone proves that the commission did rather more, not less, than what was to be expected of it in the conditions of its activity at the time.

The development of public education in Russia after the institution of the commission is evident from the adjacent table. Besides the main and lower schools, the other institutions of learning (i.e., boarding schools, household, and rural schools) are added in as well.

These figures cannot be wholly relied upon, but they doubtless have a certain relative significance. Judging from them, the number of students reached a maximum in the sixth year of the reform (1791), the number of schools in the eighth year, and the number

YEAR	SCHOOLS	TEACHERS	STUDENTS
1786	40	136	4,398
1787	165	395	11,088
1788	218	525	13,539
1789	225	576	14,389
1790	269	629	16,525
1791	288	700	17,787
1792	302	718	17,500
1793	311	738	17,297
1794	302	767	16,620
1795	307	716	17,097
1796	316	744	17,341
1797	285	664	15,628
1798	184	752	16,801
1799	281	721	17,598
1800	315	790	19,915

of teachers in the ninth. Subsequently all these figures begin to fall sharply. In the last year of Catherine II's reign, true, they again return to the old maximum, but again they fall sharply in the first year of Emperor Paul's reign. Then, the number of students again begins to rise swiftly.

The pupils in Catherine's schools were very unevenly distributed by sex. Although the main and lower schools were intended for boys and girls equally, the old view about feminine education, along with a fear of sending girls to such a school, where there were apprehensions about harm even to boys, prevented the society from seizing this opportunity. Out of the 176,730 pupils who went through school in the 1782–1800 interval, only 12,595, or 7 percent, were girls. Besides, a large part of that number belonged to the capital city. For example, of the 1,121 girls attending the schools in 1796, 759 were in the St. Petersburg province; that left only 362 in the rest of Russia.

Compared with the school statistics for 1727, the figures just cited represent a substantial stride forward. But with respect to the entire population of Russia in that day, even these figures prove quite negligible. Taking 26 million as the population of Russia in 1790, we come up with the result that there was one student (in a secular school) for every 1,573 members of the entire population. This figure alone suffices to show that Catherine's school was "public" only in name, and that the popular masses, prior to the nineteenth century, were deprived of any of the cultural influence of schooling.

It cannot be said that the question of rural [elementary] schools did not come up at all in Catherine's time. On the contrary, this question was raised more than once and was quite distinctly formulated. As early as 1768, two or three deputies of Catherine's commission for drafting a code began to talk about an elementary school for the lower classes. These deputies' proposal, however, evoked decisive resistance. One of their opponents found that schools for peasants "are absolutely inappropriate, because the tiller of the land absolutely should not have other sciences not befitting his condition, besides reading and writing"; and as for reading and writing, "they can have them even without the institution of schools for them, as it has been up to now." In the opinion of this deputy, the school would only distract the peasant from farming, which had to remain for him the only school. Advocates of the public school, however, did not find it difficult to prove that the author of the *Instruction* herself was on their side. After all, among the countless commissions elected to consider the special questions prompted by the deputies and by the *Instruction* there was a "commission on Schools," organized under the "Great Assembly." By the spring of 1770, this commission had presented a completed prospectus for the establishment of rural schools. Its prospectus recommended, following the Prussian example, the introduction in Russia of compulsory literacy instruction for all male children. Each village or large hamlet was to open one school for each 100 to 250 families. All expenditures on schools were to be borne by the parishioners. Supervision of the schools was assigned to clergymen, and those appointed to be teachers were the deacons, sacristans, or, finally, laymen.

"The ideas of the schools' commission on the establishment of rural schools," wrote D. A. Tolstoi, a minister of Alexander III, "were so sound that they outdistanced not only their own time but ours as well. To this day we have not arrived at the conviction that the only true means of universal education of the people is compulsory primary schooling. . . . It is easy to imagine what beneficent consequences would have ensued from the government's adoption more than a century ago of the principle of compulsory education. Now almost all the Russian people would be literate, like the Germans, and the general level of the country's education, which would affect its entire situation, both spiritual and economic, would be far higher."

. . . In any case, under Catherine the matter was confined to the singular efforts of individual people. One could have counted up to a dozen rural schools opened in various *gubernias* and accommodating as many as 250 peasant children. But aside from the fact that this was only a drop in the bucket, almost all these schools were immediately closed again. The lower school in Russia remained a matter for the future, a matter for the end of the nineteenth and the beginning of the twentieth century. The eighteenth century was barely able to put the secondary school on its feet.

PAVEL N. MILIUKOV

Voices of the Land and the Autocrat

C ATHERINE AND PETER—contemporaries were already
comparing these two names as symbols of two successive eras
of Russian cultural history. Contemporaries also realized that the
era of Catherine was not only a *continuation* of Peter's but also
constituted a sharp *contrast* with it at the same time. They even
thought up a vivid metaphor for the contrast, and it became common currency among writers of Catherine's age: "Peter created
Russia's body, but Catherine endowed it with a soul."

From Pavel N. Miliukov, *Ocherki po istorii russkoi kul'tury* (Paris:
Sovremennye Zapiski, 1930), III, 293–328. Used by permission of the Execu-
tor of the Estate of Professor Pavel N. Miliukov. Translated by Norman K.
Sloan.

Needless to say, the observation was not subtle and reflected the naïve personification of social phenomena characteristic of the world view of that time. But it formulated, in a rough way, the extremely important sociological fact that, indeed, constitutes the principal feature of the age and for that reason alone could not elude the attention of those contemporaries. The age of Catherine is an era in the history of Russian social self-consciousness. The "soul" of the new Russian society, in fact, began to remember and to take cognizance of itself at that time. It was then that the prehistoric, tertiary period of Russian social life ended, and it took on the appearance and the forms in which it is known to our time. The old, antediluvian forms either died out forever or, condemned to extinction, emigrated to the lower strata of the social atmosphere.

We know that such was actually the fate of the old social selfawareness that had developed in the fifteenth and sixteenth centuries and had borne a predominantly nationalistic character. Cast aside by the victory of the new culture, it was not replaced at once by a corresponding new awareness. The new culture won out primarily through its technical superiority, which made it an indispensable weapon of the new state and a requisite condition of a more developed economic life. Having won out, that culture acquired the sympathy of the ruling class, to which it gave an attribute that was conveniently conspicuous, providing for the first time a sharp external line of demarcation between "nobility" and "baseness." Finally, and again from the very outset, the new culture secured the following of the influential classes which derived from it special, and previously unknown, material, aesthetic, and intellectual pleasures, from gourmet dining and free attitudes toward women to card games, music, stage shows, and entertaining books. All this, however, did not provide enough material for a new direction in social self-awareness, fundamentally different from the old.

Such material was provided by books, the moment people ceased to look for simple amusement in them. Originally, it is true, people looked to them only for rules of personal conduct. But from that

first step—from rules of etiquette or prescriptions for individual morality—the transition to the next step, to recognition of the importance of social theory and the necessity of conscious social conduct, was painless and was accomplished without notice. . . . We know that from the 1750's on, the influence of bookish morality and social theory ceased to be confined to individuals and embraced an entire social circle, to be sure still a very limited one: the circle of the aristocratic youth who had passed through higher education. Thus, the Empress Catherine had the good fortune to ascend the throne at a time when the ground was already cleared for the acceptance of the last word in modern European literature, for the assimilation of the basic notion propagandized by that literature —that the social order, in the interests of "humanity," can and must be rebuilt according to "rational" principles.

At that point, the role of the critical ideas fashioned in the new Petrine culture became absolutely different from what it had been. In the common broad and turbid tide of the new cultural life from Peter's time to Catherine's, two elements that were in essence mutually hostile had been but faintly discernible: the new criticism and the new privileged social tradition. Without having been separated, all aspects of the new culture were indiscriminately accepted under the common blanket of the state power, which was carrying out the reform. In this regard, too, a complete turnabout was effected under Catherine. The elements of criticism were sorted out and constituted the basis of a new public opinion, which consciously and sharply opposed the new culture monopolized by the privileged classes. The new culture as sanction for the existing social order, then, stood in complete contradiction with the new culture as basis for a conscious attitude toward life. For some time, the regime vacillated between the two hostile concepts of the new culture. But the vacillation did not last long: the regime willy-nilly took the side of social strength against social impotence.

Then representation of the elements of criticism passed from th regime to intellectual public opinion. This differentiation of th mutually hostile elements of the new criticism ended the peri

of "the official triumph of the critical elements," as we have characterized the period from Peter to Catherine. Russian public life entered a new phase, which has not concluded to this day.

The sea change in Russian life just noted occurred in especially vivid and prominent forms, partly because it was taking place in a setting that was still very uncomplicated, in the relatively limited circle of people who were affected by the new culture; partly also because that sea change found its graphic expression in the change of disposition of the Empress personally. Catherine, herself initially imbued with critical ideas, at the very outset became convinced of their contradiction with the existing social order, which she was obliged to protect. The contradiction did not particularly disconcert her, because the critical ideas at the same time were beginning to seem to her useless for practical life and impotent against Russian reality. The French Revolution opened her eyes and forced her to join battle with the dreams of her youth, as these were truly dangerous to the continued existence of those phenomena of life (above all, serfdom) against which the criticism was aimed. The realization that critical ideas were not merely superfluous but dangerous to the surrounding reality amounted to a civil rite of confirmation for them. At that point there began the unbroken tradition of Russian social-critical thought.

Having turned from an ally into the conscientious opponent of the critical elements, the regime, in keeping with the spirit of the time, could no longer confine itself to a simple material, physical struggle against them. Ideas must be fought in the name of ideas; it was necessary to find a base in principle for a positive, not merely a negative, program of action. The base was found . . . in the idealization of the past. It is impossible to view this idealization as a simple restoration of contact with the national self-awareness of the sixteenth and seventeenth centuries. . . . The idealization of the past in Catherine's time turned out to be an absolutely new phenomenon, not resting on any tradition of the past whatever. On the contrary, while the old tradition had been alive, as long as the past was too close, no idealization of it was possible. Only a

forgetting of the past could form the basis of its *literary* restoration.
We shall see that at the beginning the restoration went hand in
hand with the work of critical thought and even served as one of
its techniques. Only as critical thought was cast into the opposition
did the literary idealization of the past begin to serve as material for
conservative political theory. Thus, the conservative ideology, like
the opposition, carries on an unbroken tradition of its own from
Catherine's time. For contemporary nationalism, just as for contemporary social criticism, Catherine's era serves as the epoch from
which each dates its conscious existence. There, in rough outline,
is the original watershed between the two streams.

By now it is evident, from what has been said, that even if Catherine did not personally invest the material body of Peter's new
culture with a "soul," she still did play a large role in the history of
that soul. Catherine attracted to critical ideas, Catherine cool to
them, Catherine hostile to them—all these metamorphoses of the
Empress' personal disposition were tightly interwoven with the
first steps of conscious social life in Russia. To understand the two
streams properly, it is necessary to investigate them both in parallel.

First of all, let us consider some chronological data. Catherine's
date of birth (1729) placed her midway between two generations
in Russia: that of Elizabeth, who was born in the second decade
of the eighteenth century and whose school years corresponded approximately with the opening of the Corps of Cadets (1732), and
the young generation, born in Elizabeth's reign and adolescent by
the time of Catherine's own coronation. The school years of the
latter generation coincide approximately with the opening of Moscow University (1755). . . . The first, insofar as it lived a cultured
life at all, lived by the ideas and tastes of the age of Louis XIV; its
interests were predominantly literary-aesthetic. The second generation began to think and feel at the very moment when abrupt
change of mood had taken place in Europe, signaling the transition
to a revolutionary era. Catherine's generation was midway between
the two. It grew up in that interval of relatively indistinct public
mood when the transition from Louis XIV to the revolution was

just ripening in the best minds and was not yet fully grasped even by them. Literature and poetry were already giving way to "philosophy" and politics. But the new philosophical and political ideas had not yet been carried through to their ultimate logical conclusions. Rousseau and Diderot, Helvétius and Holbach—in brief, all those who struck a chord of social and philosophical protest—had not yet appeared or had not yet attracted the attention of the educated circles. Voltaire was still occupied primarily with literature. Deism satisfied the common mood in philosophy, and constitutionalism in political thought. But suffice it to remember that the representative of the one was Voltaire and the other Montesquieu, and one can see that those teachings were not presented in the form of strict, completed doctrine. Nor would that social milieu in which the fashionable ideas of fashionable philosophers and political theorists were being spread have tolerated any doctrine. Thought found its way into that milieu—the glittering aristocratic salons—exclusively in the form of frivolous witticism, just serious enough to take on the appearance of a theoretical defense of the scatterbrained court life against the "pedantry" of all kinds of doctrines and systems, but light enough, still, not to overtax the minds even of those ladies who were acquainted with the printed word only through the prayer book.

The vast literary talents of Voltaire and Montesquieu, in alliance with the passion of the former and the profundity of the latter, were needed in order to squeeze the contraband new world view into such a tight framework. But even in such a condition, the new views could find a good-natured reception only when heavily diluted and, consciously or not, distorted to fit the stereotype of the very social milieu for which they were intended. Literature allowed itself to shatter only those foundations that had already been shaken in that milieu. When undermining the strength of certain prejudices that had survived from the past, the fashionable writers too often sought support in an alliance with other prejudices that were stronger still, and thus they "fawned upon Lucifer to rid themselves of Beelzebub," as d'Alembert tartly observed. The theoretician of political forms (Montesquieu) platonically admired the "republic" of the Greeks and Romans, not foreseeing the possibility of encountering it in the Europe of his day, and just as platonically shot his arrows at "despotism," reserving to it a place exclusively in Asia. At home he was content with a hierarchical monarchy, limited by the privileges of the nobility. And it was for the same nobility, for "the top two or three thousand," that the preacher of tolerance (Voltaire) whetted his sarcasm, frankly preferring the frivolous freethinking of the gentry to the committed fanaticism of the bourgeoisie and the Jansenist "pedantry" of the *parlements*. For him, mankind was divided into the "rabble" and the "gentlemen," *canaille* and *honnêtes gens,* a division quite similar to our Russian *podlost'* and *blagorodstvo*. He consciously confined his mission to those belonging to "good company." "We will have done enough, if all well-born scorn superstition." The people will always remain stupid and ignorant: "they are cattle who need only the yoke, the whip, and some hay." The monarchial regime had to be his ally in the fight against the clergy and the *parlements*. It was necessary to convince the government that the "philosophes" were the natural allies of kings and were engaged with them in one and the same cause.

Those who speak of the "betrayal" by Catherine of the views of her youth must not forget that those views were first assimilated by her in that watered-down, noncommittal form. The "betrayal," by the way, was an everyday act for the first heralds of "philosophical" ideas. Having perpetually repudiated his own works, having hastened to confession and communion after each quarrel with the Church, having flattered kings, the Pope, and the Jesuits, having regularly composed madrigals to the king's mistresses, having drawn forth, finally, on his deathbed, from his own secretary, a Protestant and a Mason, after twenty-four years of living together, the bewildered question, What, after all, did he believe in? —Voltaire could not have been an especially strict teacher in questions of conscience. It is even not difficult to guess that it was that lack of strictness that made Voltaire Catherine's "teacher" in the science of "sound thinking" and common sense. The fact that Voltaire's science was something else altogether, and that in it sound thinking was only a tool and a method, were something to which the Empress, somehow, had never paid special attention. She knew, of course, that when talking with Voltaire it was necessary to mention tolerance as often as possible and to reject superstition. But those slogans, dangerous to their defenders in a Catholic country, were taken for granted in Peter's Russia. Here it would have been far more difficult to defend intolerance and traditional faith. That is why, after a fifteen-year correspondence, the Empress still did not understand perfectly clearly with whom she was dealing; Voltaire's death deprived her only of the "god of laughter." Shocked by the outbreak of the French Revolution, Catherine stubbornly held up her "teacher" as a reproach to the revolutionaries. So gently, merrily, and insouciantly could he joke about serious matters in good company: was it not tactless of those "bootmakers and cobblers" to carry the stimulating causerie of their "best writers" out of the salon and onto the street? And it was only when convinced, finally, by the inexorable logic of events of the identity of word and deed that Catherine ordered the bust of her "teacher"— her last one—removed from the Hermitage gallery.

The nature of the written correspondence between Catherine and Voltaire gave no forewarning of such a sorry end. Theirs was a most firm and stable relationship, since on both sides it was based on calculation. The seventy-year-old philosopher and the thirty-five-year-old novice proved to have had ample experience of life and disappointment in the past, too much so not to cherish mutual illusions and to understand implicitly what each needed from the other. In his intimate correspondence with d'Alembert, Voltaire admitted that "philosophy has nothing special to boast about in such disciples" as "the fair Cato." But, be that as it may, the Empress' patronage enhanced his prestige in Europe, and Voltaire, without a twinge of conscience, elevated Catherine above Solon and Lycurgus, exalted her soul and mind, admired her wise laws and brilliant ceremonies, and even her little hands and feet. Catherine, for her part, was terror-struck by the thought that Voltaire might take her at her word and come to visit her in Russia; she hastened to assure him that "Cato is good only from a distance." But from that fine distance, she artfully exploited Voltaire's pen for officious communiqués to Europe. The scales of advantage tipped to the Empress' side, rather than to the writer's.

It is more difficult to decide whether or not Catherine was *from the very beginning* of her career such a politician in her relations with the representatives of the critical ideas. True, an indirect answer can be found in the circumstance that she made herself a politician in general very early. Let us recall her admission in the *Memoirs* that she made it a rule for herself, when still the Grand Duchess, to court everyone, so that each might be an ally in the event one was needed. But toward Voltaire, in particular, her attitude was somewhat different, since she was partly obligated to him, under that same rule. Before there was any occasion for her to seek an ally in him, she found in him a tutor in the art of giving [intellectual] pleasure. Her interest in serious reading developed from this. What attracted her in Voltaire and Tacitus was, first of all, the lessons in empirical psychology, which coincided with her own pessimistic observations of the motives of human conduct. "I started to see things in a more gloomy light and learned to look, in everything that went on before my eyes, for the deeper explanations in a diversity of interests." That is how the Empress herself summed up the practical results of her serious reading. From the ironies of Voltaire and Tacitus, she obviously drew the ethical conclusions of La Rochefoucauld.

Catherine no doubt grasped precisely that fact and was utterly sincere when she admitted that Voltaire had taught her to read and to think and that he had had an enormous influence on her in the period when her mind and character were being formed. That is why she, in her relations with Voltaire—and with him alone—in the early stages showed the timidity and indecisiveness of the pupil and seriously sought his approval. Only after gaining that approval too easily and undeservedly did she realize its worth. That was her first lesson in suspicion of "philosophy" and philosophers. The "teacher" thereafter ceased to awe her; but the king of European public opinion and the "entertainer" retained the Empress' sympathy.

The question of the specific influence upon Catherine of the *ideas* of the "Enlightenment" philosophy of her time is far more complicated than the question of her personal relations with "philosophes." There is no doubt, first of all, that her early pessimism about people was for a long time combined with optimism about ideas. Why, having lost faith in people, Catherine continued to believe in ideas is something we have yet to explain. But it is a fact that she indeed believed in them and was willing to suit her actions to them. To rebut this by citing the earliest instance of contradiction between the "principles" and the conduct of Catherine—her ambiguous stance between Voltaire and the Orthodox religion—would be absolutely unfounded. In that case, the conflict of "interest" with principles was quite easily resolved by her very assimilation of philosophy. Was not the actual change of faith itself proof of freedom from the "superstition" in which the old Protestant, Catherine's father, wallowed? And on the other hand, did not Voltaire assert that any owner of five or six hundred peasants had to admit the necessity of a religion of eternal suffering and retribution beyond the grave? Obviously, teacher and pupil were in full accord about the evaluation of both the social significance of religion and what in Catherine's language was called *momeries*.

In matters of state administration, of course, it was not so easy to harmonize "principles" with "interests." The historians of Catherine have turned their attention to a dictum in Bayle's dictionary that, in their opinion, must have settled in the mind of the future Empress: "The rules of the art of statecraft are contrary to strict honesty." But we know from Catherine's own remarks when she was still Grand Duchess that she refused to be reconciled to that maxim and set herself a straightforward goal: to reconcile honesty

with politics. She found the means for doing so in the idea that
to be honest is more to the ruler's own benefit. The idea of the
advantageousness of good principles runs conspicuously through
all those interesting notes, which limn for us a portrait of the
Grand Duchess with all her strengths and weaknesses, the very
same ones that subsequently characterized the Empress. Here
we find in a perfectly distinct, recognizable form all the rules of
the future reign. The ruler must, in Catherine's opinion in the
notes, do good and love the truth, since that "will make him
pleasing to God and man." He must be concerned for the glory
of the country, because it is his own glory. He must make the
lords and the courtiers contented and rich, because his own grandeur depends on that. He must candidly state his purposes, "if
truth and reason are on his side," since his arguments, probably,
"will take the uppermost in the eyes of the masses." He must announce the law that he intends to promulgate beforehand, then
listen to the public's views about it, so that the law will turn out
successful and there will be no need to rescind it. The courtiers
must be forced, *out of flattery,* to tell the truth, to make it to their
advantage, since otherwise the ruler risks being deceived—the
most demeaning situation that Catherine could imagine.

From the chosen standpoint, however, one thing could not be
denied: the *possibility* that "principles" would diverge from "interests," and Bayle's rule would be needed. The same penciled
notes forsee two such cases—the very same ones for which posterity
was to condemn Catherine. In one of them, the chief issue of her
domestic policy, Catherine even then grasped clearly the entire difficulty of her situation, but still hoped for the possibility of a compromise. "It is contrary to the Christian religion and justice to
make people (who all are born free) into slaves. The church in
Germany, France, Spain, and elsewhere has freed all the peasants
(who previously had been serfs). To manage a similar sharp turnabout would be a poor way to win the love of the landowners, who
are filled with obduracy and prejudices. . . . But here is an easy

. . . means: to decree that with each sale of an estate to a new owner, the slaves are declared free. In a hundred years, all or most lands will have changed owners: *voilà!* The people are free."

In the other awkward case, in the area of foreign policy, Catherine was obviously more prepared to incline toward the side of "interests." "They say that in any matter there are two possible outcomes: the just or the unjust; usually, the advantage leans toward injustice. In the question of Courland, justice required that the children of Biron be given that which God and nature had given them.[1] If the desire is to look out for advantage, one should (unjustly, of course) keep Courland for oneself, take it away from Poland, and annex it to Russia. Who would guess that a third way will be found—a way to do an injustice without advantage? Courland was given to the Saxon prince, and thereby the Polish king was strengthened. . . . The question is asked, Is a powerful neighbor really more advantageous for Russia than the happy anarchy in which Poland finds itself, thanks to which we rule the roost there as we please? . . . If you want to be unjust, after all, then you have to derive some profit from it."

So Catherine's faith in the "applicability" of general principles to life was based on the conviction that, in most cases at least, the application of good principles is advantageous. Catherine made her commitment to administration by ideals, as she expressed it in those same notes, "with eyes open" and on condition that administration by ideals not only would not contradict but, on the contrary, would coincide with her personal "interests." Were it to fail to coincide, Catherine was expressing in advance her readiness to reject it. Thus, if Catherine's judgment deserted her with respect to ideas, it was not, at any rate, on that point, the reckoning of advantage, but in the question of the "feasibility" of ideas when presuming them useful.

---

1. Ernst Johann Biron (or Bühren), 1690–1772, the favorite of Empress Anna Ioanovna (1730–1740), had been made duke of Courland which was a fief of the Polish commonwealth. From 1697 to 1763 the kings of Poland were also hereditary dukes of Saxony.

In her view of the feasibilty of an idea, Catherine proved to be the daughter of her time, a fanatic of her station, and a victim of her temperament. The idea of the wise legislator's omnipotence was one of the basic axioms of the Enlightenment. But for Catherine, that idea was not a simple tribute to the times. For her, it was inseparably linked to a trust in the omnipotence of the Russian ruler. "What can oppose the boundless power of the absolute monarch who governs a warring people?" the Grand Duchess asked in those same jottings. Catherine had brought that idea with her to Russia, and with it she consciously and patiently laid out her path to the throne. Upon reaching her goal, she boldly laid hands on the mechanisms that had beckoned with their immensity from afar to her craving for glory and power.

She had hoped in that station to implement "good and righteous principles." To implement them, she needed precisely *that* station. But in such a station, only "a personality endowed by nature with useful talents" could realize such principles. Where such a personality could make a "brilliant career," another would only be "laughable." We are again quoting from the notes here: even in the reign of Elizabeth, Catherine considered herself to be the only worthy bearer of great ideas in high office. Belief in the power of ideas and in the boundless power of office, in turn, were for her inseparably tied to faith in herself; she derived from her own psychology what was lacking in the other sources of her faith.

Even back in Elizabeth's reign, the French ambassador L'Hôpital found Catherine to be a "hothead." One might even stress: specifically the "head," not the "heart," the imagination, not the emotions. Evidently, Catherine herself was in full accord with that definition of her "predominant capabilities." There was once a conversation in her presence about what she might have been, had she been a private citizen and a man. The diplomats vied with one another in anointing her as a minister of state or a commander of armies. The Empress decided it: "You are all mistaken; I know my hot head; I would risk everything for glory and, in the rank of lieutenant, would lose my life in the very first campaign."

Instead of all the merits with which Grimm adorned her in 1774, Catherine acknowledged that she had one that she could thank for being "worth something"—"an ability to want passionately that which she wanted." "One must be firm in one's decisions," she said on another occasion. "It is better to do badly than to change opinions: Only fools are indecisive."

It cannot be said that Catherine was unaware of the danger of such a temperament in a ruler. "Success is to the mind what youth is to the temperament," we find in those same notes. "It brings all the passions into play. It is a lucky man who does not allow himself to be carried away by this stream." In those last words, one can hear misgivings, as it were—well founded, as time has shown—that Catherine herself would be unable to contain herself when the situation called for it. But she knew her weaknesses —and, as a politician, she wanted above all to take advantage of them, if it was impossible to eliminate them. Obsession was inevitable, but obsession is also strength. In the absence of such strength, self-assurance could replace it to some extent. "I can congratulate myself on the beginnings of popularity," she wrote in Elizabeth's reign. "I must not, of course, trust it, despite the outward signs; but that does not prevent me from behaving as though I were confident of it. They praise me only when, and to the extent that, they are displeased with the Grand Duke; I am still too young to be loved; but I must act as though I believe I am loved." We see here a complete program of politics, deriving its strength from the outward appearance of success.

Given the complexity of Catherine's disposition, it is very difficult, obviously, to tell in each separate instance where her conviction leaves off and politics takes over. Perhaps it would be most accurate to suppose that politics operates throughout, and in some cases the wellsprings of her politics are convictions, which she holds to be right and advantageous.

In any case, Catherine was to apply the politics *herself,* with her own mind and on her own initiative. In the matter that was to serve as the pedestal of her glory, Catherine recognized no predecessors or collaborators. She was second only to the "first" Peter; but in *her own* affairs she was primary and singular. In her *Instruction* she wrote these daring words, so slavishly quoted by the deputies of the commission: "God forbid that, after the completion of this legislation, there should be on earth a people more just, hence more prosperous; the intention of our laws would not be fulfilled—a misfortune I do not wish to live to see." That mood of Catherine's is emphasized more vividly by a contemporary allegorical engraving that commemorated the promulgation of the *Instruction*. In the center of the picture, on an elevation, stands Catherine in a calm, confident pose, not at all reminiscent of the canter at which, in her jocular phrase from her notes, she was supposed to sally forth between the chilling skepticism of Panin and the eager encouragements of Grigorii Orlov in the first years of her reign.[2] The places of those two, flanking Catherine, were taken in the allegory by Minerva and a youthful Mars, his heel resting on a chained enemy. The people mill about beneath the Empress' feet: a sea of heads, longing to look upon Catherine, looking at her with expressions of love and hope, striving to imprint on their memory the golden lines of the *Instruction,* unfurled before them. At the side, above that sea of faces, a pyramid rises on which "The Happiness of One and All" is inscribed, along with the date, 1766, and on which rests the imperial crown.[3] In comparison with the pyramid, a statue of some ancient lawgiver, standing atop a column behind the pyramid, seems quite small. Finally, overhead, in clouds of smoke, a winged figure of Glory is already hastening to carry the good news of the new era of "the happiness of one and all," dated 1766, around the world.

The basic idea of the allegory is clear. It was Catherine's "good fortune to find good and true principles," but those principles were

2. Reference is to Count Nikita I. Panin, 1718–1783, the highly educated tutor of Grand Duke Paul and chief minister for foreign affairs of Catherine II, and to Grigorii G. Orlov, 1734–1783, her lover who, as officer of the Guards Regiment, engineered the coup that raised her to the throne.

3. The same emblem was depicted on the medals handed out to the deputies. [Author's Note]

being realized because Catherine was putting them into practice. And if subsequently she should have to admit that the principles had remained unrealized, not for a minute would she think to doubt the principles or her own ability to realize them. At least, she will never openly admit this and will place the blame on others. "My ambition was not bad, but possibly I took too much upon myself, in the belief that people can make themselves sensible, just, and happy."

There was but one thing that Catherine could not allow: for people to be able to make themselves sensible, just, and happy under some other system, exclusive of her own, especially under a system that would admit of the possibility for them to attain that goal using their own resources. Catherine saw her reformer's role as absolutely personal. This determined her attitude toward all the contemporary systems that were built on the principle of self-help. There were two such systems in Russia in Catherine's time. Both were rather clearly discernible in the mood of the young generation that had grown up prior to the Empress' coronation. One is known to us as the theory of *natural law*, which soon would be able to celebrate the fiftieth anniversary, not only of its existence, but also of uninterrupted academic instruction in Russia. Since the time of Gross, who taught natural law to Kantemir at the Academic University, a succession of generations had studied that discipline with Pflug in the Corps of Cadets and with Dilthey and Langer at Moscow University.[4] But a man of "good society" was not obligated to "read through all the books and assiduously learn everything taught in the schools": it would suffice for him to have "naturally sound thinking." We shall soon see how Catherine dealt with the theory of natural law from the example of Beccaria. Her attitude toward the other system of fundamental views, which had made its appearance in Russia later but still before her time

4. The German version of natural law jurisprudence and philosophy (based on the works of Grotius, Pufendorff, Chr. Wolff) was a compulsory subject in secular and ecclesiastical schools throughout the eighteenth century.

and independently of her, the religious-ethical world outlook of Freemasonry, was even more negative and superficial, as we shall see later. If at first there were no sharp clashes between the Empress and representatives of the two philosophies, it was only because the representatives themselves, in the first generation, proved to be not as outstanding or consistent as their theories required. . . .

And we shall now understand how Catherine was to regard Voltaire's formidable rival, Rousseau, who, with the system of social contract that he had originated, ruled the science of natural law of that day. His system left too tight a corner for the favorite personage of the eighteenth century, the wise lawgiver. Catherine did not choose to have a personal encounter with the unsympathetic philosopher, and the recluse thinker turned down an invitation from Grigorii Orlov to visit his estate. With that, his relations with Russia ended. At the same time, an ardent admirer of "the great man, and the beneficent mankind that persecutes him," the jurist Beccaria, was destined to enjoy a resounding success in Russia.

Beccaria's book appeared at the very time when Catherine was drafting her *Instruction*. It was well nigh the only one of her sources in which Catherine could detect notes that were absolutely alien to the salon decorum of her favorite preceptors. But Beccaria was a zealous votary of one of them (Montesquieu); Catherine needed him, since she could borrow from him his prospectus of the future humane court. Thus it is all the more curious to see the meticulousness with which all the features that place Beccaria in the ranks of Rousseau's admirers have been removed from the borrowed text. When reading the *Instruction*, it is impossible to guess that the basic nerve of all Beccaria's reasoning is missing. According to his social contract theory, the minority usually fences itself off from the majority with such a contract, and centuries of suffering and poverty are needed before the contract can be redrafted in favor of the dispossessed majority. The thinker, ahead of his time, discloses this radical flaw in the law, which consists in its protection of a privileged minority. The enlightened despot can hear the voice of the thinker and use his power in the interests of the majority and thereby anticipate the result of natural historical developments.

> We usually leave the development of the most important decisions either simply to the course of time or to the discretion of those very individuals who stand opposed to the promulgation of wise laws. These have the aim, in essence, of making benefit universal, while the minority endeavors to retain full power and ownership for itself, allocating nothing to the others but impotence and want. Therefore, only by going through thousands of errors in the problems that determine the most essential conditions of life and liberty, only after enervating agonies engendered by evil, which has reached an extreme, will we arrive at the correction of the disorders that dismay us. Only then will we know those palpable truths that, by their very simplicity, elude the attention of men who are not sufficiently advanced. . . . Let us open the book of history, and we shall see that the laws, which in essence constitute and must constitute nothing other than a contract of free individuals, have always been an implement for the passions of the few, or have been the result of a casual and transitory necessity. In no case have they been the fruit of calm research into human nature, which strives to make us know that the task of our life is to grant the highest prosperity to the largest number of people. Those few states are fortunate that have not waited for the slow movement of human interrelations and the vicissitudes of life to bring first the rule of evil and then a gradual development of good, but have hastened the establishment of good with wise laws. And the philosopher who has had the courage to take from his unnoticed and even neglected study the first seeds of beneficial truth, which for a long time still will remain unfruitful, and to cast them among the people, deserves universal respect.

It proved not difficult to turn this fiery speech about age-old barriers to conscious social life into the inoffensive "happiness for one and all" decreed forthwith. One need only cast out the premises and the basic principles of Beccaria's reasoning and blur his concrete historical observations, and we end up with the corrected text of

Catherine's *Instruction*. Here is how the correction was made (by Catherine or by her advisers?):

BECCARIA

Only one legislator, representing in his person the entire united society and holding all power in his hands, has the right to make laws on punishment.

The right to institute these laws belongs exclusively to the legislator, representing all society, joined by a mutual contract.

Unlawful undertaking against the life and liberty of a citizen is among the greatest of crimes; and that heading encompasses not only murders committed by individuals from among the common people, but also the kind of violence committed by individuals whatever their origins or honors.

To this kind of crime (infringement of the safety and liberty of citizens) belongs not only the murder and theft committed by common men but also that committed by lords and judges, whose influence operates over a great area and with great force, destroying any idea of justice and duty among the subjects and instituting in its place the rule of the strong.

(Beccaria's version continues:)

There is no freedom where laws permit a man to cease, under certain circumstances, to be an individual and permit him to be turned into a thing; in such a case, strong men would use all their guile to extract from the multitude of civil relations only those that are established by law in their favor. To achieve that purpose means to discover the magic wand that turns citizens into howling beasts. In the hands of the powerful, that wand is a chain, shackling the actions of weak men. That is why in certain states, evidently disposing of full liberty, the rule of force is concealed, or else it unexpectedly burrows into some nook the lawgiver has forgotten, where it develops unnoticed. . . . The privileges of the nobility constitute a large part of the laws in various states. I shall not go into the question here of whether the hereditary division of nobility and the people is useful to the government or whether it is necessary in a monarchy: is it true that the nobility constitutes an intermediary power, restricting the abuses of the two extremes (all of which is Montesquieu's opinion)? . . . Supposing it is right that inequality is inevitable in a society, is it then just for it to be expressed in a differentiation of groups, not individual persons; for it to be focused in one part of the state, not to suffuse it throughout; for it to continue uninterrupted, and not be born and destroyed from minute to minute? [5]

Perhaps these were those *axioms à renverser les murailles* that Catherine's advisers had excised from the final draft of the *Instruction*. Our native theory of natural law had already been familiarized with those burning topics and had replied to them more or less innocuously. For example, Zolotnitsky's guide had reasoned quite calmly about "household servitude," both "absolute" and "non-absolute," easily finding for the former "a place in the natural state itself" and wavering only with regard to the latter, which, as it were, "does not occur in the natural state from the beginning of the simple society by reason of the inherent equality common to all." But the common equality was no barrier to deriving the origin of privileged estates from "the natural state." "Although all men in the natural state are equal among themselves, not all of them are worthy of equal repute, honor, and praise. For they are called equals only for the fact that they have rights and obligations, but not everyone has those excellences upon which the claim to repute, honor, and praise depends."

At the proposed gathering of the deputies, all these ticklish questions, raised by life but hushed up by politics and schoolroom theory, were to float to the surface. But there was no way of avoiding the meeting. Catherine had just decided it was necessary to publicize "in the marketplace" the draft laws that had laid claim to perpetuity. She had just read Beccaria's lucid comment

5. This viewpoint was openly defended at the sessions of Catherine's commission by several deputies (especially Ursinus, of the city of Dorpat). [Author's Note]

that "mankind would be fortunate if the laws were prescribed all at once by the monarchs whom we now see on the thrones of Europe," and that in such a case the "always candid voice of the people" should be heard, that it was being silenced by second-rank officials, "the more cruel because they are less well off" (the idea of the "intervening wall" appealed especially to the Empress, as witness the *Instruction*). Catherine's "philosophical" turn of mind, finally, could not lag behind that of her predecessors on the throne, who had, without any theories at all, supported the tradition of the seventeenth century: calling together deputies from various estates to compile a Code. Endless commissions labored in vain through the entire first half of the century over that impossible task. The last of them (1754), after fruitless efforts to compel the chanceries to work with it, conceived the idea (in 1761) of reinforcing itself, "after the example of the previous Code drafted in 1649" with people elected from among the nobles and merchants. In the first half of the century all attempts of that sort (1722, 1728, 1730) had failed: instead of "good and wise men," the provinces sent to Petersburg the old and the crippled, partly because they took a formal attitude toward the government's demands and regarded the sending of deputies as an irritating obligation, and partly because there were no suitable men among the landowners who remained to live in their villages. At mid-century, the provincial society had not yet taken shape: it made its appearance only as the result of the successes attained by the estates in the Age of Catherine. But still, officers who had been abroad (in the Seven Years' War) and who had been to school were beginning to turn up more often in the provinces. Now and then they brought with them, besides capital-city fashions and lax morals, printed books and subjects for "learned and weighty conversation" about poetry and literature, in brief, about more or less abstract matters. Beginning, in 1761, with the elections for the Commission of 1754, the Senate deemed it possible to speak to the provincial electorate in language that up till then had been quite unusual: working on the code is not an obligation but a social duty. "As the writing of the Code for the governance of the entire state is quite necessary, the labor of the entire society on the councils is required for this," and therefore "the duty of any son of the fatherland is to help in this with advice and deed." The Senate hopes that those elected not only will not refuse but will willingly bear "all the hardships and sacrifices," and not simply "in order to receive rewards for extra exertions" but also "in the hope of leaving an indelible memorial to themselves for future generations." Such is the language of Catherine's commission.

The deputies invited by Elizabeth began work in Catherine's reign. To the two titles of the draft law drawn up through official channels (the judicial and the criminal laws—tradition has it that the latter struck Elizabeth with their harshness and deterred her from signing the draft), they added a third, on the rights of the estates, largely similar to the deputies' mandates and to the draft laws on the estates worked out by Catherine's commission. Now, these deputies and the commission had to give way to Catherine's.

Thus it was that Catherine received both the end (codification) and the means (the participation of elected deputies), and even the general orientation of [its] work (the reform of criminal legislation in a humane spirit, and of social-class legislation in an aristocratic spirit), ready-made from her predecessor. Nevertheless, if she said and thought that she was undertaking something altogether new and to that day unprecedented, this cannot be explained *only* as deliberate deception stemming from egotism or as well-meaning delusion through an ignorance of precedents that are now better known to us. Catherine actually could assert that she was opening up an absolutely new path, and not because she was proclaiming "Happiness for one and all" as the highest goal of legislation. Assertions of that sort could have been heard, I daresay, from the regime that convened the assemblies [*zemskie sobory*] of the seventeenth century (then too, those elected from all the land were supposed to tell about "all their needs and hardships . . . and reflect upon all the good, so that all men of the state might live in security and happiness"). But she was the first to want to base *her own* legislation on a conscious theory, on that "truth" that "flashes like lightning in the long and gloomy night that stupefies men," in Beccaria's felicitous phrase. Whatever the motives of the young princess were, whether seeking the "trust of the people," "love," or "glory," we can believe that her heart beat more strongly when she read these lines from that same Beccaria: "The words of a wise man are too weak to stand against the clamor and shouts of people guided by blind habit . . . [but] if the truth could, despite the endless obstructions that separate it from the monarch, even against his will, reach his throne, he must realize that it is expressing to him the secret desires of the entire people; he must realize that his glory will drown the glory of conquerors and that a just posterity will raise him higher than the peaceful Tituses, Antonys, and Trajans." The "words of the sage" had reached Catherine's throne; the "secret wishes of the people" will also reach it. Catherine was right: it was not an "evil ambition" to erect the pyramid of her legislation higher than Trajan's column.

The instructions of the deputies from the provinces brought Catherine out of her heaven and down to earth. And she became ever more solidly implanted on that earth as the drama under her direction unfolded before her. When a short time had passed, her *Instruction* began to look to her like "prattle." She preferred the sober, businesslike contents of the "statute on the Provinces" to that chatter. What part had the deputies' cahiers and the activity of the commission convened by Catherine played in this turn-about?

When reading these cahiers now, we can see for ourselves that they opened up for Catherine a truly horrible picture. When she convened the commission, she knew men, but she still did not know Russia. Russia was screened off from her by a small circle of the young nobility, more or less permeated, or capable of being

permeated, with the same theories and ideas that engrossed the
Empress. In the provinces, the men of this intellectual circle were
casual guests. By choosing as their deputies those of them who had
not turned up among the deputies from the central institutions,
the provinces camouflaged their natural opinions and tastes somewhat. But they could not camouflage them for long. In the cahiers
and the debates, the cosmetics gradually wore off, and the un-
adorned reality came to the fore. It would be absurd to assert that
this reality had nothing in common with theory. For all its de-
ficiencies, the political theory of the eighteenth century was nonetheless sufficiently subtle and flexible not to fall short in the explanation of Russian reality. The practicing legislator, after reading through all the deputy mandates, could not write a better and
closer-to-life page than the page by Beccaria (see pp. 131–132),
which was the one that, in view of that closeness, had to be excised from the *Instruction*. But the serious application of *such* a
theory to practice required a greater break than the Empress
might have expected on the basis of her acquaintance with the
court-centered circle of the Russian nobility. It was possible to
converse with *that* circle about the most dreadful things. We have
seen how people here were able, without the least embarrassment,
to reconcile the advanced theories of natural law with Russian
reality. It was another matter when Russian life itself began to
speak in its own behalf. At that point, there was no longer
room for compromise; it was necessary to make a choice. And
the choice, in view of the conditions of the time, could not be in
doubt.

What, actually, did this commission say and observe, as it lit
up Russian reality like lightning in the dead of night and sig-
naled the start of a new era, if not of "happiness for one and all,"
at least of conscious social life in Russia?

The cahiers showed, first of all, that all the state and public
successes achieved by Russia through the centuries were confined to superficialities, and that in its depth this life had not
come far from that picture we saw in the pamphlet of Ivashka

Peresvetov.[6] Neither the court nor the administration had yet reached into the village. The juridical and administrative authorities established by the government had not penetrated there, and the population, regardless of class, remained without any protection of law. Because of the absence of that protection, the struggle of the strong and the weak there went on in the forms characteristic of the most primitive society. "No matter how many laws are prescribed, with the threat of the most cruel penalties, the deep-rooted internecine insolence and willfulness which is the paramount evil of society will not be destroyed; whether the strong do it to the weak, or the rich to the poor, *whoever is able to do it to whomever, he will wipe him out.*" "It is always better for the weak one to give in to the strong than to start a prolonged and, for themselves, ruinous case." Such observations found their way into cahiers not once. Against this "paramount evil" was directed the unanimous howl, which the cahiers bring from the countryside. The provinces were aching to receive, first of all, courts and government that would be *close* to the population and accessible to it. The voters clamored to be given an opportunity to execute and witness all the documents of civil law in their own neighborhoods, to have their own local surveyors draw the boundaries between disputed lands, to find close at hand, in the nearest town, the necessary information in legal documents, which until then were stored exclusively in the Patrimonial Archive of the ancient capital. The nobility attempted to bring it about so that small rural disputes about trampled crops, timber poaching and all kinds of thefts could be decided by a swift, verbal trial, with the application of immediate sanctions on the spot, according to fresh evidence. . . .

The population also wanted to go to school near home, and receive medical care or obtain credit: it demanded the institution of provincial schools, banks, pharmacies, and doctors. Then, almost

6. Ivan S. Peresvetov (dates unknown, sixteenth century), author of several political works in which he advocated a professional army based on a landholding service nobility.

just as unanimously, but nevertheless in a secondary position as compared with the main substantive demand for a nearby court and administration, the nobility's cahiers demanded that this court and administration be established along the lines of the *nobility's elective self-government*. The forms proposed by the nobility differed. Some wanted the assistant *voevoda's*[7] to be elective, others wanted to restore for that the office of the Petrine *Landsrichter* or to create a new post of "trustee"; still others wanted to retain the "leader" elected for the voting for deputies; and some proposed dividing the province into districts and appointing "land judges" in each, with full administrative-judicial authority. One cahier even remembers Ivan the Terrible's *gubnye* [elected local] institutions. It was generally assumed that there would be meetings of nobles for the selection and control of elective officers to assist criminal investigation and prosecution. In some cahiers, the nobility's class-consciousness went no further than this. But more often we encounter signs that even the provincial aristocracy, following that of the capital, was beginning to be aware of its privileged status and to be suffused with a corporate class spirit. First of all, the pedigreed nobility strove persistently to close itself off from the new bureaucratic nobility of the Petrine Table of Ranks. The older fraternity did not want to recognize nobility by rank, but only by letter patent (i.e., by imperial bestowal). They were especially displeased that the parvenus were "making a great disturbance in the purchase of villages" and driving up the price. Beside the considerations of profit, however, what came through here was a new sensitivity in the nobility toward questions of class honor. If some electors still were making a fuss, according to the old custom, about a monetary fine for "dishonor," others were by then protesting: "the nobility cannot equate its honor with money." Noblemen considered it demeaning to sit in the same room with "riffraff" and demanded the setting

7. *Voevoda*—originally army commander. In the eighteenth century the title referred to the head of a major administrative division or larger town below that of province or provincial capital.

aside of special premises for themselves in governmental chanceries. Out of the same feeling, they protested against frisking at sentry posts and against searches and arrests on their own estates. In connection with that same class spirit, a concept of the honorability and obligation of public service, especially in an elective capacity, was developing. Whereas some cahiers made much beforehand of the official salaries of the future judges, others announced outright: "As does the Marshal [of the local nobility], so must the judges serve the public out of love of honor alone, and for the good of the public." Nobles were chosen for elective office "not as a job, but only because any son of the fatherland will not foreswear to perform this duty for the common good and tranquility (1761 Senate Instruction, p. 311)." True, this conception of the matter was obviously prompted from above. "Regardless of grade or rank," one cahier proclaims, "each one, deeming it a necessity, as a patriot of the fatherland, must serve society for a specified time *as it is prescribed in the present manifesto on the election of a marshal and a deputy.*"

The nobility eagerly endeavored to "distinguish" itself from the other classes through the expansion of the old privileges and the granting of new ones. It demanded exemption, as an exclusive right, from all those encumbrances in the transfer of owners' rights over peasants and land that still remained intact from the old Muscovite service regulations. It wanted to obtain full freedom of testament, which, however, from the viewpoint of the natural law of the time, "can scarcely be considered a natural method of transferring one's own possessions to another." The nobles wanted also to free their property of the taxes and duties imposed by the new Petrine legislation (restriction of the right to own forests, mineral riches, distilleries; the tax on bathhouses). And they clamored especially for the prohibition on the ownership of serfs by other classes and about reserving their own serfs to themselves by strict new measures. The fine for harboring a fugitive should be increased from 10 to 100 or 200 rubles; the government should facilitate the prosecution of fugitives or even take it upon itself; peasants who were lost or had been banished by the landlord should be credited toward the owner's quota of recruits.[8]

We have seen that Catherine, while still Grand Duchess, was prepared to accept a compromise with the serf owners in the peasant question and foresaw their resistance. In subsequent conversations and correspondence (with I. P. Yelagin, D. A. Golitsyn), she became definitely convinced that it was useful for the peasantry to enjoy ownership of property and that it was even necessary for the economic development of the country, but that it was impossible to give the peasants freedom and the right to property immediately, through a general law, either on the lands of the landlords, where complete freedom had to be given, or on the imperial lands, where a general reform would endanger landlords. The matter led, the first time, to the preparation of a small experiment on Grigorii Orlov's land. "Property and liberty" here were to be brought about in the form of a hereditary lease for a definite rental, on the model of the Baltic peasants (and even in this form the proposal remained on paper only). Further, a modest inquiry was made of the newly instituted Free Economic Society: in what, specifically—movable chattels or real estate—should peasant property consist? Finally, Catherine inserted a few mild excerpts from Montesquieu, but half of them were deleted from the *Instruction* even before its issuance. There was, however, some mention of safeguarding the person and property of the peasant against the arbitrary acts and coercion of the landowners. Before the answers on the subject were forthcoming (the Economic Society had raised the question somewhat more boldly than Catherine), Catherine had to be convinced that the mere talk about any changes whatsoever was considered dangerous and that, instead of compromise, the nobility required unconditional and solemn affirmation of its rights of ownership.

8. Serf owners had to furnish recruits (usually one for every 150 souls at every conscription call). As military service was virtually lifelong (twenty-five years) and followed by automatic emancipation, conscription meant a loss of manpower for the landlord and constituted an economic burden for the village and estate, hence the desirability of accumulating "credit" toward the conscription quota.

The cahiers stated that "people and peasants are now slackening somewhat in their obedience to their landlords," that "many, especially in the nighttime, are not in their homes and conceal themselves in places known to no one" or "out of fear spend half a year or more in the cities," since fugitive serfs, "such of them as their masters catch in their homes, are cruelly tortured, put to the torch, their throats cut, or chopped into pieces, and their homes burned." In view of this, the nobles "most humbly request that, in preservation of the ancient ordinance, the nobles' men and peasants remain subject to their lords, and that this be confirmed in the draft of the new code with the statement that the landlords' power over their men and peasants, enacted in ancient times, not be taken away irretrievably, and that as it has been until now, let it be in the future." The 500 peasant petitions that Catherine had brought with her to Moscow from her trip along the Volga in time for the opening of the commission's session were an all too eloquent illustration for the information contained in the cahiers. The remarkable, petulant retort Catherine made to the poet Sumarokov ("And at times they"—meaning the landlords—"are butchered by their own people," and so forth) proves that the Empress by no means imagined the rural community of classes to be a happy idyll. But at first the practical result of this clear understanding of the situation proved to be only a prohibition of peasants' complaints and of military expeditions. We know that Catherine did not like to waver in matters of policy.

Another grave blow dealt by reality to the humane intentions of the Empress was the cahiers' treatment of her attempts to mitigate criminal procedure. As early as 1763, Catherine had ordered that in the case where the offender confessed, the judge would not put him to torture (to discover his accomplices or other crimes with which he had not been charged) and that officials of small towns in general would not resort to torture. From the districts of Novgorod, Belozersk, Opochetsk, and Chukhlomsk came the answer: the demand to torture as before, and statements that "it is inescapable so as not to legalize even more cruel and merciless practices." The Alatyrsk nobility explained to the Empress that only an "enlightened and politicized people" would confess without torture, "but in the case of the Russian people, when someone does evil, he already has such a stony heart and deceitful spirit that he will not tell the truth—not only to the priest but also under questioning, when he is being tortured." And the semi-literate Danskov nobility, in a throwback language, stammered in the train of the others: "And in cases of those condemned under Her Imperial Majesty's laws to public punishment with the whip and the death penalty, it would be pleasing to arrange (the execution) in deterrence of others in those hamlets and villages where someone has committed some crime . . . so that all within the *Sotnia*[9] and the parish might come together to that execution on that day, and all without exception might be at the announced place to observe the offenders and malefactors and their punishment and execution . . . so that through that fear unlawful misdeeds might better be eradicated . . . that the fear and rumor lodged in their hearts by the criminal might come before their eyes and their punishment might be understandable to each. . . ."

Alas, on this occasion the shouts of the Russian provinces should have reminded Catherine of Beccaria's original text, which she had softened in paragraph 208 of her *Instruction*: "One must act upon the jaded spirits of a people that has just emerged from the wild state with impressions that are very powerful and palpable; a bolt of lightning is needed to startle the lion, for a shot from a rifle may only irritate him. But as the people develops *in conditions of social intercourse,* its impressionability grows as well, and the severity of punishment must lessen along with it." If called to account, the Empress could only have responded with her answer to Sumarokov when he remarked that "our low people have not yet had any noble feelings. And they cannot, in their present state." Thus the question automatically arose of what depended on what: a change in the "conditions of life" on the

9. A "hundred"—i.e., administrative unit of about one hundred households.

development of "noble feelings," or, conversely, the development of the "feelings" on changes in the "present state"? Catherine for the time being remained of the liberal opinion: the "body" had to be freed before the "spirit."

Our characterization of the situation that determined the fate of the Commission on Codification would be incomplete if we ignored altogether the area of Catherine's activity in which it was easier for her to decide between "interest" and "justice." I am referring to the sphere of foreign policy.

As we know, the paths of Catherine's domestic and foreign policy intersected. The commission was closed down (or, more accurately, adjourned), because the first Turkish war started [10] and absorbed all the Empress' attention. Catherine's tastes and aspirations found easier and more gratifying application in the new sphere of activity. The glory of a conqueress proved less elusive than legislative laurels. The *appearance* of strength here was easier to convert into a source of strength. That is why the reign, which had begun with a demonstrative pageant of critical ideas, later turned onto the path of a policy of conquest.

Here too, of course, Catherine linked up with the earlier tradition. She completed the tasks set by Muscovite policy back in the fifteenth century. The aims were indeed the same. And the means at times were strikingly similar as well. I have in mind the support for the Orthodox party in Poland, which was sufficiently weak to be unable to sustain itself with its own resources and therefore served as a constant pretext for Russian intervention.[11] It seemed as though fruit that had ripened for centuries was falling of its own accord into Catherine's lap. Actually, however, this was not quite so. Some scholars even assert that Catherine had extended

10. The war lasted from 1768 to 1774 when it was ended by the signing of the Treaty of Kuchuk-Kainardji.

11. The non-Catholic population—Orthodox, Protestants, Jews—of Poland was discriminated against politically and socially. These religious minorities, the so-called Dissidents, sought protection and found support among the neighboring powers (Prussia, Russia) whose intervention and meddling sapped the authority and power of the Polish government.

a hand toward fruit that had not yet ripened, and for this reason came away with only part of the whole. In any case, there is no doubt that her personal influence (more precisely, the influence first of Orlov, then of Potemkin) in foreign policy made itself felt with extreme cogency. The chief result of the indulgence in a passion for conquest was an acceleration of the *pace* of events, which created a very unfavorable situation for deciding questions that came up. Too many of them came up at once, and future prospects gravitated into the realm of pure utopia. The "hot head" made its presence felt here, too. Circumspection and slowness, two of the principal features of the old Muscovite policy, were completely absent from Catherine's policy.

To give a more graphic idea, let us mention the rapid succession of events in the interval of time we are now discussing. Catherine made her debut in politics with peaceful intentions. They already harbor the future belligerent program, since very soon it is observed that the support of peace is, in Europe's eyes, a *new* goal of an *independent* Russian policy, which breaks with the system of old alliances and begins a new era in Russia's international posture. Catherine then is pulled inexorably into the rut of the old Muscovite policy. The first, too easy, successes befog her mind.[12] The victories won, by excessively indiscriminate means, in the issue of the Dissidents place the very government in difficult straits. Russia cannot hold onto the position it has occupied, face to face with alarmed or antagonistic powers and with the national awakening in Poland, agitated by the Russian insolence. "Our strength can do everything," as Prince Repnin himself, the agent of Russian power, characterized this situation from Warsaw, "but it is not only through this that we affirm the faith of the nation in us and in our influence here, but, on the contrary, we utterly destroy it, leaving a wound in the hearts of all the reasonable and worthy men who alone can, through their judgment, give leadership to the nation.

12. Reference is probably to the election of Stanislas Augustus Poniatowski as king of Poland (1763), the securing of guarantees for the Dissidents, and the maintenance of the constitution that perpetuated Poland's weakness.

. . . Such an opinion, naturally, produces extreme mistrust and hence will powerfully obstruct us in assembling into a party dependent on no one but us the trusty and worthy men on whose character and influence with people we can rely. If we assemble our party of men who have no honor in the nation, then they will be more of a burden to us than a benefit, having no credit; and so we will be compelled to do everything by force. And from this there will result that on the first occasion that our attention or our forces are turned in another direction, Poland, bearing the severity of our yoke only out of impotence, will seek to take advantage of the situation in order to rid itself of it. . . . In explaining this, I venture to propose that our interests, for the duration of any involvement with the Porte, require that we beforehand establish internal order in Poland, so that we might in case of necessity give it the strength that we see fit . . . or else it cannot be useful to us."

These words proved to be prophetic. The earliest consequences of the policy condemned by Repnin were not long in making themselves felt. The disorders in Poland prompted the Turks to declare war. Russia foresaw it, but attempted sedulously to prevent it—and had to wage it without having had time to prepare properly. Catherine was not despondent. She made up for the lack of troops with the celebrated reminder to Rumyantsev: "The Romans did not ask how many of the enemy were against them, but where they were." Rumyantsev proved more than equal to the task: Larga and Kagul bailed the Empress out of trouble and backed up the claims of the Russian diplomats. But these were the effects of a minute, with years yet to come; and the Russian troops, despite a brilliant beginning, were unable to move from the Danube into the heart of the country. Nor did their Roman valor help them. Despite this, the demands presented to Turkey were so great that, contrary to its own wish to conclude a peace, the Porte let the war drag on. Finally, in order to get out of the sticky situation, Catherine was compelled to make up for the outcome of the Turkish war with a concession from Poland—and for this to consent to the partition with the other neighboring powers. Thus, the result of the abuse of Russian power in Poland turned out to be the hasty liquidation of the Polish question by the European consortium.

By the time of the opening of the commission's sessions on codification in the summer of 1767, no one had yet thought of such a forced outcome of the Russian diplomatic victories in Poland. Europe, it seemed, had bowed down before the unexpected unveiling of Russian might. The Empress' position within the state also had gained strength. After the collapse of the Orlovs' matrimonial plan,[13] which had caused annoyance with them among the Guards officers, Grigorii Orlov could no longer intimidate Catherine with his influence on those circles that had elevated her to the throne. Panin's claims[14] to power were cleverly eliminated by bringing him close to hand—as Catherine later advised Louis XVI to do with Lafayette. The reputation as an enlightened legislatrix that Catherine dreamed of gaining was ensured for her beforehand by Voltaire. Finally, the "kindness and love of the people" that Catherine was counting on acquiring through her attention to the "popular welfare" and "justice" proved to be the traditional trappings of the high rank she held: Catherine did not know whether to be angry or touched when, during a trip, some village women set up candles before her, crossed themselves, and touched their foreheads to the ground. In brief, a substantial part of the external inducement toward wise legislation vanished the moment easy success began to divert the Empress' attention toward matters of foreign policy. When the commission convened, the mood was very different from that which prevailed at the time it had been conceived.

The commission turned out to be a cumbersome, complex, and hard-to-drive machine. It did very serious work—and did it very respectably. But it was not quite the work for which the Empress

13. Allusion to the alleged plan of Grigorii Orlov to become the officially recognized husband of Catherine II.

14. As tutor of the heir, Grand Duke Paul, Nikita Panin is believed to have advocated that Catherine be proclaimed regent during her son's minority.

had destined it. The mood of the assembly was very businesslike, and the level of preparation for work and of comprehension of its own interests was very high. But aside from that, members who had a defined ideology were a rare exception. However, to deduce from this, as the son of the commission's marshal, Bibikov, deduced, that "the minds of the greater part of the delegates were not yet prepared for this and were quite far away from the degree of enlightenment and knowledge that were required for such an important affair as theirs" would be unfair. A brief description of the debates and views of the assembly will show it.

The first thing that interests us when we look into the minutes of the commission meetings is the role played by the noble intelligentsia with which we are already familiar. We see, actually, in the roster of commission members almost all the names we encountered seven years earlier in the pages of the first Russian journals. But a great disappointment awaits us. The star role in the commission belongs not at all to this flower of the aristocratic youth. The young nobles behave with extreme restraint, speak seldom, for the most part remain silent on questions of principle, and meticulously, as it were, avoid expressing themselves. The readiest explanation can be sought in the fact that the noble intelligentsia, often occupying high posts at the court and in government, felt that it was at home on the commission and was deferring to its guests. But there is another nuance here. The officials of the capital, obviously, were better acquainted with the behind-the-scenes story of the commission. They acted only when necessary, out of one special consideration or another, and left it to the provincials to carry on the heated debate over principles, from which they in any case did not expect important practical results to emerge. There were occasions, however, when they deemed it necessary to express themselves and even to condescend to polemics with the rank-and-file members of the assembly. In such cases, the representatives of the first generation of the Russian intelligentsia disappoint us still more. If they expressed liberal thoughts, one can almost always assume that they wanted to please the Empress or

were directly carrying out her secret assignment. And if they spoke for themselves, their speeches almost always amounted to a cautious defense of the nobility's claims in all their breadth. Time, obviously, had contrived to cool their ardor. We recognize here a generation that had busied itself with journalism for its own diversion and had introduced into the abstract theory of natural law some practical emendations. We begin to understand why the generation of the 1750's did not inscribe its names in the history of Russian society and disappeared altogether from the memory of posterity. In order to find their names, it is necessary to exhume Novikov's dictionary and Dmitrievsky's memoirs. But even there we recognize only that all these gentlemen of the bedchamber and dignitaries had been promising at one time in their youth. Not a word is said about the fulfillment of their promise.

Having renounced active ideological propaganda, the noble intellectuals nevertheless felt it awkward to openly defend class privileges. Other people were the fundamental and unconditional defenders of the nobility on the commission. They associated themselves with one of two extreme types: that of Prince Shcherbatov,[15] the only theoretician of the nobility, who debated with heat and knowledge against the Empress' vaunted liberalism but was in tune with her secret sympathies for the "ancient names," and that of the inveterate rustic Mikhail Glazov—the prototype of Markov the Second [16]—who couldn't speak without cursing and who regaled the assemblage with his angry outbursts and his nonsensical argumentation.

The main animation and interest were imparted to the debates by the presence in the assembly of large groups of urban deputies opposed to the nobility. It is difficult to say to what extent this had been intended, but these representatives of the middle order of

15. Prince Mikhail M. Shcherbatov, 1733–1790, author, historian, and official. He was the spokesman for the old noble families and the large serfowners in the Commission of 1767.

16. Nikolai E. Markov, born 1876, arch-conservative deputy in the Third and Fourth Dumas (1907–1917)—called "the second" to distinguish him from another deputy of the same name.

men proved to outnumber the noble deputies (207 to 160). At stake for them were their most vital interests, impinged upon by the claims of the nobility. The draft worked out by the preceding commission had already tightly squeezed the commercial-industrial class in favor of the nobility. Now, seeing the mandates and the opinions of Catherine's deputies, the urban deputies "noted with sorrow that a great oppression was being prepared for the Russian merchantry" and readied themselves for a serious struggle. The powerful upsurge of industrial life in Catherine's time often sharpened the antagonism between the commercial-industrial and landowning classes and often created new strains. In the village, there was considerable development of seasonal industries, cottage manufactures, and the wholesale purchase and reselling by rich peasants of the peasants' produce. Here the fight was over the role of wholesale buyer, which the merchants wanted to wrest away from the peasants and the peasants wanted to keep for themselves. In the other direction, from city to countryside, the middleman's role of the small dealer was developing. By all rights, it belonged to the merchantry, but it continually slipped away from it, thanks to the itinerant rural peddlers and the tradesmen at the fairs. In both cases, securing the role of middleman in trade for the *peasants* was to the direct advantage of those who owned them. They imposed high quit-rents on such peasant-tradesmen, or else invested their own capital heavily in their businesses. It is understandable why the noble deputies, not sparing the dark colors when describing the laziness, dissoluteness, and all other manner of sins of their peasant serfs, suddenly became their ardent defenders against the onslaughts of the merchantry and began in equally vivid colors— even with "great transports of the soul"—to depict the sorry state of the peasantry. There was another point on which the interests of the nobility and the merchantry were by then in direct confrontation. As soon as factory production began to show profits, there appeared a mass of factories founded by landowners and operated with serf labor. This kind of landlord-serf factory threatened the Petrine factories with ascribed labor with serious disruption.[17] That is why, on the question of the ownership of factories, a lively exchange broke out in the commission. Both sides demanded a prohibition, and they could not get together on any compromise whatsoever. This single circumstance placed the townspeople in permanent and persistent opposition to the demands of the nobility.

There was yet another group on the commission, not as numerous as the above, and not so homogeneous in its interests. It occupied an intermediate position, on different questions joining now with one of the above groups, now with the other. It comprised the *odnodvortsy*[18] and civil servants of the lower ranks. They were turned against the nobility by its claim to be sealed off by the high wall of the monarch's bestowal of nobility from a mass influx of all kinds of *raznochintsy*[19] into the nobility through government service. But that very hope of becoming noblemen themselves often aligned this group with the nobility. The merchants' desire to confiscate all trading and craft shops from the *raznochintsy* set them against the merchantry. The *raznochintsy*, meanwhile, needed the revenues from industrial occupations more than did the peasants; here the number of individuals who had lost their land and were compelled to feed themselves through manufacturing was far greater.

On only one question were the representatives of the various classes unanimous among themselves and in agreement with the Empress' views. The Baltic, Finnish, Ukrainian, and Smolensk

17. Peter the Great, permitted to adscribe peasants permanently to factories and mines, created what became virtually a class of industrial serfs.

18. *Odnodvortsy,* literally single homesteaders, originally a class of petty military servicemen settled on the frontiers of the Muscovite state. In the eighteenth century they had sunk to the status of free peasants. Cf. T. Esper, "The Odnodvortsy and the Russian Nobility," *American Slavic and East European Review,* XVIII (1959), 124–134.

19. *Raznochintsy,* literally men of various rank, denoted those who were neither peasants nor members of the service hierarchy. The bulk of this group was made up of children of the clergy and of townspeople who had received some education. Cf. Ch. Becker, " 'Raznochintsy': the Development of the Word and Concept," *American Slavic and East European Review,* XVIII (1959), 63–74.

deputies had not come to the commission with the intention of considering Russia's affairs as their own. Rather than the "happiness of one and all" they preferred the preservation of the old privileges, granted to them in the treaties on the basis of which they had once upon a time been annexed to Russia. Catherine clearly understood the situation and had long before drawn up a plan of action for herself. "To violate (the privileges) by abolishing all of them suddenly would be improper; to call them [the regions] foreign, however . . . is not only a mistake but can be termed genuinely stupid. . . . These provinces ought to be brought by the easiest methods to the point where they are Russified." These words from an instruction to the procurator-general [of the Senate] were written in 1764. But in the commission, Catherine had to sing a different tune. She had been offended in her enlightened principles. "To let the Livonian laws be better than ours will be—never! For our rules were written by philanthropy itself, and they have no rules to show us, and, more than that, some of their enactments are filled with ignorance and barbarism. And so they solemnly request self-protection: we want to be punished with death; we request torture; we request that cases in court be never adjudicated because of interminable slander. . . . It is left for the enlightened world to judge such absurdities." Catherine intended to instill such attitudes in the commission "in whomever is most favorably disposed, but it would be better if it were someone of quality." However, the Empress' delicate work was not needed. The assembly was no less offended by the demands of the deputies from the border regions than was the Empress. But it expressed this affront more coarsely and candidly. The "vanquished" must not have an advantage over the "victors"; but a lord can do as he wishes; hence, the laws must be the same for all. Such, in its main outline, was the argumentation of the speakers in the assembly. Catherine could not help but sense how these deputies, retarding all her plans in questions of internal policy, were prepared to untie her hands and went even farther than her in the nationality question. This was a foretaste of the success that awaited the Empress in the opinion of the public, once she would transfer her dreams and efforts to the field of foreign policy.

Such was this complex milieu. It was not adapted, perhaps, for the accomplishment of Catherine's tasks, but it was quite able and prepared to endeavor to accomplish its own. Once Her Imperial Majesty deemed the deputies "worthy, not only to declare their needs, but also to be the judges of the nationwide affairs under consideration," they, of course, did not find it "possible for a citizen to be silent." It was quite natural, of course, that they conducted the discussion of "nationwide affairs" from the viewpoint of their own group interests. And this was what deprived the Empress and her deputies of an opportunity to come to an agreement.

The Empress attempted more than once to guide the assembly, through her own intelligentsia, toward discussion of the questions that interested her: torture and serfdom. But the former question evoked almost no response at all among the deputies—unless one counts a few accidental slips of the tongue by the provincials in favor of corporal punishment. This elicited sharp calls to order from the noble intelligentsia and sarcastic reminders about the ideas of the *Instruction*. On the question of serfdom and restriction of the landowners' authority, the bellwether was again an intellectual nobleman, the provincial Korob'in, inspired, it seems, by higher authority.[20] To the nobility's annoyance, the deputies of the other estates treated Korob'in rather sympathetically. But such a storm came forth from the nobility's side that it must have convinced Catherine once again that the most modest attempts by her on the question of the serfs would come up against the most obdurate resistance. Catherine did, however, make another attempt. In the draft on the rights of nobles worked out by the special commission, an implication of the possibility of setting up a new type of "free villages" was tacitly introduced. It was proposed that they be provided with various privileges with respect

20. Catherine later entrusted to Korob'in the protection of the "rights of the nobles." He often voted with the noble intelligentsia that was close to the throne. [Author's Note]

to legal status. But the nobility, and specifically the intellectuals, on this occasion preferred not to take the hint, which actually was not particularly clear.

In the deliberations on the "draft of nobles' rights," finally, the main class groups at the assembly joined in a full-scale battle. It must have shown the Empress graphically what could and what could not be obtained from the commission. The very first effort made by the Marshal—Bibikov—to confine the assembly to a *summary* evaluation of the draft—evoked a protest from both contending groups. A small group of writers and intellectuals from the nobility requested, briefly but resolutely, "time for reflection." The representatives of the *raznochintsy,* whose interests were especially injured by the draft, even more insistently argued that "If it [the draft] is in conformity with the statute of our state, *and, what is more—if it is in agreement with natural reason* [from which the *raznochintsy* derived their demand for the equality of all nobles!] —then we shall affirm and decree it unshakably. But if, on the contrary, we find in it anything that can be harmful for the entire fatherland and general security, let us submit our representations." The marshal yielded, and a decisive battle began. In it, all the delicate questions were brought up again, and with them all the serious disagreements that had divided the deputies. But by now the warring parties had identified their members and were acting as solid groups. The intellectual nobility, defending privilege, put forth as their leader Aleksei Naryshkin, whom we already know as a staff member of Kheraskov's journals.[21] A tightly knit group of thirty-six men was behind him on all questions, large and small. Far more imposing were the groups of *raznochintsy* and townspeople, who fought for access into the nobility and for protection

21. *Poleznoe uveselenie* (Useful Entertainment), 1760–1762; *Svobodnye chasy* (Idle Hours), 1763; *Nevinnoe uprazhnenie* (Innocent Occupation), 1763; *Dobroe namerenie* (Good Intention), 1764, played a leading role in disseminating Western literature and ideas among the Russian educated nobility. Kheraskov, their main sponsor or editor, was at the time director of the newly founded University of Moscow whose students contributed actively to the journals.

of the commercial-industrial bourgeoisie against noblemen's factories and peasant kulaks. There could be no thought of further agreement on the substantive questions in the assembly, where numerical superiority belonged to the implacable enemies of the "rights of nobles." The mood of this majority and the impossibility of going with them in the direction desired by the government were especially vividly evident in the story of one ballot, which at the outset seemed entirely casual but by its outcome exerted a decisive influence, perhaps, on the fate of the commission.

In the session of August 7, 1768, the noble deputy Prince Ivan Viazemskii made a proposal that was outwardly conciliatory. He found that the draft of the nobles' rights took away nothing from those who *at the given moment* owned something, and that all the *raznochintsy* who "up to this time" had attained the required rank in service would doubtlessly end up in the nobility, and it only remained to petition the Empress about reviewing the membership and compiling a general roster of the nobility. But in the conception of the intellectual nobility, "reviewing" merged with the sorting of nobles into grades and with closing off further access into the nobility. Viazemskii's proposal had no doubt been inspired by the Empress. But it was introduced, like many similarly inspired proposals, so cautiously that in the beginning it attracted nobody's special attention. This, however, proved dangerous for the final outcome of the motion. At the end of the following session, which heard perfectly reasonable arguments from two urban deputies to the effect that the compilation of lists was a matter for the Heraldry Office; that the assembly should only establish *rules* for attaining nobility and not concern itself with *who* was going to end up in the nobility and who was not; that, finally, Viazemskii's motion was plainly ambiguous and tended toward the removal of civil servants and officers from the nobility, the *raznochintsy* and urbanites voted down the Viazemskii motion by a vote of 102 to 18. Then, at the next session, members of the noble intelligentsia group who had been absent from the previous one appeared, among them such rare visitors to the commission and such intimates of the Empress as Grigorii Orlov, Kozitskii, and Lev Naryshkin. The Viazemskii motion was resubmitted on the clumsy pretext that the Heraldry Office was demanding lists from the commission, that the commission itself could not supply them and had to beseech Her Imperial Majesty to give them. There were 140 sponsors of the Viazemskii motion, including as many as ten Tatars. A new vote was scheduled for the next session. Before the vote, the marshal invited the deputies to give special thought [to it] and "during the issuance of the ballots did not fail to remind people that those who agreed with Viazemskii should place the ballots in the 'yea' box." After all these explanations and reminders, there were still to be found 158 stalwart daredevils who preferred the nay box to the yea one. There were 242 ballots cast for Viazemskii.

The adjournment of the commission sessions four months later was not, of course, directly connected to the incident just described. There was quite a respectable pretext for this. Out of 160 noble deputies, 92 had to go into the active army, a sufficient excuse for an interruption in the commission's work. But the Viazemskii episode must have shown that the commission was of absolutely no use as a *machine à voter*. As a source of information on the state of the country "with whom we are dealing and for whom we must care" it had already done its job. It was far more convenient to make use of the business reports and the deputies' labor in the countless special commissions picked by the "great" one. Thus, the calling once again of the great commission would have been only an encumbrance on the Empress' personal initiative. And we know that she had no desire to surrender this initiative, especially now, when she was convinced of the stubbornness with which the various class groups were defending their interests. The era of "the happiness of one and all" had ended. When Catherine's taste for legislation returned, she would seek other authorities and set herself other, more modest goals. But she would always remember the failure of her "enlightened" legislation, when circumstances brought her into collision with the direct manifestations of the autonomy of Russian society.

ALLEN McCONNELL

The Autocrat
and the Open Critic

A Tartuffe in a skirt.
ALEXANDER PUSHKIN, Historical Notes

Catherine . . . required of Russians nothing contrary to their conscience or civil tradition. . . . Her proud, noble soul refused to be debased by timid suspicion, and so vanished the dread of the Secret Chancery. With it left us also the spirit of slavery, at any rate among the upper classes. We accustomed ourselves to pass judgment. . . . Catherine listened to our opinions, and there were times when she struggled with herself, but she always overcame the desire for revenge—a virtue of great excellence in a monarch!
N. M. KARAMZIN, Memoir on Ancient and Modern Russia

The Empress of Russia is very proud, very ambitious, and very vain.
FREDERICK THE GREAT to KAUNITZ, 1770

Reprinted from *The Journal of Modern History,* Vol. XXXVI, No. 1, March 1964. Copyright © 1964 by the University of Chicago. Originally published under the title "The Empress and Her Protégé: Catherine II and Radishchev."

*Elle changera la face de cette contrée, la nation russe devien-
dra une des plus honnêtes, une des plus sages, et une des plus
redoutables contrées de l'Europe, du monde!*

DIDEROT to MME DE VANDEUIL, October 23, 1773

IN MAY 1790 an anonymous book, *A Journey from St. Petersburg to Moscow,* severely critical of serfdom and autocracy,
appeared in Russia's northern capital and was soon brought to the
attention of Catherine the Great, then in her twenty-eighth year of
triumphant rule. She read the book carefully, making marginal
notations, and observed that the author "had learning enough and
has read many books." Catherine, who confessed to Grimm that
whenever she saw a new quill her fingers itched to write, understood the desire to make a name through letters. She recognized a
fellow intellectual.

But she found that the book was also seditious: "The purpose of
this book is clear on every page: its author, infected and full of
the French madness, is trying in every possible way to break down
respect for authority . . . to stir up in the people indignation
against their superiors and against the government."[1]

She noted the author's "bilious black and yellow view of things"
and speculated on his reasons for writing the book: "It is a safe
bet that the author's motive in writing it was this, that *he does not
have entrée to the palace.* Maybe he had it once and lost it, but
since he does not have it now but does have an evil and consequently ungrateful heart, he is struggling for it now with his pen"
(p. 240).

She soon guessed the author through his references to Grotius,
Montesquieu, Blackstone and modern jurisprudence. Catherine had

---

1. A. N. Radishchev, *A Journey from St. Petersburg to Moscow,* trans.
Leo Wiener, ed. Roderick Page Thaler (Cambridge, Mass., 1958), p. 239.
Catherine's marginal notes to her copy of the *Journey* are given on pages
239–249. This translation hereafter will be cited by page number in parentheses.

sent Radishchev and eleven other elite Russian youths to the University of Leipzig twenty-four years before to prepare them to become jurists and she had a long memory (p. 241). She suspected Radishchev after she had read only thirty pages. Twelve days later she had finished the *Journey* and, made no more indulgent by the intervening signal naval victory over the Swedes, she called Radishchev "a rebel worse than Pugachev," the Cossack leader of a terrible rebellion, 1773–1774. As one proof, she observed that "he praises [Benjamin] Franklin"![2]

She forwarded her notes to Sheshkovskii, the dread head of the Secret Chancery, who arrested and questioned Radishchev. The unhappy author, plainly astonished by all this, made an abject and absurd confession that he had written an "insane" book through his reading of Raynal and others and had sought merely to gain literary fame.[3]

Radishchev was tried by the criminal court and the Senate and was condemned to death. Catherine commuted the penalty to ten years' exile in Siberia. The trial of her protégé, whom she had decorated for distinguished service and had promoted to head of the St. Petersburg Customs, several months before the arrest, is one of the darkest spots in her reign, and illustrates how far she had lapsed from her early published liberal aims.[4]

Radishchev was convicted for publishing a book which—except for insignificant additions—the censor had passed. He was condemned on the basis of plainly inapplicable laws on conspiracy—no collaborator could be found. He was also condemned for treason, a charge patently false, and for incitement to rebellion, which,

2. *Dnevnik A. V. Khrapovitskago, 1782–1793* (St. Petersburg, 1874), pp. 338, 340.

3. A. S. Babkin, *Protsess A. N. Radishcheva* (Moscow and Leningrad, 1952), pp. 170–171. Babkin's book is the best collection of materials on Radishchev's trials and related matters.

4. For a contrary view see E. Shmurlo, "Catherine II and Radishchev," in the *Slavonic and Eastern European Review*, XVII (1938–1939), 618–622. Shmurlo condemns Radishchev's "naïve and childish attacks against autocracy" and almost agrees with Catherine that he was a "madman." She had "no right not to punish him."

by showing the urgent need for reforms, the book was written to *prevent*. Catherine read a summons to revolution into the very pages that expressed dread of serf vengeance—as if illiterate serfs, not serf-owners, were reading the book!

The trial and harsh penalty were all the more shocking in that they violated many of Catherine's own principles contained in her widely publicized *Nakaz* or *Instructions to the Commissioners for Composing a New Code of Laws* (1767), which within four years had appeared in twenty-three versions, including one or more in almost every European language.[5] The *Nakaz* called for the publicizing of trials, a minimum of two witnesses, no punishment for words as compared with deeds, and warnings against treating as treason mere disrespect for the sovereign (pp. 471–484). The dismay of liberal Russians at the heavy penalty may be seen in a letter of Count Semion Vorontsov, Russian ambassador to England, to his brother, Count Alexander Vorontsov, Radishchev's friend and protector: "The condemnation of poor Radishchev hurts me deeply. What a sentence and what a commutation for a mere blunder! What will they do for a crime or a real revolt?" [6]

Catherine was plainly frightened by the French Revolution; her references to Radishchev's "infection" with French ideas show she feared that these could be contagious even in the literate nobility, her chief source of support. Little wonder that she feared Radishchev more than Pugachev, the illiterate Cossack whose rabble was quickly crushed once her armies were freed from wars in Turkey

5. The authorized English translation of 1768 is given in W. F. Reddaway, *Documents of Catherine the Great* (Cambridge, 1931), pp. 216–309. Reddaway's introduction is considerably more perceptive than the lengthy studies on the *Nakaz* and Catherine's politics by Georg Sacke, *Die Gesetzgebende Kommission Katharinas II* (Breslau, 1940) and his other works cited therein. The Russian and French versions are given in parallel columns in N. D. Chechulin (ed.), *Nakaz Imperatritsy Ekateriny II, dannyi komissii po sochineniiu proekta novago ulozheniia* (Moscow, 1907). My citations are from Reddaway's translation, unless otherwise specified, and indicated in parentheses by italicized numbers referring to paragraphs. I have retained the spelling and emphasis of this text.

6. *Arkhiv Kniazia Vorontsova* (Moscow, 1870–1890), IX, 181.

and Poland. In addition to fear, she felt insulted personally—as well she might—and by someone to whom she had given the signal privilege of service at court in the Corps de Pages, a university education, and steady advancement in the civil service.[7]

Radishchev's motives in writing the *Journey* are more complex than Catherine's on reading it. Catherine thought Radishchev sought to gain an entrée at court to vent his bile or to lead a rebellion. Pushkin, Radishchev's first biographer, called the *Journey* a "satirical call to rebellion," a "criminal" work, yet gave credit to Radishchev's refusal to compromise with the evils of his time and his "knight-like scrupulousness." Radishchev's son Pavel, writing in 1858, denied the criminal or revolutionary intent of the book and called it simply a collection of useful observations on life in Russia, except for the radical "Ode to Liberty."[8] For Pavel, as for subsequent Russian liberal historiography, Radishchev was a friendly reformer, seeking to warn his sovereign, the "philosophe on the throne." Soviet historiography since the 1930's has taken the view of Catherine herself and later conservative writers—for entirely different reasons—and claimed Radishchev as the *chef de file* of Russian revolutionaries, scornful of the possibility, even the desirability, of reform.[9]

To understand Radishchev's attitude toward Catherine, one must note their common philosophical assumptions, and the many parts of the *Nakaz* that formed points of departure for Radishchev's

7. For the effect of the French Revolution and Swedish war on Catherine at the time of Radishchev's trial, see Roderick Page Thaler, "Catherine II's Reaction to Radishchev," *Études slaves et est-européenes* II, fasc. 3 (Autumn 1957), 154–160.

8. For a discussion of Pushkin's two works on Radishchev see my "Pushkin's Literary Gamble," in *American Slavic and East European Review,* X (December, 1960), 577–595. Biographies of Radishchev by his sons, Pavel and Nikolai, are given in *Biografiia A. N. Radishcheva napisannye ego synoviami* (Moscow and Leningrad, 1959).

9. A lengthy review of the historiography of Radishchev's *Journey* is given in Kariakin and Plimak, "O nekotorykh spornykh problemakh mirovozzreniia A. N. Radishcheva," *Istoricheskie zapiski,* LXVI (1960), 137–205 (see also my "Soviet Views of Radishchev's *Journey,*" in *Slavic and East European Journal,* XXII [Spring 1963], 9–17).

Journey; the latter was partly an attack on the *Nakaz* (its defense of autocracy) but mainly a criticism of Catherine's failure to carry out the Nakaz's promises.

The Empress and her protégé had a large common stock of Enlightenment ideas. Both were formal members of the Orthodox church, Catherine ostentatiously, Radishchev quietly; but both were deists at heart, Catherine privately in her correspondence with philosophes, Radishchev openly in the *Journey*. Both knew Bayle thoroughly, and both favored religious toleration; Catherine practiced it toward Protestants in the Baltic, Catholics in White Russia, and Jesuits expelled from western Europe. She constructed mosques in St. Petersburg and the Crimea, and on the sixth of January every year presided over a *banquet de tolérance*. At the same time, both gave credit to Helvétius. Radishchev noted that Helvétius, whom he had read in Leipzig at the suggestion of a passing Russian diplomat, taught the Russian students "how to think";[10] Catherine was not only pleased to have his *De l'esprit* translated—a work burned by the public hangman in France—but she was also flattered by his dedication of *De l'homme* to the enlightened northern rulers, Frederick II and herself. Catherine, like Radishchev, made utilitarian ideas an important argument against inhuman punishments, tortures, obscurantism, clericalism, and superstition.

Both Catherine and Radishchev admired Voltaire. Catherine corresponded with the patriarch of Ferney and so flattered and misled the head of the philosophe party—who prided himself on his practical sense and intimate knowledge of Russia—that his relations with her, according to a recent excellent study, displayed "the depths to which a violent partisan can descend."[11] Radishchev

10. For a study of Helvétius' influence on Radishchev and his fellow student and mentor at Leipzig, Fedor Ushakov, see my "Helvétius' Russian Pupils" in the *Journal of the History of Ideas,* June–Sept. 1963, pp. 373–386.

11. Peter Gay, *Voltaire's Politics: The Poet as Realist* (Princeton, N.J., 1959), p. 172. The correspondence is available in French in W. F. Reddaway, pp. 1–213.

cited Voltaire with admiration all his life, and in exile wrote a mock epic, *Bova,* in imitation of *La pucelle.*

Montesquieu was for Catherine a "breviary of rulers"; she boasted that she had based her *Nakaz* largely on him. Radishchev hailed the author of "the immortal book on the laws" and wrote a *Historical Song* in imitation of *Considérations sur les causes de la grandeur et décadence des Romains.*[12] Both admired Beccaria's *Dei delitti e delle pene.* Catherine often cited his principles in the *Nakaz* and, in a country where her predecessors had had tongues torn out for slander, largely abolished the use of torture in prisons. Radishchev had admired Beccaria since his days at Leipzig university.

Like most philosophes, both Catherine and Radishchev admired classical antiquity for its men of civic virtue. After his visit to Russia in 1773, Diderot called Catherine a ruler with "the soul of Brutus and the charms of Cleopatra," and referred to her in his letters as "Cato." He could hardly have pleased her more. Catherine wrote to Grimm that at night she used to read Plutarch, favorite of eighteenth-century men of letters, "to hearten myself." [13] A recent biographer, generally hostile to Catherine, nevertheless noted that the Roman historian Tacitus, in his scathing portraits of Roman emperors' tyranny, "inspired her with a hatred of despotism." [14] She boasted of her *"âme républicaine"* before coming to the throne, and observed that liberty was "the soul of everything; without thee everything is dead." [15]

Radishchev was equally devoted to Cato, the classic example of patriotism, self-respect, and fortitude, and he recommended in the

12. A detailed analysis of Montesquieu's axioms used in the *Nakaz* is given in the preface to Chechulin, *Nakaz.* Fifteen of the first twenty chapters are based on Montesquieu.

13. For Catherine and Diderot see Maurice Tourneux, *Diderot et Catherine II* (Paris, 1899); see also L. G. Crocker, *The Embattled Philosopher: A Life of Denis Diderot* (East Lansing, Mich., 1954), Chap. 16, "A philosopher queen," pp. 373-400.

14. Ian Grey, *Catherine the Great* (Philadelphia, 1960), pp. 56-57.

15. *Sbornik Imperatorskago Rossiiskago Istoricheskago Obshchestva,* VIII (1871), 84. Hereafter cited as *"S.I.R.I.O."*

Journey that anyone living under an intolerable despotism should, before compromising with tyranny, follow Cato's example (p. 123). According to Plutarch, Cato had said while stabbing himself, "Now I am my own master." Radishchev named Tacitus as one of the three greatest historians of all time.

Both Catherine and Radishchev read widely in Russian as well as classical history. Catherine restored history to an important place in the curriculum of the Academy of Sciences and encouraged work in the government archives. She wrote historical dramas based on heroic pre-Mongol Russian rulers and refuted European historians who would not include Russia as a part of Europe.[16] Radishchev also studied Russia's past, but drew quite different conclusions from it, namely that Russians had known free and self-governing republican rule in pre-Mongol times and were still capable of it.

When one turns from the ideals and rhetoric of the age to practical questions, one finds that Catherine and Radishchev were unalterably opposed. True, Catherine knew as well as Radishchev that the position of the serfs was intolerable. Early in her reign she had made the peasant question a subject for discussion throughout the land, and the legislative commission deputies argued it further. From the height of the throne Catherine set forth the novel idea that the serf is just as much a human as his lord, that he also has a right to rational existence, and thereby, in the words of the leading historian of serfdom, she "inscribed her name forever in the history of the peasant question in Russia."[17] Even after the terrible Pugachev rebellion, Catherine could see clearly that repression of the serfs was no solution. She wrote to her procurator-general, Prince Viazemskii, "If we do not agree to reductions of the [serf-

16. For her support of historians see Hans Rogger, *National Consciousness in Eighteenth-Century Russia* (Cambridge, Mass., 1960), pp. 241–243, 263 (see also Alexandre Koyré, "Catherine II, historienne de la Russie médiévale," in Institut de France, Académie des inscriptions et des belles lettres, *Comptes rendus des séances* [Paris, 1944], pp. 458–472).

17. V. I. Semevskii, *Krest'ianskii vopros v Rossii v XVIII i v pervoi polovine XIV veka* (Saint Petersburg, 1888), I, 228.

owners'] cruelty and to amelioration of a position intolerable to humans, then they will rise up against our will sooner or later." [18]

Yet Catherine spread the area and intensified the oppression of serfdom.[19] Serfs were prohibited from even complaining against their lords to the sovereign, and they were sent to Siberia for "continued impudence"—as determined by the serf-owner. Subsequent revocation of this decree remained ineffective. Russia's victorious armies brought serfdom to parts of former Ottoman territory and to Polish lands hitherto largely free from it.

But serfdom, the most distressing social evil for Radishchev, was only one of the many ills he saw in his day and recorded in his *Journey*. To understand fully Radishchev's frustration and despair, one must note the fine hopes Catherine held out in her *Nakaz,* and how reality mocked them.

Catherine's liberal first draft of the *Nakaz* had no chance, given the Russian nobility's power and jealousy of its privileges. She later wrote in a memorandum of 1779 that she had showed her draft to Panin who said *"Ce sont des axiomes à renverser des murailles."* He and others in her entourage struck out more than half of what she had written.[20] Among the stricken parts were provisions for establishing peasant courts, liberating the families of violated serf women, and prohibiting any free person from enserfing himself.[21] A French diplomat at her court at the time noted her dilemma: "This princess feels only too well that she is in absolute dependence on the magnates of her empire, whose wills she cannot and dare not often counter for fear of the funereal consequences which might result." [22]

18. P. Bartenev, ed., *Os'mnadtsatyi vek,* III (1869), 390.

19. The best brief account of this process is Geroid T. Robinson's *Rural Russia under the Old Regime* (New York, 1932), Chap. 2, "The triumph of the servile system."

20. *S.I.R.I.O.,* XXVII (1880), 175.

21. A. S. Lappo-Danilevskii, "Ekaterina II i krest'ianskii vopros," *Velikaia Reforma* (Moscow, 1911), pp. 163–190. Reprinted on pp. 267–289.

22. Despatch of Rossignol, *S.I.R.I.O.,* CXLI (1912), 251. Sacke has challenged the traditional view of Catherine's insecurity and weakness as well as any conceivable sincerity on her part in wishing for reforms. He asserts

But if her real power was thus severely circumscribed and her "autocracy" was in name only, she clung resolutely to the name. She conceded nothing in her claims to supreme power. The *Nakaz* begins with a frank and vigorous defense of autocracy: "The sovereign is absolute. The extent of the empire necessitates absolute power in the ruler. Any other form of government would have ruined it." Thus she applied Montesquieu's theorem: *"un grand empire suppose une autorité despotique dans celui qui gouverne."* But she softened Montesquieu's *"despotique"* to *"souveraine"* in the French version. The Russian version used the word *"samoderzhavnyi,"* literally "autocratic" but having the older connotation in Russian history of a ruler independent of foreign control, rather than above the laws.[23]

Given this initial assertion of autocracy, the rest of the *Nakaz* logically remained conditional upon the sovereign's will, but the document still had many encouraging paragraphs that expressed the humane and philanthropic spirit of the age. The word "citizen" (*3*), suggesting the right to participate in government and be ruled by laws, was used in a Russian document for the first time. Laws, not the will of the sovereign, are called the "foundation of the state" (*20*) and they were to be confided to the care of the Senate and the courts (*25, 23*). The courts were urged to an unprecedented responsibility—remonstration against any of the sovereign's laws "repugnant to the fundamental constitution of the state" (*24*). All citizens were to obey the same laws (*34*) and this equality before

---

her complete domination of the legislative commission through her bureaucracy, through insuring elections of toadies, through control of agenda and checks on debates, through threats, bribes, etc. In short it was "absolutely subjected to her." These theses are documented, but he sees no contradiction between them and his admissions that these toadies became so independent, astute, and determined that she had to dismiss them as dangerous, and that a contemporary, Castéra, could speak of the "revolutionary attitude of the deputies" (Sacke, pp. 116, 150, 154).

23. Chechulin, *Nakaz*, 3. *Esprit des lois,* VIII, xix. For the meaning of *"samoderzhavnyi"* see Richard Pipes, "Karamzin's conception of the monarchy," *Russian Thought and Politics* ("Harvard Slavic Studies," IV [Cambridge, Mass., 1957]), 35-58.

the laws required institutions "to prevent the rich from oppressing those who are not so wealthy" (*35*). Provisions were made for more lenient treatment of debtors who went bankrupt honestly (*236, 358, 341*). The first supplement to the *Nakaz*, anticipating the modern welfare state, promised "maintenance and means of cure" to the sick or weak and work for beggars who have the use of their limbs.

Her chapters on punishments and the administration of justice (Chaps. 8–10) showed her as a champion of Enlightenment ideals. At a time when in France blasphemy could bring the death penalty, Catherine advocated merely the blasphemer's temporary exclusion from the society of the faithful (*74*); at a time when even in England the death penalty could be used for scores of offenses, Catherine would have it used only for one who killed or tried to kill (*79*). She advocated publicity of court proceedings despite the advice of those, like Diderot, who felt that decisions of the courts stifled the laws and should never be quoted, since law and reason sufficed.[24] She held that laws condemning a man on the deposition of only one witness were "destructive of liberty" (*119*); at least two witnesses were "absolutely necessary" (*120, 189*). The use of torture, so normal and indispensable in the minds of most officials at that time—and in many lands today—was deplored as a sure method of condemning an innocent person of weak constitution and of "acquitting a wicked wretch, who depends upon the robustness of his frame" (*194*).

A major innovation for the whole continent of Europe was the axiom without which no liberty or security of the person is possible: "No man ought to be looked upon as *guilty*, before he has received his judicial sentence; . . . in the eye of the law, every person is innocent whose crime is not yet *proved*" (*194*). Such an assertion, so contrary to police practice in Eurasia from the Pacific to the Atlantic, an assertion made from the height of autocratic power, was remarkable in European politics.

Along with these impressive declarations of high judicial prin-

24. Reddaway, p. 324, note to paragraph 101.

ciples, so dear to the philosophes, went a concern for the less dramatic but very important problem of agriculture. Catherine noted that the whole economy depended ultimately on the land and the peasant. There is of course no hint in the *Nakaz* of the eventual limitation, much less the abolition, of serfdom except for a brief paragraph: "A great number of slaves ought not to be enfranchised all at once, nor by a general law" (*257*). No more people should be reduced to slavery "except the *utmost* necessity should inevitably oblige us to do it," and then it should be done only for "the interest of the state" (*260*). Despite her italics, the qualifier opened the way for her enormous extensions of serfdom to the south and west.

Catherine worried about the slow but deadly effects of high infant mortality and depopulation in a sparsely populated, immense empire (*265*), but she did not mention the major cause for these evils, serfdom. She did, however, skirt the subject by criticizing oppressive absentee landlords who tax their peasants "without the least regard to the means" of the unfortunates (*269*). Such a country eventually will be deserted by its inhabitants (*275*). In true physiocratic fashion, she noted the connection between failing agriculture and failing commerce (*294*), and she set forth in one of her few paragraphs italicized all the way a maximum of self-interest often paraphrased by Radishchev as an argument against serfdom: *"Every man will take more care of his own property than of that which belongs to another, and will not exert his utmost endeavours upon that, which he has reason to fear another may deprive him of"* (p. 296).

The most remarkable provisions of the *Nakaz*—a limitation on the sovereign's power by her own initiative—were those to protect free speech. Warning against vagueness in defining high treason, she noted that "the liberty of a citizen is endangered by nothing so much as by judicial and oblique accusations in general" (*467*). Vague laws on high treason will produce "an infinity of different abuses" (*469*). "Words are never imputed as a crime, unless they *prepare,* or *accompany* or *follow* the criminal action" (*480*). Great care must be taken in examining alleged libels because of the "danger of *debasing* the human mind by restraint and oppression" (*484*).

If one paragraph had to be taken to illustrate the high liberal rhetoric of the *Nakaz* it would have to be the 520th: "All this will never please those flatterers, who are daily instilling this pernicious maxim into all the sovereigns on earth, *that their people are created for them only.* But *We* think, and esteem it *Our* glory to declare, 'That *We* are created for *Our* people.' "

Radishchev's immediate reaction to the *Nakaz,* which was published while he was at Leipzig, is not known. He does not seem to have taken any interest in serfdom until he began the *Journey* in the early 1780's. But his hatred for autocracy began early. In his own footnote to his translation of Abbé Mably's *Observations sur l'histoire de la Grèce,* made in 1773, autocracy is called "the state of affairs most repugnant to human nature. . . . The injustice of the sovereign gives the people, who are his judges, the same or an even greater right over him than the law gives him to judge criminals." [25] The censor did not reprimand Radishchev, who was paid from imperial funds for his work!

By the summer of 1790, with the ancient French monarchy tottering and the National Assembly threatening further reduction of the king's power—Catherine had told Grimm in November 1789 that the deputies were Pugachevs!—the Russian Empress could no longer tolerate attacks on the principle of monarchy. Moreover, she felt, quite rightly, that Radishchev had made a personal attack on her method of rule and her character.[26] The veil over this personal condemnation was transparent, if one substitutes a woman ruler and a male pilgrim for the characters in a dream that Radishchev's traveler has in the *Journey.*

25. A. N. Radishchev, *Polnoe sobranie sochinenii* (Moscow and Leningrad, 1941), II, 282.

26. For a contrary view see David Marshall Lang, *The First Russian Radical: Alexander Radishchev (1749–1802)* (London, 1959): "There is no reason to doubt his sincerity when he [Radishchev at his trial] strenuously denied harbouring any feelings of personal hostility or disloyalty toward the Empress" (p. 190).

In the fifth chapter, "Spasskaia polest," the traveler has a dream in which he is "a tsar, shah, khan, king, bey, nabob, sultan, or some such exalted being." The throne and its trappings are then described with precise details to resemble the one in Russia's Senate.[27] Courtiers anxious to catch his glance surround the throne, and at a distance stand a multitude of various attires and facial features, obviously the peoples of Catherine's multiracial empire.

When the sovereign yawns, confusion and despair seize the courtiers; when a sneeze contorts his face into a smile, joy fills all hearts and paeans of praise begin: "One said in a low voice: 'He has subdued our enemies abroad and at home, he has expanded the frontiers of the fatherland, he has subjected thousands of men, of many races, to his power.' Another exclaimed: 'He has enriched the realm, he has expanded internal and foreign commerce, he is patron of the arts and sciences, he encourages agriculture and industry'" (p. 68). The chorus spoke the simple truth, for Catherine had done these things, although it is an exaggeration to speak of her encouragement of agriculture beyond the realm of theoretical discussions and dissemination of information. But for Radishchev the armed expansion, expanding frontiers and subjecting of thousands (in Poland and Turkey), was deplorable, not glorious—the result of "the murder called war" (p. 73).

Other courtiers called the ruler "merciful and just," the law's "first servant," a "wise legislator" renowned for clemency who "founded vast cities" rivaling those of antiquity in solitary spaces. These were terms in which Catherine probably thought of herself, and in comparison with her predecessors they were true. But a caustic remark followed. The ruler's reaction to the courtiers' paeans of praise was ludicrous: "my soul rose above the usual circle of vision, expanded its essence, and, embracing all, touched the threshold of divine wisdom."

Then comes a dramatic contrast. A pilgrim, a lone woman in simple garments who kept her hat on while all other heads were

27. See L. B. Krestova, "Son v glave 'Spasskaia Polest' *Puteshestviia iz Peterburga v Moskvu* Radishcheva," AN SSSR. Otdelenie literatury i iazyka, *Izvestiia*, XVI, vyp. 4 (1957), 352–353.

bare, attracted the sovereign's attention. A courtier, queried about her by the ruler, dismissed the intruder as a "witch who . . . gloats over grief and affliction; she is always frowning, and she scorns and reviles everyone; in her abuse she spares not even thy sacred head." The pilgrim called to the ruler, who involuntarily approached her, despite the courtiers' attempts to prevent this by force. The pilgrim touched the ruler's eyes and took off a "thick film, like horny skin," a symbol of flattery. She said she had been sent to heal him by "The Almighty, moved to pity by the groans of thy subject people" (p. 71). She warned the ruler that his subjects "are always ready for thy defeat, if it will avenge the enslavement of man." If the ruler again became blind to their plight, "avenging thunderbolts will be ready to strike thee down."

Menacing as this language was, it seems certain that Radishchev had Catherine in view as the ruler and himself—without the divine command, of course—as the truth-speaking pilgrim, who concluded, "everyone who criticizes the sovereign in the fullness of his autocratic power is a pilgrim in the land where all tremble before him. . . . But such stout hearts are rare; hardly one in a whole century appears in the world's arena" (p. 72). Catherine noted that the *Journey*'s author, "our babbler" would "pipe a different tune" if he stood closer to the sovereign (p. 240). In this Catherine was prescient, for Radishchev, trusting in the *Nakaz*'s paragraphs on the laws cited above, and probably expecting merely banishment to his estates, was unprepared for and demoralized by his arrest, solitary confinement, and condemnation to death, which would leave his small children orphans.

In the dream the ruler, his eyes now opened, sees all the horrors that had been concealed from him, particularly those of "the murder called war." "My glittering garments seemed to be stained with blood and drenched with tears. On my fingers I saw fragments of human brains; my feet were standing in slime." His commander-in-chief, sent forth to conquer, was wallowing in "luxury and pleasure." These remarks stung Catherine (240) who after all had not attacked Sweden, but been attacked by Gustavus

III. Potemkin, the obvious target of the last sally, was often "wallowing in luxury and pleasure"—but he was also a first-class general.[28]

Equally unfair were Radishchev's attacks on her architectural achievements as lacking "even the slightest particle of taste" and belonging "to the age of the Goths and Vandals," and on her commands to explore distant lands. If the ruler in the dream when cured of blindness saw a captain sent to sail the farthest seas coasting near the mouth of the harbor, Catherine had bold voyagers who sailed the Pacific despite severe hardships and mutinies. With more justice, but without any charity, Radishchev alludes to the ruler's lustful private life, his pouring out largesse upon "the clever sycophant who knew my desires and pandered to my weaknesses, the woman who gloried in her shamelessness." By standards of her day for royalty, Catherine's amours were not shocking; to an admirer of Roman virtue, they were monstrous.

The indictment most painful to Catherine must have been the charge of hypocrisy. Misapplication of the laws, delay, venality, mercy "bought and sold"—all of which had been worse before Catherine and all of which she sought to combat as best she could —made the ruler pass among the subjects for "a cheat, hypocrite and wicked play-actor" (pp. 72–73). " 'Keep thy mercy,' thousands of voices shouted, 'do not proclaim it to us in high-sounding words, if thou dost not intend to carry it out. . . . We were peacefully asleep. . . .' "

Radishchev attacks autocracy throughout the remainder of the *Journey*. Autocrats desire "universal conformity in thought" so that they may safely enjoy power and "wallow in voluptuousness" (p. 128); they permit prostitution (p. 129); they think themselves gods and that "everything they touched became good and radiant"; they make pompous external display, which is no longer impressive or justified when a nation is enlightened (p. 163). This last

28. For Potemkin's *folles journées* in his headquarters in Iassy and Bender, see A. Petrushevskii, *Generalissimus Kniaz' Suvorov* (St. Petersburg, 1884), I, 371. For Potemkin's achievements as general and statesman see G. Soloveytchik, *Potemkin* (New York, 1947).

was a challenge to the *Nakaz*'s defense of the court's need for prodigality and magnificence (579). Freedom of thought is "terrifying to governments," for the freethinker will "tear off the mask and veil" of the "idol of power" (p. 169). In a parody of the Beatitudes, Radishchev mocks autocrats' favoritism: "Blessed are the magnates in autocratic countries. Blessed are those who are decked out in ribbons and orders . . . whose exterior fills all with awe" (p. 214).

The most savage attack on autocracy, albeit not personally aimed at Catherine, is in the "Ode to Liberty" contained in the *Journey* chapter "Tver'." In words closely following those of Helvétius, Radishchev pictures "the king" in all his arrogant cruelty:

> Raising his haughty brow and grasping his iron scepter, the king seats himself augustly on the throne and sees his people only as base creatures. Holding life and death in his hands, he says: "When I laugh, all laugh; if I frown threateningly, all are confounded. You live only so long as I permit you to live" (Stanza 11).

Catherine need not have felt that this was aimed at her. She did not despise her subjects and was not personally cruel. And she had written in the *Nakaz* that rulers are created to serve their peoples, not vice versa (520). The ode's passages attacking clerical superstition and priestly power that "tramples upon the earthly powers" did not apply to Catherine's Russia. She herself had done the trampling—upon the Orthodox church. But Catherine could hardly tolerate the glorification of the regicidal Oliver Cromwell, distant as he was in time, for he had "taught generation after generation how nations can avenge themselves" and "had Charles executed by due process of law" (Stanza 22).

Given these attacks on autocracy, and the justification of popular revolution against tyrants, Radishchev's disfavor would have been certain. But he also attacked serfdom and implied that if reforms were not forthcoming a revolt would be justified through man's natural rights of self-defense. Although Catherine herself had warned her procurator-general of just such a rebellion if serfdom were not eased and had hinted at serfdom's abolition in the *Nakaz* (257), she was too frightened by the menacing example of France to realize that Radishchev's book was intended to help *avert* such violence by timely reforms, not to glory in the prospect of serf vengeance. Radishchev proposed in a "Project for the future," which the traveler discovers by accident, the best program for gradual serf emancipation that had been set forth by any Russian; in breadth and concreteness it was rarely surpassed in the remaining seventy years to the Emancipation of 1861.[29] But Catherine read Radishchev's vivid warnings as inflammatory appeals. Radishchev cited the "crude pretender" (Pugachev) whom serfs had followed when, maddened by oppression they "sought more the joy of vengeance than the benefit of broken shackles" (p. 153). After describing an inhuman serf-master, the traveler concludes, "Destroy the tools of his agriculture, burn his barns, silos and granaries, and scatter their ashes over the fields where he practiced his tortures; stigmatize him as a robber of the people . . ." (p. 160). Noting that "all those who might be the champions of freedom are great landed proprietors," he despaired of their hearts: "freedom is not to be expected from their counsels, but from the heavy burden of slavery itself" (p. 191), that is, from a desperate rebellion.

In his angriest condemnation of his own class, Radishchev predicts a terrible revolution in a century's time, and affirms its justice.

> Oh, if the slaves weighted down with fetters, raging in their despair, would, with the iron that bars their freedom, crush our heads, the heads of their inhuman masters, and redden their fields with our blood! What would the country lose by that? Soon great men would arise from among them, to take the place of the murdered generation; but they would be of another mind and without the right to oppress others. This is no dream; my vision pene-

29. V. I. Semevskii, "Krest'ianskii vopros v literature Ekaterinskago vremeni," *Velikaia Reforma* (Moscow, 1911), I, 237. Kariakin and Plimak argue that Radishchev's plans for reform set forth in the *Journey* were meant solely to illustrate reforms' futility and the inevitability of revolution.

trates the dense curtain of time that veils the future. . . . I look
through the space of a whole century (p. 209).

Radishchev was arrested, held in solitary confinement, tried in
secret without defense counsel, and condemned to death. Every
aspect of the trial violated the axioms of the *Nakaz* cited above.
The charges of treason and fomenting rebellion were baseless.
Radishchev protested his innocence of such charges but repeatedly
stigmatized his own book as "insane" and "deluded." Catherine
seems to have realized the punishment was brutal; she commuted
it to ten years' Siberian exile. Radishchev spent six years in Ilimsk
(he was allowed to take over a year to reach his destination) and
upon Catherine's death he was allowed to return to his estates by
Paul I. Upon the accession of Alexander I to the throne in 1801,
Radishchev was summoned back into imperial service to help
draft a new code of laws. After less than a year's service he committed suicide for reasons not yet known, but apparently because
a superior on the commission again threatened him with Siberian
exile for his liberal views.

In his last years, Radishchev's views came closer to Catherine's.
The French Revolution began the process. The emphasis throughout the *Journey* had been on popular sovereignty and the rights
of peoples, although he was aware of the historical abuses of power
by peoples (pp. 81, 83, 200). The French Revolution was already
distasteful to him in 1790; in France "license and anarchy have
reached the utmost possible limits" and the National Assembly,
"proceeding just as autocratically as the king before it, laid violent
hands upon a printed book" (p. 186). France was "still hovering
over the abyss of the Bastille!" When in Siberia, Radishchev wrote
Count Vorontsov of the *"folies françaises"* and when back on his
estates wrote of the Directory as *"l'hydre pentacéphale et omni-
hostile."* [30] Robespierre was as bad as Sulla, the Roman dictator
noted for his bloody rule.[31]

Such accusations directed against popular license, the national

30. *P.S.S.*, III, 404, 521.
31. "Pesn' istoricheskaia" [Historical song], *P.S.S.* (1938), I, 77–122.

Assembly, the dictator, and the Directory did not mean that Radishchev condemned the French Revolution on the same grounds as Catherine did. Radishchev had praised Mirabeau, the moderate constitutional monarchist (p. 231) whom Catherine would have hanged "not once, but many times over" (p. 249), and she condemned the revolution as an exercise in popular sovereignty that is wrong in principle; Radishchev condemned it because it became a despotism, because it crushed liberty and scorned the rule of law.

Radishchev was pragmatic enough to realize that there were times in history that called for an autocrat. The same Roman Emperor Augustus whom he had condemned in the *Journey* because he "put troublesome freedom to sleep, and wound flowers around the iron scepter. . . . Thence came slavery" (p. 200), Radishchev praised in his *Historical Song* for ending the evils of bloody civil strife. And in a poem, "The Eighteenth Century" (1800) written four years after Catherine's death, he praised her and Peter:

Peace, justice, truth and liberty from the throne shall flow,
Which Catherine and Peter raised up, that Russians might prosper.
Peter and thou, Catherine! your spirit lives with us still.[32]

Radishchev's sharpest change in outlook concerned Russia's wars. He ceased to condemn Russia's conquests and instead wrote an unfinished epic, "Angel of Darkness," on the Cossack conquistador, Ermak (who had led a daring band in the winning of much of Siberia for Russia), and an unfinished historical sketch, "On the Acquisition of Siberia." Far from condemning "the murder called war," he wrote Vorontsov after the peace with the Ottoman Empire in 1792 that Carthage was destroyed after three wars and that Russia would crush the Crescent after her own third "Punic war" which would begin *"d'aujourd'hui à demain"* and bring Russians, at last "after a thousand years," to the walls of Constantinople.[33]

32. "Os'mnadtsatyi vek," trans. David Marshall Lang, *op. cit.,* p. 251.
33. "Angel T'my," *P.S.S.* (1941), II, 165–168; "Sokrashchennoe povestvovanie o priobretenii Sibiri," *P.S.S.,* II, 145–166; letter of April 4, 1792, from Ilimsk, *P.S.S.* (1952), III, 437–438.

But Radishchev's shift to conditional acceptance of autocracy and to full approval of autocracy's bold assertion of Russia's historical foreign policy aims to the south—condemned as vain, costly in peasant lives, purely personal, bankrupting and strategically disastrous by other aristocratic spokesmen[34]—did not mean that Radishchev drew anti-liberal conclusions. He was not ready to abandon his earlier ideals of a better society or to accept the Napoleonic formula, *"La liberté c'est un bon code civil."* In an unpublished "Project of a Civil Code," written for Alexander's legislative commission, Radishchev reiterated most of the goals put forth in the *Journey*—equality of all classes before the law, abolition of the Table of Ranks, trial by jury, religious toleration, freedom of the press, emancipation of manorial serfs, habeas corpus, and freedom of trade. Catherine herself had advocated most of these and actually carried out freedom of trade and religious toleration. Radishchev, according to his son Pavel, went on to add a generous view of Catherine's Charter to the Gentry of 1785, which created at *gubernia* level autonomous corporations of the nobility endowed with legal personality and recognized their rights as being independent of the interests of the state.

> Radishchev said that in her provision for elections of their officers by the gentry, Catherine II had laid the foundation of the future constitution of Russia. He proposed that, abandoning unlimited monarchical power in Russia, they should introduce democratic institutions. Let the Tsar still be great, but let Russia remain free (like England).[35]

34. Prince M. M. Shcherbatov called the second Turkish war "shameful" and "a grave for Russians"; Radishchev's mentor and protector, Count Alexander Vorontsov, deplored the annual levies of recruits and higher taxes for the wars that derived from the Empress' vanity, not Russia's true interests. His brother, Count Semion Vorontsov, opposed the Turkish wars on strategic grounds and said he would give "thirty Crimeas for Helsingfors and Sveaborg." See for these and similar opinions, George Sacke, "Die sozialen und wirtschaftlichen Voraussetzungen der Orientpolitik Katharinas II," in *Vierteljahrschrift für Sozial- und Wirtschaftgeschichte,* XXXII (1939), No. 1, 26–36.

35. This tenth point of Radishchev's "Project," which was contained in the manuscript of Pavel Radishchev's article, did not appear in Pavel's

Thus by the end of his life, Radishchev, a foe of serfdom to the last,[36] had nevertheless come to a more charitable view of the Empress he had so scathingly condemned in his major work. Soviet historiography for a generation has presented the two as diametrically opposed: Radishchev the implacable revolutionary, the ardent democrat, the foe of war versus Catherine II, the hypocritical and ruthless despot, the vain and cynical imperialist. Liberal historians, from Pavel Radishchev to David Marshall Lang a century later, have found Radishchev friendly to her and misunderstood by her. Conservative writers have taken Radishchev's own characterization of his book as "insane" and influenced by foreign writers—testimony given when temporarily broken and demoralized—and generalized it to his whole life and outlook. All of these views contain partial truths and all underestimate the complexity of Radishchev's intellectual development and particularly the change from criticism of Catherine to praise for her.

After his experience of utter loneliness and powerlessness in prison, after realizing that the French Revolution was developing in the direction of tyranny, rather than toward the American Revolution's reliance on laws, constitutions, and self-government, and after his personal introduction to the immensity of the Russian empire built by autocracy, he turned realistically to support of what he hoped would be a reforming monarchy. Given the absence of a strong middle class or a large enough liberal wing in the aristocracy, Russian reformers had no other choice in combatting serfdom; and indeed it was a tsar, native-born, beholden to no

---

published version. It was discovered by a Russian scholar in 1912. See N. P. Kashin, "Novyi spisok biografii A. N. Radishcheva" [A new copy of a biography of Radishchev], *Chteniia v Imperatorskom Obshchestve Istorii i Drevnostei Rossiiskikh pri Moskovskom Universitete,* CCXLI (1912), Book 2, sec. iii, 22.

36. See, e.g., his bitter remarks on returning to his estates in the "Description of My Estate" [Opisanie moego vladeniia], *P.S.S.* (1952), III, 169–197, esp. 186. The view of Radishchev's leading biographer, G. P. Makogonenko, that Radishchev has "no condemnation of serfdom in his works after the *Journey*" is erroneous (G. P. Makogonenko, *Radishchev i ego vremia* [Moscow, 1956], p. 519).

one, and master of a bureaucracy much stronger than Catherine's, who finally overrode stubborn serf-owner opposition and liberated the serfs, seventy-one years after the *Journey,* and almost a hundred years after the *Nakaz.*

PART THREE

The Ruler

SERGEI V. BAKHRUSHIN
and SERGEI D. SKAZKIN

Diplomacy

RUSSIAN DIPLOMACY between 1726 and 1762 prepared the ground for the solution of the basic foreign policy problems that confronted Russia from the end of the seventeenth century. "In the north was Sweden, whose strength and prestige were declining precisely because Charles XII had attempted to penetrate into the interior of Russia. . . . In the south were the Turks and their tributary, the Crimean Tatars, now a mere fragment of their former glory. . . . Then there was Poland, which was in a state of

Sergei V. Bakhrushin and Sergei D. Skazkin, "Diplomatiia evropeiskikh gosudarstv v XVIII veke," in *Istoriia Diplomatii,* edited by V. P. Potemkin (Moscow, 1941), I, 283–295. Translated by Mary Mackler.

complete collapse . . . unable under its constitution to take any action on a nationwide scale and therefore doomed to become the
easy prey of her neighbors. . . . Beyond Poland was another country, which also seemed to be in a state of hopeless collapse at the
time—Germany. Since the Thirty Years' War the Holy Roman Empire had existed only in name. . . . The Prussian dynasty was already beginning to come forward as a rival of the Austrian dynasty." "The world situation had never been more favorable to tsarism's plans of conquest than it was in 1762. . . . The Seven Years'
War had split Europe into two camps. England had broken the
power of the French on the sea, in America, and in India, and had
then abandoned her continental ally, Frederick II, king of Prussia, to his fate. Frederick II was on the brink of ruin in 1762."

Such was the international situation at the time of the formation
of Catherine's new government. The Department of Foreign Affairs was headed by one of the most educated and intelligent statesmen of the time, N. I. Panin, about whom Catherine II wrote
immediately after her accession to the throne, "the most skilled,
the most intelligent, the most diligent man at my court." The in-
corruptible Panin, as one British diplomat called him, had "no
aims other than those that furthered his Empress' prosperity and
honor and strengthened the government in Russia." Though he
may have been "one of the politest of men," whose vocabulary,
if one is to believe his ill-wishers, did not contain the word "no,"
he was firm and consistent in carrying out his policy where serious
issues were concerned.

From the very beginning, Catherine personally took a major and
very active part in shaping foreign policy. Not one serious question
in that area was decided or one important step taken without her
direct participation. "I want to do the governing myself, and let
Europe know this!" she said to Potemkin. From a very early age
Catherine had been involved in major politics through court intrigue, and she already had a good deal of experience in diplomatic affairs; she subsequently developed her considerable diplomatic capabilities to perfection. She was highly accomplished in the

art of pretense, a skill considered basic for diplomats in the eighteenth century, and frequently later. "Anyone who judges a matter by the personal reception he has received is making a big mistake," she used to say, having herself in mind.

Catherine was also highly talented in using the terminology of the Enlightenment, which she employed adroitly to cover up her own ambitious designs. She dressed up her violation of Poland's sovereign rights and her preparations for that country's partition as defense of the "freedom" of the Polish people. " 'Enlightenment' was tsarism's slogan in Europe in the eighteenth century," Engels wrote.

Yet this was not where Catherine's main strength as a diplomat lay. Being an intelligent woman, she understood that respect for the country she ruled was the source of respect for her. In her diplomatic acts she put herself forward as spokesman for national policy, never separating herself from Russia. "I am the Empress of Russia," she wrote in connection with the Danish court's claims to participation in the guardianship of Grand Duke Paul Petrovich, claims which she took as a personal affront, "and I would not be fulfilling my people's hopes if I were so base as to turn over the guardianship of my son, the heir to the Russian crown, to a foreign state, which has insulted me and Russia by its extraordinary behavior."

So often did she reiterate opinions such as these that in the end she convinced herself that they were correct, and this added conviction and forcefulness to all her actions.

Catherine worked closely with Panin for nearly twenty years, though she did not trust or like him, believing him to be an advocate of a limited form of monarchy. In November 1780, Prince Bezborodko replaced Panin with "powers for all negotiations." A gifted and hardworking official with an aptitude for drafting reports, Bezborodko was essentially an executor of the Empress' will, no more than that. Formally, he was Catherine's secretary. Count Ivan Andreyevich Osterman succeeded Panin as vice-chancellor. He had a celebrated father but was himself devoid of all talent, an "automat," "stuffed with straw," who did nothing and carried no weight at all. He was the "ranking official" in the College of Foreign Affairs in title only. At that time, Potemkin was party to all the "political secrets." Catherine was fond of saying that Potemkin was her "pupil" in politics, but actually, she herself fell under the sway of his exciting and brilliant diplomatic schemes.

At the time of Catherine's accession, the prime task confronting Russian diplomacy was restoration of Russia's international prestige, which had suffered badly during Peter III's reign in consequence of his withdrawal from the Seven Years' War and the sudden shift of alliance from Austria to Prussia. Under pressure of public opinion, Catherine's government broke off the military alliance with Frederick II, but it did not violate the peace treaty. This cautious policy satisfied none of the belligerents; whereupon Catherine offered to act as an intermediary. Her offer was rejected and the Treaty of Hubertusburg was concluded without Russia's participation.

Catherine's position with regard to the adversaries in the Seven Years' War was an indication of the new direction in Russia's foreign policy, which now aimed at enabling Russia "to follow her own system in keeping with her own true interests and not to be constantly dependent on the wishes of a foreign court." The government was very well aware of the damage done to Russia's interests and prestige by the "linking of the affairs of our empire's political system to outside powers," who only sought "to take advantage of us." "We will change the system whereby we are dependent on them [the courts of Versailles and Vienna]," Panin declared, "and in its stead we will set up one which will permit us to act without hindrance in our own affairs." "Time will show everybody that we are not dragging along in anyone else's wake," Catherine wrote at the beginning of her reign. And she directed all her efforts toward making the West European powers serve the interests of the Russian Empire and help her achieve aims which had been on the agenda since the reigns of Alexis and Peter I, namely, reunification with the Ukrainian and Byelorussian lands that were still under Poland's rule; consolidation of Russia's position in the Baltic region; and advance to the Black Sea. The principal obstacle to the implementation of this program was France, who was supported by Austria. France's entire policy in eastern Europe had for a long time leaned on Poland, Sweden, and Turkey, who were intended to serve as a bulwark against Russia's growing influence. In addition, France wished to keep Russian merchant capital from penetrating into the Near East to the detriment of French trade.

Because of the death of Augustus III the Polish question came up first. Catherine instructed her agents to ensure the election of a king who "would be useful to the interests of the empire and who could not expect to win the title with anyone else's help." Even before that, steps had been taken toward rapprochement with Prussia with a view to "wresting" Frederick II "out of the hands of France," that is, preventing an alliance between Frederick and Russia's chief enemy. Prussia was the natural enemy of the German emperor, but, as Engels wrote: "This enemy was still too weak to get along without the help of France or Russia—particularly Russia—so that as he freed himself from dependence on the German Empire, he became more dependent on Russia." The rapprochement between Russia and Prussia led to a defensive alliance, concluded in April 1764 in St. Petersburg. Secret articles in the treaty provided for Prussian financial assistance to Russia in the event of war with Turkey, for unity of action in Sweden, and, finally, for the prevention of changes in the Polish constitution, inasmuch as both parties to the treaty were interested in maintaining the political weakness of the commonwealth. The alliance with Prussia enabled Russia to influence Poland's affairs, to restrain Turkey, "to maintain primacy in the north" and "play a leading role in Europe without serious expenditures on Russia's part." This was a major achievement of Russian diplomacy and it was the first result of Panin's foreign policy of seeking friendship with Prussia; Panin's appointment as "first member of the College of Foreign Affairs" at the end of 1764 was official recognition of this program.

In 1766, Russia concluded a commercial treaty with Great Britain. In this instance, too, the price of the Russian government's agreement was Britain's identity of views on the Polish question. There were other, more extensive, political considerations that bound Britain to Russia: both countries had the same enemy—France. Consequently, Russian and British diplomacy acted together in Sweden, too, which was allied with France. Employing very much the same methods as in Poland, Russia and Britain tried to maintain the archaic form of Sweden's state system, giving support in the Diet to the Anglo-Russian party, on which both governments had spent and continued to spend considerable sums of money. Large subsidies were also paid to the Swedish government in the hope of preventing the renewal of the Franco-Swedish alliance. Denmark also contributed to these expenditures, starting in 1765, in return for the secession to her of the Holstein possessions of Grand Duke Paul Petrovich. In the treaty, Panin included a paragraph on assistance in the event of war between Russia and Turkey.

Panin attempted to unite the separate agreements with the individual states on matters of North European policy in a single "Northern system." Russia's ambassador to Denmark, Baron Korf, had made a suggestion in 1764 calling for "a notable and strong alliance of powers to be formed in the north," with Britain's participation, against France and her ally Austria. The "Northern alliance" was to include Russia, Prussia, and Denmark as "active powers," and Poland and Sweden as "passive powers," with the preservation of peace being all that was required of the latter. Its purpose was to "remove Russia from constant dependence" on other powers and to give her "a large share of the leadership in common affairs," especially in the north. However, the idea of the "alliance" was not seen with favor in Berlin. Frederick II was perfectly satisfied with what he had already obtained from the alliance with Russia and had no desire to undertake new commitments that might enhance his ally's international power.

Despite the failure of the Korf-Panin plan, Russia did manage to free her hands sufficiently with regard to Poland. The Russian autocracy's pretext for intervening in that country's affairs and subordinating it to its will was the alleged need to protect the interests of the non-Catholic population of Poland (the Dissidents). Russia and Prussia, supported by Britain and Denmark, had already in 1764 demanded that the Polish Diet grant equal rights to the Dissidents. At the same time, they protested against every measure that might have strengthened Poland's political system. In 1766, Russia and Prussia demanded the preservation at all costs of the "liberum veto," which was the most harmful archaism in the Polish constitution. They resorted to bribery widely, but took more decisive steps, too: units of Russian troops never left Polish territory. In 1767, the Russian ambassador, Repnin, succeeded in uniting the Dissidents as well as some Catholics who were dissatisfied with the Polish government in a confederation (an alliance of the gentry). Under the guise of assistance to that confederation, Russian troops marched into Warsaw. This forced the Diet to enact a law granting the Dissidents equal rights with the Catholics. At that same time, Russia undertook to guarantee the old Polish constitution, without the repeal of which Poland could not begin to emerge from the continuous anarchy that was so advantageous to her neighbors.

Austria and France turned to Turkey in an effort to prevent Russian policy from making further gains. At the end of 1768, Turkey, under direct pressure from the Austrian and French ambassadors, declared war on Russia. It was in connection with the Turkish war that the issue of partition of Poland came to a head. The idea had been discussed in Russian and Prussian diplomatic circles practically since 1763. Catherine had sounded out Berlin about it several times. No sooner had the Turkish war begun, than Frederick II openly proposed a partition plan. He hinted that Russia could not only be compensated for her military costs at the expense of Polish territory, but could also obtain help against the Turks from Prussia and Austria. Catherine and Panin very skillfully postponed giving a direct reply to this, despite the Prussian king's importunity, for they wanted to probe their ally's intentions more exactly and if possible to get him to reduce his demands. Only Austria's conclusion of a defense alliance with Turkey in the summer of 1771 compelled the Russian government to make haste with the partition. By the beginning of 1772 the interested powers reached a preliminary agreement, which was made final in August. Russia received the Polish part of Livonia and part of eastern Byelorussia. In return for this, she curtailed her demands regarding Turkey. Under the Treaty of Kuchuk–Kainardji of 1774, she received Kinburn, Kerch, Yenikal and Azov, and obtained recognition of the independence of the Crimea. The last article of the Treaty of Kuchuk–Kainardji, however, enabled Russian diplomacy to intervene in Crimean affairs, and eventually led to Russia's annexation of the peninsula in 1783.

By the late 1770's, Catherine, having received all she could expect from the alliance with Frederick II, began to move away from Panin's Prussian orientation and to seek new paths in her European policy. Aware that the state which she governed was very strong, the Russian Empress determined to play a decisive role in the affairs of Central Europe and to realize the dream she had had since the first year of her reign—"to be arbiter of the destinies of Europe." The war of the Bavarian succession that broke out in Europe [1778] between Prussia and Austria provided her with a convenient pretext. Frederick expected military aid from his Russian ally, but Catherine chose the role of powerful intermediary instead. She sent a threatening statement to Vienna, demanding that Maria Theresa "satisfy fully the German Princes' just demands." At the same time Catherine's representative in the Prussian camp "behaved like a minister with full authority, come to dictate the law to Germany in the name of his own court." Thus, it immediately became apparent that "Russian signs of friendship for Prussia merely served as a pretext for Catherine to interfere in Germany's affairs in order to extend her influence to all of Europe."

The Peace of Teschen, 1779, which ended the war, was a triumph for the Russian Empress, who acted not only as an intermediary, but also as a guarantor of the situation established by the treaty. From then on, to use a contemporary expression, Russia was a kind of "co-member of the Empire," and could participate "at will" in Germany's affairs. The German princes besieged Catherine with requests; they appealed to her to settle their quarrels and misunderstandings, sang her praises "for the peace granted Germany, lauded her as their savior and implored her to continue her good deeds as guarantor of the German constitution and not to abandon for one moment its benevolence toward it." As a matter of fact, a special German department was set up in the College of Foreign Affairs in St. Petersburg to serve as a channel for exerting Russian influence in Germany. The aged Frederick II tried to ingratiate himself with the "northern Semiramis," in the hope of establishing with her cooperation an alliance of the German princes under his leadership and of forming a strong anti-British coalition.

Catherine's foreign policy aims were not limited to Germany. England was trying to utilize Russian forces in the war with America and even offered to concede the island of Minorca in return for this. Catherine, however, preferred to prescribe international law rather than to fight for someone else. In connection with the British-American war, Russia issued the famous declaration on naval armed neutrality of February 28, 1780, which established the right of neutral ships to defend themselves by force of arms on the high seas. The majority of countries, except for Britain, against whom it was directed, subscribed to the declaration.

The Peace of Teschen and the declaration of "armed neutrality" clearly showed the extent of the claims of Russian diplomacy and the significance Russia had attained in international affairs. They also testified to withdrawal from Panin's "Northern system." The year 1780 marked the beginning of closer relations between Russia and Austria. Catherine II's meeting with Emperor Joseph II in Mogilev that year dealt a "frightful blow to the influence of the Prussian king." At that meeting it was resolved that Russia and Austria would take the "same position" with regard to Turkey and

Poland, and a defense alliance was sealed by the exchange of hand-written letters. The following year Panin was given leave to go abroad.

Now Russian diplomacy, directed by Catherine herself and by the all-powerful Potemkin, concentrated on the Turkish problem and the so-called Greek project. Its goal was not only territorial aggrandizement at Turkey's expense, but the expulsion of the Turks from Europe and the restoration of the Greek Empire, the crown of which was intended for the Empress' grandson Konstantin Pavlovich. Moldavia and Wallachia were to constitute a buffer state, to be called Dacia, and Austria was to receive the western part of the Balkan peninsula. "Constantinople as the third Russian capital, with Moscow and St. Petersburg," Engels wrote, "would have meant not only moral domination over the eastern Christian world, but would have been a decisive step toward domination over Europe as well."

Russian diplomacy was making gradual preparations for this "decisive step." Measures were taken to weaken the resistance of France. A commercial treaty concluded with France at the end of 1786 greatly improved relations between the two countries; among other things France ceased to conduct anti-Russian agitation in Constantinople. Finally, Catherine's celebrated trip to Tauris (Crimea) was intended to demonstrate Russia's readiness to wage war for the Black Sea, while Emperor Joseph II's participation in that trip sealed the anti-Turkish alliance with the Austrian Empire.

The Porte did not wait to be attacked. In 1787 she declared war against Russia, at England's instigation. In accordance with the Mogilev agreement of 1780, Austria acted in alliance with Russia. Unexpectedly, Sweden entered the war, wishing to take advantage of the situation to regain the Baltic territory lost during Peter's reign. England and Prussia, who were now hostile toward Russia, prevented Denmark, who was Russia's ally, from joining in the war between Sweden and Russia. There was a time when St. Petersburg itself seemed to be in danger. In the final count, however, under the Peace of Wereloe, in 1790, Sweden had to give up any idea of altering the frontiers. The Swedish war and Austria's conclusion of a separate peace upset Catherine's plans for Turkey. The campaign against Constantinople could not be undertaken and the Treaty of Jassy in 1792 merely advanced Russia's frontiers to the Dniester River and confirmed the one-sided act of annexation of the Crimea.

To sum up, Russian diplomacy during Catherine's reign accomplished in the main the tasks inherited from the seventeenth century. Peter the Great's achievements in the Baltic region were consolidated; the territories inhabited by the Byelorussians and Ukrainians, peoples related to the Russians, were reunited with Russia. Russia obtained a firm foothold on the Black Sea. Finally, the Russian Empire won a decisive voice in the affairs of Europe as a whole. "All the essential features," to quote Engels, of tsarism's policy in the nineteenth century "were already clearly visible" in Catherine's foreign policy—the advance toward the Balkan peninsula, the "weakening of England's naval superiority by means of restrictive international rules," intervention in the affairs of the German states.

Russia's increased international prestige in the eighteenth century was also evident in the gradual recognition of the imperial title her rulers had taken (by the German Empire in 1744, by France in 1762, and by Poland in 1764). At a time when western Europe was being torn asunder by inner contradictions, backward but "united, homogeneous, young, and rapidly growing Russia, practically invulnerable and completely inaccessible to conquest," succeeded in acquiring an outstanding position among the other European powers.

Russian diplomacy's achievements in the latter part of the eighteenth century were not restricted to foreign policy. They included an important role in the development of the principles of international law. The act of armed neutrality provided the foundation for a universally recognized international naval law. The Convention of 1783 with Turkey established the principles of consular law, which also received international recognition.

A number of new diplomatic techniques were introduced under Catherine II. Political propaganda in foreign countries was placed on a broad footing. Specifically, Catherine's correspondence with Voltaire, Grimm, Diderot, and the other Encyclopedists served propaganda purposes. Catherine kept a watchful eye out for foreign publications that might be detrimental to Russia or to her own position as Empress of Russia. She managed to stop the publication of Rulhière's book about the palace coup of 1762. At her behest the *Antidote* was published in Amsterdam to refute Abbé Chappe d'Auteroche's book about Russia, etc.

Among the new diplomatic approaches was the inviting of foreign diplomats to join the Empress on her trips through Russia, for example, to inspect the waterway from the Baltic Sea to the Volga in 1785 and to the Crimea in 1787. During these trips the most delicate diplomatic matters were raised and often settled in informal talks with the Empress or with Potemkin. The French ambassador Ségur relates very verbosely in his memoirs how he took advantage of these trips to plant the idea of Franco-Russian friendship. Thus, during the trip of 1785 the ground was laid for the conclusion of the Franco-Russian trade treaty, later ratified in Kiev en route to the Crimea. Direct contacts with foreign sovereigns were another important diplomatic approach during Catherine's reign. Catherine conducted a lively, "private" correspondence with Frederick II, striving through it to influence that allied state's policy as well as to elicit needed information. She did not stop at correspondence, but arranged personal meetings. For example, she insisted that Prince Henry, Frederick II's brother, come to St. Petersburg from Sweden when he visited that country in 1770. In 1780 Catherine met with Joseph II of Austria in Mogilev. In 1787 she managed to have him join in the trip to the Crimea despite his obvious wish to avoid such a meeting and the great obligations it would impose on him. During these meetings between "crowned heads" serious matters of international policy were settled amid the entertainment, meals, and banter.

Of the traditional diplomatic methods, Catherine II made especially wide use of demagogic agitation among the Russian Orthodox populations of foreign countries. The reader already knows how tsarist diplomacy utilized the issue of the Dissidents to intervene in the affairs of the Polish commonwealth. During the first Turkish war Catherine's government managed to provoke a rebellion on the Aegean islands. The Treaty of Kuchuk–Kainardji with Turkey included, for the first time, articles concerning the religious rights of the Christian inhabitants of Turkey. Catherine followed the same pattern in the Crimea. In 1779, under the guise of rescuing them from Tatar violence, the local Christians—Greeks and Armenians—forcibly resettled on the coast of the Sea of Azov. In a word, everywhere with regard to Christians, "Tsarism would pose as a 'liberator'" in order to achieve its own aims.

By the second half of the eighteenth century Russia no longer differed from western Europe in diplomatic etiquette. Incidentally, Russian practice brought greater precision to some of its details. For example, in 1750 Elizabeth Petrovna decided to grant audiences only to ambassadors and "ministers plenipotentiary," while ordinary ministers and residents had to present their credentials to the College of Foreign Affairs. Under Catherine II an innovation intended to emphasize Russia's high position among other European states was introduced: on being officially presented to the Empress, foreign ambassadors were expected to speak in French, the international language of that time, whereupon the Empress would reply in the same language. But if the ambassador spoke in his native tongue, Catherine replied in Russian, though, as is well known, her Russian was not quite correct. When Lord Buckingham greeted Catherine in English, Catherine replied in Russian. Buckingham's successor, McCartney, however, wishing to gain the Empress' favor, spoke in French.

The requirement that ambassadors kiss the Empress' hand at the presentation had the same purpose—to uphold the prestige of Russia. In 1762 this provoked a conflict with the Austrian ambassador

Count Mercy, who at first refused to go through with this cere-
mony on the ground that it was not customary at the court of
Vienna. He then demanded a commitment that the Russian ambassador in Vienna kiss the hand of the Austrian Empress, but he
finally had to yield.

Catherine's government was also very punctilious about the form
of address of the Empress. In 1766 the French court refused to add
"Impériale" to "Majesté," claiming that this would be contrary to
the rules of the French language. Catherine's reply in the form of
a resolution was not without dignity: "It is against the rules of the
Russian language and protocol to accept credentials not presented
with the proper form of address."

With regard to diplomatic precedence so typical of the seventeenth century, only as much of it as was recognized by West
European custom was retained. In fact, observance of diplomatic
etiquette was less strict in St. Petersburg than in other European
capitals. But when the French government advised its representatives "everywhere to insist on precedence over the Russians, voluntarily or by force," Panin instructed Russian ambassadors "to
defend their places, voluntarily or by force." Panin defined his
views on the importance of etiquette as follows: "Etiquette strictly
regulates forms of correspondence between states precisely because
it serves as a measure of the mutual respect for each other's
strength."

The complexity of diplomatic activity in the latter part of the
eighteenth century put on the agenda the reorganization of the
institutions in charge of foreign relations. Under Peter I, the College of Foreign Affairs was still a comparatively small institution
(in 1718 it had a total of 120 employees). In 1762, the number of
employees had risen to 261 and the budget was over half a million
rubles. The College had a president, usually with the rank of chancellor, and a vice-president and was divided into (1) the secret, or
political, department, with two officials in charge of European and
Asian affairs, respectively, and (2) the public department, with var-

ious individuals in charge of "the treasury," "current affairs," and "postal affairs" and which also included a "ceremonial department." Decisions were supposed to be made collectively. Actually, the president and vice-president were in control, even though in 1781 Catherine issued a decree stressing that all matters should be handled collectively. The College accompanied the court on its long visits to Moscow (under Peter II and Elizabeth Petrovna), leaving behind only a "St. Petersburg office" to take care of current matters.

The importance of foreign policy in the affairs of the state required that all matters pertaining to that domain be concentrated in an institution with access to the sovereign, without whose sanction not a single decision could be taken. Such was the purpose of the Supreme Privy Council, established in 1726, where, along with other matters, were presented and discussed "ambassadorial reports and dispatches." There was a close tie also between the College of Foreign Affairs and the "cabinet" which Anna Ivanovna established in 1731. In 1756, in connection with the start of military operations against Prussia, Elizabeth Petrovna, at the suggestion of Bestuzhev-Ryumin, formed a special "conference at the Imperial court," consisting of trusted dignitaries, for the purpose of guiding the movement of the troops "with the necessary speed and force." The conference discussed foreign policy matters as well as military affairs. In 1768, under Catherine, a special council was established in connection with the Turkish war to discuss military and political affairs. The council was supposed to decide only general issues, without going into details. But under an empress who personally decided all the basic questions of foreign policy, it never played an important role.

The collective organization of the administration of foreign policy, established in the eighteenth century, despite the shortcomings that emerged, continued into the nineteenth century. As a matter of fact, Alexander I's Manifesto of September 8, 1802, which established ministries, hardly affected the College of Foreign Affairs, which continued to function under the minister and his deputy. However, its importance declined gradually and the minister's personal power increased. The College was finally abolished by a decree of April 10, 1832 and replaced by a Ministry of Foreign Affairs.

MARC RAEFF

In the Imperial Manner

I F ONE WERE TO SINGLE OUT the periods of Russia's
greatest expansion the choice would no doubt fall on the reigns
of Ivan IV (1533–1584) and Catherine II (1762–1796). In the sixteenth century, Russia broke down the barriers restraining the
movement of its population to the east by gaining control of the entire course of the Volga and by pushing on into Siberia. In the
eighteenth century Russia secured its southern border by the ac-

Marc Raeff, "The Style of Russia's Imperial Policy and Prince G. A.
Potemkin," in *Statesmen and Statecraft of the Modern West: Essays in
Honor of Dwight E. Lee and H. Donaldson Jordan,* edited by G. N. Grob
(Barre, Mass.: Barre Publishing Co., 1967), pp. 1–51.

quisition of the northern shore of the Black Sea and, by eliminating the troublesome neighbors in the southwest and west, prepared the ground for the settlement and rapid economic development of the Ukraine.[1] It is easy in retrospect to view these events as a working out of conscious designs, ideological tenets, and consistently purposeful actions. But such a view is too much of an *ex post facto* rationalization and it harbors the danger of anachronistic judgment. The uncontrolled and spontaneous movements of population, the search for adventure and wealth, the longing for effective protection against incursions by unruly neighbors, the historical memory of past political and spiritual unity, the expectation of a great political and economic international role, the desire to contribute to the spread of Christianity and to the liberation of brethren in religion from impious domination, the seizing of unexpected opportunities—these are some of the elements which, woven into an inextricable web, account for Russia's expansion into a Eurasian empire.

How should we describe this expansion? Is it the wresting of political control over territory from another power? But how does such a definition apply to genuinely empty and free lands which still abounded in the eighteenth century (not to speak of the sixteenth, of course) on the frontiers of the Russian state? And how are we to treat the movement of peasant settlers into empty areas to escape the control of Moscow? Where does defensive action stop and aggression begin in the case of open steppe and the grazing grounds of nomadic tribes? We are the children of an age of ideology and it is difficult for us to conceive that a complex series of events resulting in a clearly definable pattern of political and economic transformation was not determined by an overarching ideological (i.e., conscious and rational) design. We speak of an "urge to the sea," the doctrine of "natural frontiers," the messianic ambitions of Russia as heir of Byzantium, Russia's "duty" to protect or

1. Throughout this essay, unless otherwise qualified, we use the name Ukraine in its modern connotation, i.e., to refer to the entire south of European Russia, between the lower Don and the lower Dniester.

liberate the Orthodox Christian peoples of the Balkans and Caucasus. Obviously, some of these ideological considerations are mutually exclusive; conceivably, of course, some were uppermost in the minds of the Russian officials at one time and some others at other times. But how can we be sure that people really thought in these terms? Are some of these ideological notions not a manifestation of intellectual concerns or economic necessities (such as nationalism, imperialism, access to foreign markets) that appeared only subsequently? We also should remember that chronologically distinct ideological elements may be at play in different areas at the same time: a "traditional" and unconscious defensive motive may explain happenings on the eastern frontier of Russia, while at the same time "modern" and "rational" geopolitical considerations determined actions in the west. One last *caveat,* the tools and methods used in the pursuit of a political goal play no mean part in determining—either negatively or positively—the outcome of a policy. Traditional methods may give a particular form and limit the scope of aims defined on the basis of "modern" and "rational" considerations.

How can we give a meaningful and historically accurate account of the "imperial" policies of Catherine II? A perusal of the decrees and laws promulgated by the Empress during the thirty-four years of her reign (and their general tenor was adumbrated in the notes she jotted down for herself when she was only the wife of the heir presumptive[2]) points to one concern that, for whatever reason, was ever present in her mind: develop the economic resources and potential of the empire, help to bring into play all the economically creative forces of the population. It is true that this had to be done without touching at the foundation of Russian society—serfdom. This strikes us as being so completely incompatible that we readily dismiss her major aim as mere sham; but in so doing we forget that neither she, nor most contemporaries, felt it as such. This was the goal behind Catherine's laws giving full security to the private

2. Sbornik imperatorskogo russkogo istoricheskogo obshchestva (Sbornik IRIO), VII (1871), 82–109.

property of the nobility, including the right to exploit at will whatever was to be found on their estates, on the surface or beneath
it.[3] The same motive underlay the legislation abolishing internal
duties, restrictions on private industrial and commercial enterprise,
as well as the measures promoting the modernization and expanding the productivity of agriculture.[4] Finally, in spite of their inade-
quacy or ambiguity, the statutes giving some measure of corporate
organization to the nobility and the towns population also helped
to promote this same goal.[5] Naturally, economic growth and a
higher level of prosperity would also benefit the government and
give to the Empress and her courtiers greater means for indulging
their love of luxury. This selfish aspect, however, in no way
negates the genuineness and consistency of purpose of Catherine's
economic legislation.

Russia's expansion to the south and southwest could further
these same ends. It is doubtful that the expansion was determined
by the needs of Russian trade or incipient extensive agriculture, as
Soviet historians like to believe. But quite clearly the expansion, it
was felt, would promote them once they became a realistic possibility. The term "expansion" is somewhat misleading in this context,
for it was not so much the political control over new territory that
was significant for economic development, but rather the settlement of people and the promotion of agriculture and trade on the
underpopulated lands of the south that had been under Russian
sovereignty for several generations. Yet, clearly, in order to be of
economic benefit, these territories had to be safe from foreign incursions and possess adequate access to waterways.

3. Polnoe sobranie zakonov rossiiskoi imperii (PSZ), 12474 (September
19, 1765), 15447 (June 28, 1782); Sbornik IRIO, XXVII (1880), 68, 186. It
was a break with the policy of Peter the Great who had reserved to the
state the monopoly over all minerals and ores and the control over the
exploitation of such resources as timber.
4. For ex. PSZ 14275 (March 17, 1775); cf. P. I. Liashchenko, *Istoriia
narodnogo khoziaistva SSSR,* I (Moscow, 1947), 418–424.
5. The so-called Charters to the Nobility (PSZ 16187, April 21, 1785)
and to the Towns (PSZ 16188, April 21, 1785).

The quest for security in the south determined Catherine's policy toward Turkey and led her to fight two wars for the establishment of Russian control over the northern shores of the Black Sea. Similar considerations explain the more aggressive penetration into the Caucasus, as well as the annexation of the Crimea. It would be more difficult to establish a connection between these trends and the blatantly imperialistic plans and moves of Catherine II, e.g., the notorious "Greek project." [6] Most likely this ambitious (and unrealistic) scheme was only a move in the diplomatic game as it was played at the time. In the eighteenth century much of political and even military life was carried on within a framework of play, as manifested not only in the rules and forms of diplomacy and warfare, but also in their aims.

Of all of Catherine's moves in foreign affairs, the partition of Poland made the deepest impression abroad and, incidentally, saddled Russia with a heavy psychological and political burden for generations to come. But from the point of view of Russia's internal affairs, as well as in terms of its style of imperial policy, it was not Poland but the push to the south that was most characteristic and significant. This push enabled Russia to settle and develop the fertile plains of the Ukraine, which in turn led to the formation of an exportable surplus and made of the Ukraine an international breadbasket. The acquisition of the Crimea proved less significant economically, although it was essential for defense and the development of Russian shipping on the Black Sea.

Unlike the conquest and settlement of Siberia, but like the first eastward advance in the sixteenth century, the expansion into the south was intimately connected with international military and dip-

---

6. Recently, historians have come to the conclusion that the project was drafted by A. A. Bezborodko and that it does not seem to have been taken seriously by anyone else, except as a gambit in the tortuous relations between Russia and Austria. See O. P. Markova, "O proiskhozhdenii tak nazyvaemogo grecheskogo proekta (80e gody XXVIII v.)," *Istoriia SSSR,* 1958, No. 4, pp. 52–78; and E. Hösch, "Das sogenannte 'griechische Projekt' Katharinas II," *Jahrbücher für Geschichte Osteuropas,* N. F. XII (1964), 168–206.

lomatic events. The Russians had first to wrest control from the Turks and their Tatar vassals, and then secure the grudging assent of the powers by treaty in order to maintain their domination. Consequently the policies of settlement and economic development of empty territories could not be dissociated from military policy; nay, military and naval considerations frequently dictated both form and goal of administrative and economic measures. The establishment of fortresses and harbors, and the organization and maintenance of garrisons to protect the area went hand in hand with colonization and the foundation of towns that would promote economic activity. As the distances over the newly acquired lands were great and the means of transportation scant, the military establishment had to procure the necessities of life on the spot. This increased the demands on agriculture and the need for settling an economically active population. Military and economic purposes could not, therefore, be separated and the colonization of the south always had a double aspect: military and agricultural. In this sense the steppes and shore of the Black Sea played a role similar to the old Roman *limes* and their Byzantine and Near Eastern successors.[7] Those organizing Russian authority in this part of the world had to be both military and administrative leaders. For this reason, too, Catherine's most dynamic and influential military adviser, Grigorii Aleksandrovich Potemkin, also took the lead in the economic and agricultural development of the region. He was truly a builder of empire and may in all fairness be counted among the great colonizers of modern times. Our main task will be to examine the ways by which he pursued his purpose, so as to be able to draw some conclusions about the style of his statesmanship and make some observations on the pattern and methods of Russian imperial policy in the eighteenth century.

The highlights of Potemkin's meteoric career can be given in

7. For this aspect of the history of the southeastern European plain, see W. H. McNeill, *Europe's Steppe Frontier, 1500–1800: A Study of the Eastward Movement in Europe* (University of Chicago, 1964).

a few words.[8] The future Prince of Tavrida (i.e., Crimea) was born in Byelorussia in 1739, the son of a somewhat eccentric retired officer of middling wealth. His father died when he was six years old and the boy was raised in Moscow under the supervision of his godfather. He attended the gymnasium attached to the newly founded University of Moscow and received several distinctions for outstanding performance. He was particularly interested and proficient in theology and Greek, and at one point he even seems to have contemplated entering the Church. He did not maintain his good academic standing and was dismissed in 1760. He then joined the regiment of the Horse Guards in Saint Petersburg. During the hectic days in June 1762 when Catherine overthrew her much disliked and incompetent husband, Peter III, Potemkin was in her entourage and apparently made himself useful to the new sovereign. His reward, however, was modest and at the time he did not achieve the prominence he ambitioned. He secured, however, an appointment to the chancery of the Holy Synod; he became the executive secretary of the Ober Prokurator, a rather important and responsible position for a man of his age and which shows that his earlier theological interests and studies did not go unwasted.[9]

Potemkin did not remain long in the ecclesiastical administration, however, and returned to the Horse Guards in Saint Petersburg. He was admitted to court and his attractive physique and good humor were noticed by Catherine II. After the outbreak of

8. The biographical data are drawn from A. Loviagin, "Potemkin, G. A.," *Russkii biograficheskii slovar'* (Plavil'shchikov-Primo) (St. Petersburg, 1905), cols. 549–670; Th. Adamczyk, *Fürst G. A. Potemkin: Untersuchungen zu seiner Lebensgeschichte* (Emsdetten, 1936); the only modern biography in English, G. Soloveytchik, *Potemkin: Soldier, Statesman, Lover and Consort of Catherine of Russia* (New York, 1947), is unfortunately useless to the historian. A number of legends are connected with the dazzling career of Potemkin; most of them have been shown to be derived from one or two malevolent contemporary Western pamphlets, cf. V. Bil'bassov, *Katharina II. Kaiserin von Russland im Urtheile der Weltliteratur,* 2 vols. (Berlin, 1897).

9. Sbornik IRIO, VII, 316–318; Zapiski odesskogo obshchestva istorii i drevnostei, ZOOID, XIII (1883), 187–188.

the first Turkish war in 1768 Potemkin joined the army on the Danube. If the Empress had no occasion to learn of any high feats of his, she did notice his absence and thought of the dangers to which he was exposed. She wrote him that she had not forgotten him and asked him not to endanger his health or life. The hint was clear. Potemkin arranged to be sent with news of victory to Saint Petersburg; there he promptly became Catherine's lover and favorite. From then on, his rise was dazzling. By 1775 he had been created count, appointed vice-president of the College of War, and put in charge of all military forces and administrative authority in the southern provinces and territories. He later became field marshal, president of the College of War, which gave him control over the entire military establishment of the empire.

Even after he had ceased to be the Empress' lover he kept his great influence over her mind and remained her most trusted and influential counselor in all matters political and administrative. He took on responsibility for developing the regions acquired by terms of the Treaty of Kuchuk-Kainardji and as governor of New Russia he became the satrap of the empire's south. He engineered the seizure of the Crimea; entrusted with the protection of the Caucasian frontier he helped to further Russia's penetration and extend its protectorate over the princelings of Abkhazia and Kabardinia. The last important act of his life was the capture of Ochakov which paved the way for the victorious end of the second Turkish war, an end he did not live to see. He died in characteristically theatrical fashion in the open air, on an Oriental rug laid out in the steppe in October 1791.

II

Since the sixteenth century the Cossacks had been in the forefront of the unplanned, gradual advance of the Russian people into the open steppe lands of the south and east.[10] Part adventurers, part

10. The best account is G. Stökl, *Die Entstehung des Kosakentums* (München: Veröffentlichunges des Osteuropa-Institutes, 1953); the most re-

soldiers, always ready to pick a good fight, especially if it promised booty, tillers of the soil and fishermen when they were not fighting, the Cossacks had developed a social organization of their own. Theirs was a kind of "military democracy" which attracted all those who wanted to escape the yoke of serfdom and the shackles of the law, be it in Poland or Muscovy. At first the Cossacks had appeared on the banks of the lower Dnieper where by the late sixteenth and early seventeenth centuries they had created a respectably strong political and military organization with headquarters at the Dnieper rapids (the so-called Zaporozhian *sich'*, or *sech'*). Eventually they had to accept the overlordship of Muscovy. From then on their social system, political organization, and even economic and cultural way of life underwent erosion at a rapidly increasing pace. Basically the pattern of this process was the following: the officers and headmen (*starshina*) secured increasing wealth and power; they associated themselves with the Russian government, obtaining rewards, estates, and ranks. Gradually this led also to their social and cultural russification in the eighteenth century and to their forgetting the traditions, way of life, and values of "military democracy"; in fact they had betrayed the "Cossack liberties." The rank and file, on the other hand, were rapidly sinking to the level of peasant bondsmen. The process was accelerated after Hetman Mazeppa's siding with Charles XII of Sweden against Peter the Great and the flight of his followers to Turkey. In retaliation, the Russian government proceeded to abolish all Cossack privileges and traditions systematically. The final blow fell in 1775 when Catherine II destroyed the last stronghold of the Dnieper Cossack liberties, the Zaporozhian *sich'*.[11]

But already in the late sixteenth century many Cossacks from the Dnieper had decided to move eastward, where they hoped to find

cent comprehensive Soviet history is V. A. Golobutskii, *Zaporozhskoe kaza-chestvo* (Kiev, 1957).

11. PSZ 14354 (August 3, 1775); N. F. Dubrovin, *Bumagi kniazia Grigoria Aleksandrovicha Potemkina-Tavricheskogo* 1774–1788 gg. (St. Petersburg: Sbornik voenno-istoricheskikh materialov, vyp. VI, 1893), Nos. 36, pp. 36–37, and 47, pp. 46–52. Hereafter this source will be cited as *Bumagi Potemkina.*

more scope for both their warlike energies and agricultural endeavors. The Russian government had favored this movement as it helped to protect the southeastern frontier of the state.[12] Thus a Cossack Host and political organization had emerged on the banks of the Don River. But as had been the case of the Dnieper Cossacks, the Don community became rent with inner dissensions as the wealthy officers endeavored to entrench themselves in their leading position on a hereditary basis, while the rank and file opposed them in the name of traditional Cossack equality and liberties. These dissensions, and the ensuing discontent, led many Don Cossacks to join the Pugachev rebellion that swept across eastern Russia in 1772–1775 and threatened to shake the very social and political foundations of the empire. For the central government the problem was, therefore, to retain the Cossacks as a valuable military organization, ready to be called upon to do garrison duty on the frontier, to fight in case of war or internal disturbance, while at the same time preserving their economic role as free peasants, capable of providing for their own livelihood and equipment. It fell upon Potemkin, as commander in chief of all irregular troops, to work out a solution.

The simple solution was to take advantage of the social and economic rift existing in the Cossack corps in order to reform and control it for Russia's imperial purposes. The Host's ataman (chief commander) had in the past wielded almost absolute power, although he was in principle elected by the entire Host. This had enabled him to pursue any policy he wished. Like their counterparts on the Dnieper earlier, witness Mazeppa, the atamans of the Don Cossacks were of doubtful loyalty. They were bent upon making themselves hereditary masters of the Host and well nigh independent rulers of the Don Cossack territory.[13] Although the Cossacks would have liked to preserve complete independence from

12. Cf. S. G. Svatikov, *Rossiia i Don 1549–1917* (*Issledovanie po istorii gosudarstvennogo i administrativnogo prava i politicheskikh dvizhenii na Donu*), (Belgrade, 1924); V. A. Golobutskii, *Chernomorskoe kazachestvo* (Kiev, 1956).

13. The instructive example of Ataman S. Efremov was vividly present in Catherine's mind, cf. Svatikov, pp. 210–216, 223.

any power, they were not willing to submit to the ataman's autocratic rule, the more since he was in fact elected by a small minority of wealthy officers. It was therefore natural and easy for the Russian government to play on this dissatisfaction to abolish the elective character and autonomous power of the ataman.

As commander in chief of all Cossack forces in the empire, Potemkin in 1775 transformed the office of ataman of the Don Cossacks into an appointive position. He himself appointed the new ataman, A. I. Ilovaiskii, whom he knew to be devoted and loyal to the empire.[14] Preserving the ataman's power in matters of military discipline, Potemkin split the traditional unity of the military and political organization of the Host by establishing the "Host's Civil Administration." This administration was directly under the governor-general of New Russia as part of the Azov province.[15] It consisted of the appointive ataman, two counselors appointed by the governor-general, and two counselors elected by the general assembly of the Host. In this manner the control of the central government and of the regular hierarchy of local administration was secured over the Host, at the same time a measure of participation and autonomy was left to the Cossacks themselves. The degree of autonomy was still greater in judiciary matters and with respect to village life. Justice was administered by a panel of five judges of which four were elected. Customary law prevailed for minor cases, but the law of the empire took precedence in cases on appeal.[16]

Most important, however, was the decision to equate the Cossack officer ranks with those of the Russian regular army, and thereby give the Cossack leadership group access to the status of Russian nobility with all its privileges.[17] This gave official sanction to the social process of differentiation that had been going on among the Cossack hierarchy in the same way as it had among the Dnieper Cossacks. In this manner the Cossack ruling group

14. *Bumagi Potemkina*, Nos. 22, pp. 17–18, and 24, pp. 20–21.
15. PSZ 14251 (February 14, 1775), 14252 (February 14, 1775); *Bumagi Potemkina*, No. 23, pp. 18–20.
16. Sbornik IRIO, XXVII, 63.
17. *Bumagi Potemkina*, No. 23, p. 19.

was deprived of any need to oppose the imperial government. Gradually, though quite fast, Cossack officers were assimilated into the Russian élite and abandoned their claims to special treatment and rights. As for the rank and file, they were satisfied not to be at the mercy of the ataman and his henchmen, of enjoying the security of imperial law, while preserving their traditional ways in local matters. In addition they could retain the illusion, or hope, that through a successful service career they had the possibility of joining the ranks of the nobility, of acquiring serfs, and of playing an active role in the life of the country.

There were further compensations of an economic nature. The wealthier officer group, by becoming part of the Russian nobility, could now acquire populated lands and they also obtained the right to purchase serfs in Russia proper and settle them on their personal estates.[18] The rank and file Cossacks retained their personal freedom, their rights to the communal lands, and experienced an alleviation of their service obligations, in particular with respect to garrison duty in border fortresses. With the decline of the threats to the security of the area, the military obligations decreased still further. Eventually, the Cossacks became a militia called upon only during time of war.[19] Furthermore, they received preferential treatment if they settled in newly acquired territories in the foothills of the Caucasus and on the Kuban, where eventually a new Host was formed along the same lines as on the Don.[20]

III

The reorganization of the Don Cossack Host was essentially a matter of domestic policy. The annexation and assimilation of

18. *Bumagi Potemkina*, No. 81, p. 89.

19. Their use as military police—especially during strikes, riots, and pogroms—which gave the Cossacks their ill-famed notoriety on the eve of the Revolution did not come about until the end of the nineteenth century.

20. I. I. Dmitrenko (ed.), *Sbornik istoricheskikh materialov po istorii Kubanskogo kazacheskogo voiska, I*, 1737–1801, gg. (St. Petersburg, 1896); and Golobutskii, *Chernomorskoe kazachestvo*, passim.

territories which had belonged to the Ottoman Empire was a different matter. There was, in the first place, plain military conquest, or cession by treaty. But more interesting in our context was the procedure followed in the case of the Crimea, a former possession of the Ottoman Empire which had become an independent state by the Treaty of Kuchuk-Kainardji, and which was annexed by the Russians in 1783. We shall leave aside the international aspect, the complicated intrigues of two contending factions of the Crimean ruling family, the Gireis, as well as the relations with the bordering Nogai hordes.[21] We shall only be concerned with the way in which the Russians—under Potemkin's direction—prepared the ground for the bloodless annexation of the rich and attractive peninsula.

The population of the Crimea consisted of several distinct national, linguistic, and religious groups. The Tatars, Moslems speaking a Turkic language, were the majority and had been the dominant group since medieval times. Next there were sizable Christian minorities, Greeks, Armenians, and Georgians. The latter two were the leading fruit growers and owned most vineyards, while the former—because of their far-flung connections—played a particularly important commercial role. Potemkin proposed to lure to Russia these valuable minorities. He had two main considerations in mind for so doing: in the first place, he correctly suspected that the migration of these elements would fatally weaken the Crimean state, making it ripe for easy absorption into the empire. Secondly, and here Potemkin was to be proven only partly correct, he thought that by settling in Russia, these minorities would play the same beneficial role for the economic development of the southern territories of the empire as they had in the Crimea.

At the direction of Potemkin, the military commander at

21. For Catherine's considerations, see Sbornik IRIO, XXVII, 221–225 for general treatment and background, B. Nolde, *La Formation de l'Empire russe* (*Etudes, Notes et Documents*), II (Paris: Collection historique de l'Institut d'Etudes slaves, XV-2, 1953), Chaps. IX and X. Also Alan W. Fisher, *The Russian Annexation of the Crimea, 1772–1783* (New York: Cambridge University Press, 1970).

the Perekop isthmus, Prince A. A. Prozorovskii, approached the religious leaders of the Greeks, Armenians, and Georgians and, playing on their traditional fear and hatred of the Moslems, persuaded them to organize a mass migration of these national groups.[22] Two additional considerations helped, no doubt, in persuading the Greeks and Armenians to go to Russia: the promise of economic benefits and privileges to be conferred upon them by the Russian government and the expectation that with the help of Russia they could work for the independence of their mother lands.[23] About 20,000 Greeks left their homes in the harbors and trading centers of the Crimea. A large number, not exactly known, of Armenians did likewise. As the Georgian group was quite small, no further information has been preserved about it beyond the fact of its migration.

As was to be expected, the migration of such a large number of people did not proceed too smoothly. The Russians could not always make good on their promises to provide adequate food, shelter, and transportation. The whole movement was arranged rather precipitously; those involved had to sell their possessions at ridiculously low prices, their plight brought about much abuse; disease set in on the road to fill the cup of bitterness to the brim. The mortality rate was very high and discontent intense.[24] But there was no turning back. As the Greeks were not used to work on farms, they eventually were allowed to settle in towns, e.g., Taganrog and Mariupol, which, in a sense, were founded especially for them.[25] The Armenians and Georgians, on the other hand, resettled on the land; not all of them, however, remained in the prox-

22. N. Dubrovin (ed.), *Prisoedinenie Kryma k Rossii* (*Reskripty, pis'ma, reliatsii, doneseniia*), Vols. I–IV (St. Petersburg, 1885–1889), in particular see II (No. 114), 318–319 and (No. 117), 320–321. Hereafter cited as *Prisoedinenie Kryma.*

23. The charter to the Greeks is in PSZ 14879 (May 21, 1779) and to the Armenians PSZ 14942 (November 14, 1779); cf. also ZOOID, II (1848–1850), 660.

24. Report of Gen. Suvorov, *Prisoedinenie Kryma,* II (No. 314), 752–753.

25. ZOOID, I, 197–204 and IV (1860), 359–362.

imity of the Crimea and quite a few moved farther west, to the banks of the Dnieper and Dniester. Eventually, those who survived assimilated and became accustomed to their new environment. The Greeks, in particular, whose ranks were swollen by their compatriots from the islands, came to play a prominent role in the economic as well as cultural life of the whole region, particularly of Odessa and Sebastopol. The Armenians do not seem to have been as successful, for they have left few traces of their contribution to the development of the Black Sea shore in the eighteenth century.

The primary objective of the mass migration, namely the sapping of the Crimean polity, was accomplished. Within a few years the Crimea could be annexed by Russia without any difficulty or resistance. The whole episode is quite interesting from the point of view of the methods used. It is reminiscent of a pattern—albeit in modernized form—that had prevailed in the sixteenth century. When after two centuries of Mongol-Tatar domination, the Russians took the offensive against the successor states of the Golden Horde—the khanates of Kazan' and Astrakhan'—they first undermined the latter's power of resistance by luring away their most active and useful subjects: noble servicemen, junior members of the ruling families. These Tatar nobles and princes were given estates and rewards, they joined the ranks of the Grand Duke's military establishment; in some cases—e.g., the Kasimov princes—they founded vassal principalities along the fluid boundaries between the khanates and the Grand Duchy of Muscovy. Eventually they converted to Christianity, became russified, and were absorbed into the Russian service nobility.[26] The Greeks, Armenians, and Georgians played a similar role in regard to the Crimea. But conditions had changed since the sixteenth century. Instead of undermining the military service class, the Russians were luring away those most active and productive in the economic life of their potential victim. But as in earlier times, the newcomers

26. Best summary in B. Nolde, Vol. I (Paris: 1952), Chaps. I–III.

bolstered the strength of Russia and pumped new blood into its economic lifestream.[27]

The policy we have just described helped to undermine the Crimea and facilitated its annexation, but it did not solve the problems involved in organizing the administration of the newly acquired territory. Unlike most other territories conquered or absorbed by the Russian Empire so far, the Crimea had neither been contiguous (except for a few short years after Kuchuk-Kainardji, and even then the boundary ran through almost empty lands) nor populated by people sharing with the Russians a common language, historical tradition, religion, or culture.

The Russians endeavored at first to disturb the existing social and political order as little as possible. Only the sovereign power of the Khan was superseded by a Russian governor, who combined military command and administrative authority. This governor, a lieutenant of Potemkin, was directly responsible to him and received instructions from his chancellery; in the final analysis, of course, he was responsible to the Empress, but in view of Potemkin's powers this was purely a formality. The troops moving into the Crimea were instructed to be on their good behavior and not to harm or offend the local population.[28] As usual, unfortunately, this order was frequently disobeyed, as witness the episodes related in our sources. The fact that special injunctions had to be given not to tamper with property and to remind soldiers and officers that the Crimea was not to be considered conquered enemy territory tells us what the normal situation was in fact.[29] Also, the local population were permitted to leave the Crimea to go to Turkey if they so chose.[30] Quite a number took advantage of this opportunity,

27. One may also note in passing the greater role played by religion and language in the eighteenth century in bringing about the separation between different national groups that had lived in the same territory.

28. ZOOID, XII (1881), No. 38, p. 265, and No. 101, p. 286.

29. For numerous illustrations see the memoirs of a member of the Russian administration D. B. Mertvago, "Zapiski Dmitriia Borisovicha Mertvago 1760–1824," Appendix to Russkii Arkhiv, 1867, especially pp. 177–178.

30. ZOOID, VI (1867) 604; XIV (1886), 149–150; XXXI (1913) 79.

sold their possessions and abandoned their estates. This resulted in a dislocation of the local economy which hastened further the decline initiated by the migration of Greeks, Armenians, and Georgians. As at the time there was no one who could buy these lands and keep them in production, the annexation of the Crimea led to the impoverishment and ruin of the province. Only generations later did Russian landowners and new settlers manage—at great cost—to restore the Crimea to its rank of the empire's garden and orchard.

One may wonder why Potemkin allowed this to happen. The explanation must be sought in the fact that eighteenth-century Russian administrators did not believe that people might abandon their homes when they felt threatened in their survival as a religious, linguistic, or cultural entity. In fact the Russian authorities were determined not only to let the local population carry on its traditional way of life, but also to draw them into the new local institutions. The Russian military commanders heading the administration of the province were to act so as not to hurt local customs and prejudices. Russian law, for example, was to be introduced very gradually and only in cases involving Russians. The administration was to secure its information about local conditions—particularly on the distribution of real estate and population—only through local inhabitants.[31] In strictly local and personal matters elected elders or traditional chieftains were to have the decisive voice.[32]

The local *optimes* could receive recognition as nobles and be assimilated to the Russian nobility. This is what happened in very numerous instances. With the introduction in the Crimea of the institutions provided by the Charter of the Nobility of 1785 the Tatar nobles automatically became members of the Tauric Assembly of the Nobility. Of course, the validation of a Tatar claim to nobility was not always an easy matter, although the Russian ad-

31. ZOOID, XIV, 149–150, 153.
32. Sbornik IRIO, XXVII, 245–246; ZOOID, XXXI, 62–63; PSZ 15988 (April 24, 1784).

ministration accepted the traditional local criteria. A special commission was set up to disentangle the complicated and often cumbersome details involved in the claims to noble status. Characteristically, this commission consisted of the local mufti, seven Tatar nobles, four native officials, and two Greeks who had been ennobled in Russian service.[33] Under the circumstances it did not prove difficult to introduce eventually the local administrative institutions provided by the Statute on the Provinces of 1775. This took place step by step, but rather fast.[34]

The native élite, treated like the nobles in Russia, were allowed to hold assemblies, elect some officials, and participate in local affairs along with their Russian counterparts. But, from a strictly nationalistic point of view (which probably did not occur to Potemkin and his contemporaries), here was the rub: to be assimilated to the nobility of the empire, to be able to participate in local affairs within the framework of the acts of 1775 and 1785 put a special premium on russification. Indeed, rapidly a large number of the Tatar upper class did become russified. This meant, however, that those who could not or would not be russified slipped in the social scale, sinking to the sad lot of peasant. It moreover created a new gap between the traditional native leadership and the local population—a cultural gap even more profound than the one which separated the Westernized Russian nobleman from his serfs. Little wonder that the feeling of national identity and cultural consciousness of the Crimean Tatars in the nineteenth century came to be closely associated with Islam and their Turkish past.

The Crimea had been annexed in the expectation of the expanded economic opportunities as well as strategic and political benefits it would bring to the empire. In this sense it was a colonial acquisition. Russian officers and officials, first of all Potemkin, of course, were granted land holdings either from empty lands or from estates that had been abandoned at the time of the Rus-

33. ZOOID, XXIII (1901), 41-43.
34. PSZ 15920 (February 2, 1784), 15925 (February 8, 1784), 15988 (April 24, 1784).

sian annexation. A new class of Crimean landowners thus came into being. Together with the russified native élite the Russian landowners became the most influential group on the peninsula. They, too, were most aggressive in exploiting the local peasant labor, importing serfs from Russia and setting up orchards and vineyards on a large commercial scale. The Russians also brought with them more "modern" and Western notions as to what constituted "civilized" activities and the most desirable way of life. In particular, they held sedentary agriculture in highest esteem and scorned cattle raising which was associated in their minds with dangerous, unruly, and primitive nomadic tribes. They therefore promoted an agricultural development which was determined by their own preconceived notions, interests, and traditions, disregarding Tatar preferences and customs, in spite of their alleged claim to work for the common good. Such a trend could only multiply the areas of friction between Russians and natives.[35]

If we look at the methods and approaches used in the incorporation of the Crimea and analyze their rationale—implicit or explicit—we are struck by their resemblance to the sixteenth century pattern in the case of the conquest and absorption of the khanates of Kazan' and Astrakhan' (to some extent of western Siberia as well). Things and circumstances had changed, of course: Russia's economy was different, the military balance overwhelmingly in favor of Russia, the religious-cultural sophistication of the Russian leadership greater. Yet, in truth, the parallel is quite close. The results, too, were similar in their ambiguity: incorporation into the Russian empire brought distinct benefits to the conquered states: e.g., eventual economic "modernization," participation in Russian culture for the élite, domestic peace and military security. But they were accompanied by the disadvantages of Russian bureaucratic centralization, and had to be bought at too high a price in economic and psychological terms, a price which many of the new subjects were unwilling or unable to pay.

35. ZOOID, XV (1889), 678–680.

IV

Closely related to the annexation of the Crimea was a set of measures which brought foreign colonists to the shores of the Black and Azov seas. After the annexation of the peninsula foreign colonists were settled there too. We have mentioned the role played by the migration of Greeks, Armenians, and Georgians from the Crimea proper. In addition, colonists from the Mediterranean were brought in to set up garrisons and relieve the regular Russian troops by protecting the newly settled territories against the nomads of the adjoining steppes.

First came the so-called Albanians, mainly Greeks from the islands and from the Adriatic and Ionian coasts, who had followed the appeal issued by Count Alexis Orlov to assist the Russian fleet during the Mediterranean campaign and who feared Turkish vengeance. They settled in military townships, in Kerch and Enikale, and the regular army units into which they were organized retained their identity into the middle of the nineteenth century.[36] In passing it may be noted that Catherine II allowed them to retain their national costume as part of their military uniforms.[37] The "Albanians" were joined by a few Italians, Corsicans, and other Mediterranean peoples, primarily from the islands.[38] Their numbers stayed small and, with rare exceptions, they did not remain on the lands originally set up for them. As soon as urban life revived on the shores of the Black Sea they moved to the towns (Odessa, for example) where their presence contributed to the formation of an active economy, and cosmopolitan intellectual atmosphere. In any event, they helped a great deal to establish a *présence "russe"* on the contested shores and to spearhead the development of a modern society there. They were also active in helping to organize

36. *Bumagi Potemkina,* No. 43, p. 43; No. 48, pp. 52–53; No. 84, pp. 90–92; No. 85, pp. 92–94; ZOOID, I, 205–226.
37. Sbornik IRIO, XLII, No. 406, p. 383.
38. ZOOID, VI, 604; XI (1879), 330–331.

the administration of the Crimea and to integrate its economy into that of the empire.

In connection with these colonists and their settlement (which was actively advertised and encouraged by the Russian authorities in St. Petersburg as well as locally) the question arises, of course, whether the real purpose was to introduce them as an active yeast in the newly acquired lands, or whether ulterior political motives played the decisive role. The latter, involving the future of the Ottoman Empire, may have continued to be an element in Catherine's thinking, even after Russia had asserted its preeminence in the Black Sea. If the Greek project was to be more than a diplomatic maneuver or the pipe dream of a few enthusiasts, these settlers could be of service in advancing political claims in the Mediterranean and in interfering in the affairs of the Porte. It was in this light that the Turks viewed these colonization moves. For our part, we are rather inclined to think that in St. Petersburg the main consideration was a desire to develop better and faster the resources of the newly acquired areas. Naturally, should the occasion present itself, the Russian government would not hesitate to make political use of the foreigners settled there. But the occasion did not present itself, except in an indirect and minor way at the time of the Greek War of Independence, and by that time the original settlers had been well integrated into the empire.[39] In any event, there is no doubt that Catherine and Potemkin thought of these settlers above all in terms of the needs of an imperial domestic policy. Clearly, the empire of the tsars had by this time ceased to be isolated politically and culturally; on the contrary, it was a cosmopolitan meeting ground on which the modern Russian culture and polity were making their appearance.

Attracting and settling foreigners was not a new policy. It had a precedent in the settling of foreigners along military lines in the Ukraine proper. But Potemkin put the finishing touches to it

39. J. Nicolopoulos, "Père et fils dans l'Aufklärung néohellénique: Les Paniagiodor-Nikovul," O EPANIΣTHΣ (Athens, 1964), XII, 254–279.

and brought to a successful conclusion a trend initiated in the preceding reign—although it should be said that Potemkin's success
was made possible by a combination of several factors that had not
been simultaneously present in the past.

The complexities of the Ukrainian situation stemmed from the
fact that it lay at the intersection of several cultural and political
cross currents. It also was a region where the Dnieper Cossack
Host had developed and maintained over a long period its peculiar
social and political institutions. Lastly, it was relatively unpopu-
lated and, therefore, attracted settlers from everywhere. All these
elements had helped to shape the notions of the separateness and
particular social identity of the Ukraine. But with the incorporation
(1654) of the Cossack Host under Moscow's sovereignty the officers
began to be russified; eventually they merged with the nobility
and joined the military and civil service of the empire. At the same
time, the loyalty of the leadership that had not become russified
had been put into question, as we have seen, by Mazeppa's defection
and the subsequent flight of the Zaporozhian Cossacks into Turkey.

To forestall the possibility of future desertions and to foster the
social and economic trends that were undermining the traditional
Cossack ways, the government of Empress Elizabeth embarked on
a policy of settling auxiliary troops that would be completely dependent on St. Petersburg. As a majority of these settlers were
recruited among the Orthodox and Slavic-speaking peoples of East
Central Europe they were called "Serbians," although most came
from the Habsburg Empire. Even though they could maintain
their customs and language, their leaders at any rate were soon
assimilated to the Russian nobility. This was not surprising, for by
virtue of their military duties and ranks, and their possession of
granted estates, the "Serbian" officers came to have the same
way of life and values as the Russian noble servicemen. We need
not go into the details of this colonization here; it has been the
subject of several detailed studies in Western languages.[40] Suffice

40. N. D. Polons'ka-Vasylenko, *The Settlement of the Southern Ukraine*
(1750–1775), The Annals of the Ukrainian Academy of Arts and Sciences

it to note that in this instance the Russian government was following the Muscovite system of granting estates (*pomestie*) in return for military service, a system that had reached its high point in the second half of the sixteenth and first half of the seventeenth centuries and had been abandoned by Peter the Great.[41]

From the very beginning of her reign, Catherine II pursued a double policy with respect to the complex multinational Ukraine (we shall leave aside the implications with regard to Russia's relations to Poland and Turkey). In the first place, like her predecessors,[42] she dismissed all claims for recognition of the distinctiveness of Ukrainian language, religion, customs, and the like. She firmly believed that the Ukraine was part and parcel of the Russian lands and that its people were fundamentally Russians—a belief, incidentally, which found validation in the assimilation of the Ukrainian élite to the Russian nobility and the undeveloped national consciousness of the common people at the time. The obvious differences in customs, legal system, attitudes, and the resulting administrative or political distinctiveness, were quite superficial, due only —the Empress thought—to historical accidents. As for Cossack particularism, it was based on the uncivilized ways of a gang of unruly ruffians who had to be disbanded for the sake of the peace and security of the region as well as of the empire. This was accomplished, as we know, when the Zaporozhian *sich'* was destroyed in 1775. The external differences between the Ukraine and Russia proper had to be eliminated gradually and the region (along with some other areas of the empire) assimilated to the pattern of the central provinces. It could be done gently, through appropriate

in the U. S., Vol. IV–V, No. 4 (14)—1 (15), Summer-Fall 1955; H. Auerbach, *Die Besiedelung der Südukraine in den Jahren 1774-1787* (Wiesbaden, 1965), (Veröffentlichungen des Osteuropa-Institutes, München, Band 25).

41. Polons'ka-Vasylenko, p. 220; cf. also E. I. Druzhinina, *Severnoe prichernomor'e v 1775-1780 gg.* (Moscow, 1959).

42. See the curious secret instructions of Empress Anne on promoting russification through a governmental matrimonial policy, Sbornik IRIO, CVIII, 26.

gradual administrative russification. This was the policy Catherine
laid down as a guideline for the central and local institutions in her
instructions to Prince A. A. Viazemskii upon his appointment as
procurator-general of the Senate.[43] In the second place, she was
very much concerned to have the potentially rich Ukraine contribute its full share to the general economy of the empire. Instead, she
noted, it was a drain on the government's resources, for the scheme
of foreign military settlements had proven quite costly and failed
to develop the local resources. This was the burden of her directives to Count Peter Rumiantsev at the time of his appointment as
governor-general of Little Russia (i.e., right bank Ukraine).[44]
From 1775 on, Potemkin's activities in the Ukraine were to bring
to successful fruition Catherine's double-faceted policy: complete
administrative uniformity and making the region economically and
politically profitable to the empire.

After the Hetmanate had been abolished and the *sich'* destroyed, the administrative uniformity with Central Russia was
completed by the creation of the governor-generalships of Little
Russia under Rumiantsev and of New Russia under Potemkin.
The latter included, in fact, more than the Ukraine in the strict
sense (for example the Kuban' and Don areas, and later the Crimea), but it extended over most of the southern steppe and frontier
areas with similar social and economic conditions. It is not necessary for us at this point to delve into the intricacies of the administrative arrangements, their subdivisions, and frequent changes of
detail.[45] Two things, however, deserve to be noted: first, that the
power wielded by Potemkin was well nigh absolute and that he
had complete control over the vast areas yet to be developed. We
shall return to this point later when discussing the character of Potemkin's authority. Secondly, we note that the administrative institutions followed closely the pattern and model of the governor-gen-

43. See § 9 of this instruction, Sbornik IRIO, VII, 348.
44. Sbornik IRIO, VII, 376–391.
45. The best summary is E. A. Zagorovskii, "Organizatsiia upravleniia
Novorossii pri Potemkine," ZOOID, XXXI, 52–82; see also relevant chapters in Auerbach and Druzhinina, cited above.

eralships (or vicegerencies) introduced in Russia proper at the time. In this manner they helped to bring about a uniformity of structure between these new territories and the core lands. The main task of these institutions was to fill up the area with people and to develop its economy; in so doing the new administration destroyed most of the significant elements of autonomous—Cossack or other—traditions and public ways of life that had survived.

The imposition on New Russia of an administrative uniformity with Russia proper cannot be divorced from the government's promoting those social processes that tended to make the social structures of the two areas of the empire alike. We can touch on this aspect only very briefly and superficially; it was very complex and extends beyond the chronological framework of this essay. The foreign settlers brought in under Elizabeth were rapidly assimilated to the normal Russian pattern. This meant that the rich officer class was acquiring estates on the same terms as the Russian nobles and was using more and more the labor of the native peasants. The latter were rapidly turning into the landowner's bondsmen. The step to full enserfment then was a short one, and it was taken before the reign of Catherine II was over.[46] As the military value of the original "Serbian" colonies had proven to be a doubtful proposition, the government did nothing to maintain or preserve their distinct regiments, so that their personnel was gradually absorbed into the regular Russian military establishment and their officers, as we have noted, drawn into the service and culture of the empire.

Potemkin tried at first to continue the old policy of attracting new military colonists. Entrepreneurs who would bring to South Russia a number of settlers would be rewarded with ranks in proportion to the number of people they persuaded to settle, ranks which carried with them the award of a specific amount of land. In this manner there came more settlers from Moldavia, Bulgaria, Hungary, Poland, Habsburg, and Turkish possessions, as well as some Swedes, Mennonites, and German peasants from the Baltic.

46. Cf. ZOOID, XXIX (1911), Part II, 59–81.

But their number was so small that they could not keep their own military units and had to be merged with existing regiments.[47]

To free the government from the costly expedient of bringing in foreigners—who had to be given special financial incentives, large land grants, and promised the respect of their customs, language and religion—and to further the other facet of Catherine's policy, that of economic development, Potemkin urged the settlement of Russians.[48] The possibilities in this respect were limited in view of Russia's chronic manpower shortage; the central provinces could not be depleted in favor of the new lands in the south. Several special social groups, however, could be tapped for this purpose. In the first place were the many Old Believers who had fled to Poland to escape the persecution of the governments of Tsar Alexis and Peter the Great. An energetic effort was now undertaken to lure them back into Russia. Old Believers were promised that local bishops would permit them to follow their ritual and consecrate their priests. In addition, they were given generous economic inducements in form of land grants, exemptions from taxation for long periods, and relief from the discriminatory capitation tax rate. They were also allowed to settle on the same terms as the military colonists, which automatically would exempt them from furnishing recruits. In return, they would have to hold themselves ready to answer calls to active duty in time of war.[49] The policy had some success, although not as much as expected, in part because of the reluctance on the part of the Church hierarchy and the loss of interest in the scheme on the part of Catherine's successors.

47. ZOOID, XIII, 127–131; II, 662–663, 665–666; Sbornik IRIO, XXVII, 350. The basic legislation and administrative framework for foreign colonists in Russia was the decree of July 22, 1763, PSZ 11879, which set up the so-called Chancery for the Tutelage of Foreign Colonists.

48. The problems involved in tracing the history of the unofficial migration of Russian settlers to the south are briefly discussed by A. Florovskii, "Neskol'ko faktov iz istorii russkoi kolonizatsii Novorossii v nachale XIX v.," ZOOID, XXXIII (1919), 25–40.

49. Bumagi Potemkina, No. 117, p. 120 (§2); No. 188, pp. 192–193; Sbornik IRIO, XXVII, 468; ZOOID, IX (1875), 285–288; VIII (1872) 212; Auerbach, p. 102.

Another group that might be tapped were the children of the Orthodox parish clergy. As the sons of priests automatically belonged to the clerical estate, and as there were fewer parishes than sons of priests, the latter were threatening to become a semi-educated clerical "proletariat." Potemkin suggested that supernumerary sextons and sons of priests be attracted to South Russia. There they could settle in agricultural pursuits, combined with some military obligations along the same lines as the Old Believers. If they preferred, however, they could enter the civil service and provide educated personnel for the much understaffed local administrative institutions, while at the same time fostering the russification of the region. In reward, the expectation was held out to them that, in view of the dearth of good administrative personnel, they might rise rapidly in the service, secure high ranks, which in turn would enable them to acquire estates and even the title of nobility with the right to own serfs. A number of children of the clergy took advantage of this opportunity and the administrative offices in the south were staffed by many from their ranks; a few eventually made very good careers in the imperial government.[50]

Finally, one should mention that the various officers and officials from Russia could bring to their newly acquired estates in the south serfs from the central provinces.[51] This was a potentially double-edged measure which did not go without some complications. Indeed, the danger was that serfs would be lured away or that owners in the central provinces would traffic in serfs to provide for the labor needs of the south. Such traffic was forbidden and landowners could transport and resettle only their own serf families.[52] How well these rules were obeyed is hard to say. However

50. ZOOID, VIII, 212; XV (1889), 613; Sbnornik IRIO, XLII, 416; *Bumagi Potemkina,* No. 117, p. 129 (§1); No. 310, pp. 268–269.

51. Although this permission must be balanced by Potemkin's purchases of serfs from private estates in the Ukraine for settlement in military units. Thereby these serfs were converted into state peasants whose lot was, by and large, much better than that of private serfs. Druzhinina, pp. 188–189 and PSZ 16605 (Jan. 14, 1788).

52. The plot of Gogol's *Dead Souls* is, of course, based on this situation.

this may have been, two things are clear: first, many serfs were moved to southern Russia, contributing to the ethnic russification of the local population (thus confusing still further the national picture for later generations). Secondly, serfdom was introduced into the Ukraine, an area that had heretofore been spared this evil.[53] The growing similarity of the social structures in the southern and central provinces enabled the russification and total assimilation of the Ukraine to make rapid strides.

The administrative organization and the social transformation fostered by Potemkin and the St. Petersburg government served to integrate the Ukraine into the economic structure of the empire. This structure, which was beginning to emerge at the end of the eighteenth century, consisted in its international aspect of a shift from the export of naval stores, industrial raw materials, and semi-manufactured products (pig iron, for example) to that of agricultural products, mainly grain. It is in this development that the Ukraine, or more generally speaking all of southern Russia, was to play the major role. Indeed, the steadily increasing number of large estates belonging to noble servicemen and high officials, the transformation of many local peasants into serfs, and the settlement of many more from the central provinces, were changing the Ukraine into a region of extensive agriculture for the export market. The foundation and development of commercial ports—first Kherson, later Odessa—served both as illustration and stimulant of this new trend.[54] This transformation conformed to what were Catherine's

53. Auerbach, pp. 108–110. It is true that for a while the strictness of serfdom was mitigated in the south by the need for labor which made the owners chary of introducing the harsh patterns that prevailed in the central provinces.

54. For the "prehistory" of this development, see D. Gerhard, *England und der Aufstieg Russlands* (München-Berlin, 1933); the three studies of H. Halm under the general title of *Oesterreich und Neurussland* give the best account and fullest documentation of the development of Russian trade in the Black Sea. They clearly point to the conclusion that the expansion of trade followed the political and administrative changes in the area and did not contribute much to bring them about. H. Halm, *Donauschiffahrt*

and Potemkin's ulterior goals, which they may only have half-consciously groped for, but which—with the benefit of hindsight—appear quite clearly. These goals reflected the basic policy concerns of Catherine which we have noted at the beginning of this essay; they may be subsumed under the fashionable terms of "modernization" and "rationalization" of Russian life in general, and of the social and economic structure of the newly acquired regions in particular. Let us consider briefly some of these goals and the way in which they began to be realized.

In the first place we might cite urbanism, that is the foundation and development of towns and cities. This fitted well into the Enlightenment's preference for urban civilization and its infatuation with town planning and architectural design, expressive of utopian rationalism.[55] Loving the grandiose and given to flashy display, Potemkin found in town planning and building a particularly satisfying outlet for his energies and ambition. He first devoted his attention to Kherson which he destined to become the political and cultural center of the newly gained lands and the dockyard for the Black Sea fleet.[56] Later he allowed the town to decline (where it remained until Soviet times) and its place was taken in Potemkin's heart by Nikolaev which was located closer to the open sea. Symbolically, Potemkin hastened his own death by his desire to return

---

und -handel nach dem Südosten, 1718–1780 (Breslau, 1943); *Habsburgischer Osthandel im* 18. *Jahrhundert, Donauhandel und Seeschiffahrt, 1781–1787* (München, 1954) (Veröffentlichungen des Osteuropa-Institutes, Bd. VII); *Gründung und erstes Jahrzent von Festung und Stadt Cherson, 1778–1788* (Wiesbaden, 1961) (Veröffentlichungen des Osteuropa-Institutes, München, Bd. VIII); Jan Reychman, "Le commerce polonais en Mer Noire au XVIIIe siècle par le port de Kherson," *Cahiers du Monde russe et soviétique*, VII, No. 2 (Avril-Juin 1966), 234–238.

55. See the suggestive proceedings of an international symposium held in Nancy, P. Francastel (ed.), *Utopie et institutions au XVIIIe siècle* (*Le pragmatisme des Lumières*) (Paris-LaHaye, 1936). Of course, J.-J. Rousseau fought against this trend, but his impact was not felt until the very end of the century, and even at that it did not prevent the continuing interest in town planning and building.

56. See Potemkin's instructions to his agent there, M. I. Faleev, ZOOID, XI, 324–377 and also XIII, 184–187; IV, 362–373.

to Nikolaev when his forces gave way at Iassy.[57] Taganrog and Mariupol' were two other creations of his, a byproduct, as we have seen, of the settlement of Greeks from the islands and the Crimea. Lastly, Potemkin selected Ekaterinoslav as the capital of the vicegerency of New Russia and gave it his particular attention and care. He hoped to make it into the "Athens" of the Ukraine. He laid out the town in grand manner, started the building of a cathedral that was to exceed St. Peter's of Rome in size, and—on paper—established a university for which he hired several faculty members, including a professor of music and of fine arts.[58] In contrast to this utopian urge to create *ex nihilo* and to build "Athens," complete with university and academy in what was still economic and social frontier country, was the resort to traditional and archaic means. For example, to speed along his building plans, Potemkin instructed his subordinates to purchase serf masons in central Russia and to bring them to Kherson. He also ordered the compulsory training of recruits in various crafts, purchased unfree craftsmen, and had them enrolled into military units where they had to work at their trade whenever ordered to do so by their superiors or local authorities.[59]

The harebrained plan to set up a university in an incompleted city amidst barely populated steppes was not the only manifestation of Potemkin's concern for education in the region under his rule. In a more realistic vein, whose effects proved to be lasting, Potemkin took the lead in establishing secondary schools. At the time of the Russian naval expedition to the Mediterranean, young Greeks had been brought to Russia; a school, along the lines of the Corps of Cadets, was opened for them in 1774 in Oranienbaum, near St. Petersburg. Other foreign Orthodox pupils were also admitted to it. In 1783 this school was transferred to Kherson where

57. Graf. A. N. Samoilov, "Zhizn' i deianiia general-fel'dmarshala kniazia Grigoriia Aleksandrovicha Potemkina-Tavricheskogo," *Russkii Arkhiv*, V (1867), cols. 1557–1560.
58. ZOOID, IV, 375, 377; II, 332; XV, 616.
59. ZOOID, XIII, 185, 186.

it served as the nucleus of a very successful secondary school, not so much for the non-Russian children as for the children of the local administrators and officers. In Nikolaev a Corps of Cadets for 300 pupils was planned; in Kremenchug a secondary school for girls was opened and supported from state funds.[60]

Closely related to these efforts at education, Potemkin helped to develop book publishing in South Russia. The mobile printing press attached to his headquarters served as the foundation of local printing presses equipped to print in several languages (Greek, Latin, French, and Russian). These presses were used not so much to print official orders and regulations, as had been intended at first, as books of general educational interest. Curiously enough, most of the books so produced were either popular Western classics or else had a theological content. They helped to spread the common storehouse of Western culture alongside with ecclesiastic learning and religious concerns among the settlers of the new region.[61]

Potemkin's recommendations for appointments to newly established dioceses are also indicative of his cultural concerns. Thus Evgenii Bulgaris, a leading scholar and active figure in the neo-hellenic movement, was made bishop of Ekaterinoslav and Kremenchug. He distinguished himself more by his efforts at establishing educational institutions than as a shepherd of his flock (whose language he barely spoke).[62] As can be readily seen, there was more than one purpose in such a choice: not only did Bishop Bulgaris promote learning and culture in New Russia, but his position in the neo-hellenic movement could become politically useful as an instrument against the Turks.

60. Sbornik IRIO, XXVII, 5, 230–231; ZOOID, IV, 374, 376; XIII, 184. The medico-surgical school in Simferopol, established in the 1790's, owes its origins to Potemkin's educational policy, cf. ZOOID, II, 331, 333.

61. ZOOID, IV, 470–472; II, 211–219. Also Georges Haupt, "La Russie et les principautés danubiennes en 1790—Le Prince Potemkin-Tavričeskij et le *Courrier de Moldavie*," *Cahiers du Monde russe et soviétique*, VII, No. 1 (Janvier-Mars 1966), 58–62.

62. ZOOID, II, 330–356; see also A. Lebedev, "Evgenii Bulgaris, arkhiepiskop slavenskii i khersonskii," *Drevniaia i novaia Rossiia*, 1876, No. 31, 209–223.

In a more sportive mood, perhaps, Potemkin endeavored to bring about diversity in agriculture and beautification of the landscape. Attempts were made to introduce the new cultures, such as sericulture, and to improve and expand existing ones, vineyards and tropical-fruit growing, for instance, in the Crimea. To beautify the region, groves were planted, parks created in the new cities, the estates and residences of the high dignitaries and administrators of the region embellished by fancy gardens and alleys of exotic trees. Potemkin contracted with several leading agronomists and gardeners to draw up and work out these projects, albeit the results were mixed and, on the whole, indifferent.[63] Lastly, obvious military needs led to the active building and expansion of fortresses and harbors, thus laying the foundation for the economic and historical roles of Sebastopol, Taganrog, and Odessa.

In all of these activities there is an unmistakable element of "play," in Huizinga's sense, of course. While Potemkin pursued fundamental long-range Russian imperial and national interests (or so it appears to us in retrospect), in the forefront of his own mind there was only the desire to enhance the glory of his sovereign, to demonstrate his own talents and power, and to indulge in his passion for luxury and magnificent display. The military context in which he acted gave him a wide stage and endowed many of his activities with an element of orderly rationality that was not devoid of aesthetic appeal. It also provided Potemkin and his aides with the physical means and manpower to carry out the most ambitious schemes. The style of Potemkin's military, administrative, economic, and building activities in the south is strongly reminiscent of the efforts made—on a more modest scale—by many Russian noblemen to introduce a rational and "civilized" way of life into their residences and on their estates.[64] In both cases the essen-

63. Sbornik IRIO, XXVII, 357, 360; ZOOID, IX, 254–255; XIII, 186; XV, 668.

64. On a truly imperial scale Potemkin behaved in much the same way as the middling nobleman, A. T. Bolotov, whose activities we know particularly well from his voluminous memoirs, did on his own estate and as steward of an imperial domain south of Moscow. *Zhizn' i prikliucheniia*

tial elements of "modernity" were vitiated by the sad fact of Russian life in the eighteenth century: that they had to be introduced by autocratic fiat and given reality by servile labor. This is perhaps the basic reason why so many of these ventures proved to be still-born and why the grandiose, but potentially useful, projects of the Prince of Tavrida turned into so many "Potemkin villages."

V

Despite its limitations and failures, from a long-range point of view, the last quarter of the eighteenth century proved to have been a period of great accomplishments in terms of the incorporation and development of the newly acquired south. This was the result not only of an almost traditional process of expansion and colonization, but also very much of the conscious policy of Catherine II and her main assistant and counselor, Prince G. A. Potemkin of Tavrida. Let us examine the methods he used and the means at his disposal; perhaps it will enable us to explain his relatively dramatic success, contrasted to the much slower and less significant accomplishments earlier.[65] Unquestionably Potemkin has few peers in the history of modern Russia in terms of the scope and significance of his work for the empire, as well as of his success; only Count Muraviev-Amurskii, in the mid-nineteenth century, comes readily to mind as a figure of comparable stature. The other architects of the Russian Empire—Speransky as administrative reformer in Siberia, General Kaufman as colonial conqueror in Central Asia, and the principals of the conquest of the Caucasus (Generals Ermolov, Vorontsov, Prince Bariatinskii)—great as were their merits, can hardly compare to the brilliant favorite of Catherine II.

Andreia Bolotova opisannye im samim dlia svoikh potomkov, 1738–1793, Vols. I–IV (St. Petersburg, 1871–1873).

65. The following represents a synthesis of the observations we were able to make in the course of our work on the documents and sources of Potemkin's activities, in particular the correspondence of his main lieutenants, V. V. Kakhovskii and I. M. Sinel'nikov, in ZOOID, X and XV, and elsewhere. A systematic summary of some of the main aspects is to be found in Zagorovskii, *loc. cit.,* and Adamczyk.

The all-powerful satrap of southern Russia exercised his authority at a distance. Potemkin either resided at the court in St. Petersburg or was to be found at his headquarters in the theater of operations. There never was a town that might have been called his administrative residence, although at first Kremenchug and later Ekaterinoslav was officially the capital of New Russia. Yet he exercised absolute control at all times. His official correspondence and reports which have been published (only a fraction of an astoundingly large amount) show that he kept an eye on every facet of the life of the regions under his administration and took a hand in deciding even the most trivial details. For this purpose he had his own private chancery, an organization of about fifty competent bureaucrats of all ranks, headed by his trusted factotum V. S. Popov, who held the rank of lieutenant-general. It was a completely personal staff, not subject to any imperial institution or dignitary, selected and maintained by Potemkin alone. This staff processed, digested, prepared the vast amount of factual information that was forwarded for Potemkin's consideration and decision. In Potemkin's name the chancery issued orders and directives to all institutions and subordinate authorities in South Russia. The degree of functional specialization among these personal officials of Potemkin's may be gauged from the fact that one of them, R. M. Tsebrikov, had been a classmate of Radishchev's at the University of Leipzig and was assigned to Potemkin's headquarters exclusively to take care of the Prince's French correspondence.[66]

V. S. Popov, who acted as a kind of chief minister, enjoyed the unbounded confidence of Potemkin, so that most matters went through his hands. To increase the channels of information at the Prince's disposal without burdening him with undue detail, Popov had the chief local officials and regional governors write to him regularly on an informal—at times quite chatty—basis. These letters give an insight into the day-to-day life of the region, the activities, problems, and concerns of its officials. They also show how devoted

66. "Vokrug Ochakova—1788 (Dnevnik ochevidtsa)," *Russkaia Starina,* 84 (September 1895), 147–211; cf. also ZOOID, XI, 506–508.

and eager the authorities were to please Potemkin in matters both official and private. One has the impression that Potemkin is the actual sovereign and Catherine II only the far-away "god" to whom they all owe devotion, but who is a remote and almost abstract symbol for most; and this in spite of Catherine's very personal style of government. The local officials communicated directly only with Popov and Potemkin, not with the central institutions of the empire—the Senate or the Colleges—to which they were formally subordinated. As a result Potemkin not only exercised firm control, but also obtained information which was usually not vouchsafed a high dignitary. The same system served also to keep a close watch over happenings in St. Petersburg during his absences (a vital element in his long political influence). He had a highly placed business agent, General Garnovskii, who took care of all his private affairs—which were extensive and involved dealing with the highest dignitaries of the empire. Besides reporting on Potemkin's private business and the execution of his manifold instructions, Garnovskii kept Popov informed of all court and diplomatic gossip and events in an uninterrupted flow of letters of which a representative sample has been preserved and published.[67] We can see how Potemkin, even at a distance, could react to practically everything that might affect his position and activities, including the choice and success of Catherine's *amant en titre*.

The fact that Potemkin combined in his person both military and civilian authority explains why he wielded such great power over so many officials and institutions. As the territories under his control had but recently been acquired and were still on a military footing (not to mention areas which lay directly in the zone of operations during the second Turkish war), his position as commander in chief and as president of the College of War gave him an uncontested power of decision. His military office permitted him to bypass the very complicated and overlapping jurisdictions and

67. M. Garnovskii, "Zapiski Mikhaila Garnovskogo 1786–1790," *Russkaia Starina*, XV (1876), 9–38, 237–265, 471–499, 687–720; XVI (1876), 1–32, 207–238, 399–440.

hierarchies of the civilian establishment. On a lower level the same was true of the governors subordinated to him who also were local military commanders. In all matters they referred to Potemkin and his chancery with which they had both formally and practically the right to communicate directly, disregarding all other hierarchies and echelons of command. One last observation may be in order at this point. Because so many policies and decisions were dictated, or could be justified, by military necessities—such as defense, preparation for war, or the conduct of military and naval operations— they were left to the discretion of local commanders and carried out in a military manner by subordinate officers. No civilian authority or central institution, the Senate for example, could make its considerations or arguments count decisively under the circumstances.

Naturally, much of Potemkin's style of administration had a distinctly militaristic character. Instructions and directives had to be executed like a military command, by the personnel of local military units; their implementation was supervised by the military and any delay or opposition dealt with in a peremptory manner. More important still was the seemingly utter disregard of a reasonable ratio between cost and result that is so characteristic of the militaristic mentality. Provided that the expected result was reached, whether in battle or in administration, any price and any means were deemed justified. An order had to be blindly executed, regardless of cost or difficulties, without taking into account local complexities and circumstances. Of course, Potemkin and his aides were quite aware of local conditions—we have seen how they were put to good advantage to further imperial interests—yet as one reads their correspondence, one senses that this awareness was rather superficial and did not extend to a genuine realization of local needs. Local conditions were, at best, treated as limiting factors, never as possible positive features to be furthered for their own sake or for the advantage their preservation might have for the empire subsequently. Like a staff officer who takes into account the relief of the terrain to direct artillery fire and troop movements, but thinks in essentially non-local terms, Potemkin made sweeping plans to achieve an overall goal without much regard for local circumstances and requirements.

In this respect Potemkin's task was facilitated by the fact that he had unlimited imperial confidence. We shall deal with his relationship to Catherine II later. But by virtue of this relationship Potemkin had almost limitless financial means at his disposal; what is more, he did not have to give a detailed account of the way he spent the sums given to him. In fact he disposed at will of countless millions of rubles that the Empress made available to him. Because of Potemkin's own habits of spending, his conception of the total and personal nature of his authority he—like an autocratic ruler—did not differentiate between personal and public expenses. His lavish entertainments were paid out of the same monies as the settlement of foreigners or the building of a new man-of-war. It proved so difficult to unscramble these accounts that, eventually, Alexander I had to write off the Prince's expenditures as part of the public debt left by Catherine II. Even the trusted Popov—perhaps for good reasons of his own—could not give an itemized account of large sums received by his chief, as is made abundantly clear by his report of the audit he made after Potemkin's death.[68]

The close intertwining of the private and public aspects of Potemkin's activities, one being used for the benefit of the other indiscriminately, may be illustrated by the following circumstance: in order to facilitate Catherine's policy of interference into the internal affairs of Poland, Potemkin acquired large estates from the husband of his niece, Count Branicki. He thus became a Polish magnate in his own right, and he then proceeded to use his new personal status for the benefit of Catherine's diplomacy. Naturally, the funds for this huge land purchase came from the Russian treasury on Catherine's personal order. In the same vein it is difficult to differentiate between his activities as private landowner in the Crimea and in the Ukraine and those as governor: the agricultural experts, gardeners, architects he hired were asked to draw up proj-

68. ZOOID, IX, 219–227; VIII, 225–227.

ects and submit plans for both the province and his personal estates. In many ways Potemkin acted as had the appanage (*udel*) princes of pre-Muscovite times who looked on their principalities as their patrimonies, administered and governed them as if they were their personal domains, without making any distinction between their private and public revenues.

In another way, too, Potemkin showed that he was practically a monarch in South Russia. While the grandiloquent display of titles was common practice in the eighteenth century everywhere in Europe, no less than in Russia, Potemkin's manner in this respect is noteworthy. His official communications—for example to the Cossack Host informing them of his nomination as commander in chief of all irregular forces and of the appointment of their new ataman, his proclamations on the occasion of the annexation of the Crimea—were introduced by an enumeration of his titles, ranks, offices, and orders of chivalry that closely resembled royal titles. The fact that he spoke in the name of his Gracious Sovereign was obliterated by this endless enumeration of his own qualities. Not unexpectedly under the circumstances, persons addressing themselves to Potemkin in official communications used formulas that came quite close to those reserved for the monarch.[69] These may seem to be trifling details, to be ascribed to an excessive degree of personal vanity on Potemkin's part, but there was substance behind this form.

Potemkin had wide powers of direct appointment, not only indirectly through his influence on Catherine II. He thus selected and appointed in his own name the ataman of the Don Cossack Host, Ilovaiskii. He conferred military offices and titles at the highest level. More significant still was the fact that he conferred ranks (*chin*), which in Russia were the principal criterion of status and privilege. And in the manner of the Russian rulers themselves he also gave estates as reward for meritorious services, as in the case of the prince of Nassau-Siegen. It is superfluous to mention that he

69. ZOOID, XIX (1896), 105–106; XX (1897), 53–54; *Arkhiv grafa Vorontsova*, XXIV (St. Petersburg, 1880), 291–293.

also awarded decorations for bravery and outstanding deeds. In one case he even conferred to a noble family the right to a specially designed coat of arms in recognition of an exploit of great bravery by a member of this family under his command.[70]

These ways and deeds made Potemkin appear rather like a monarch, a viceroy at the very least, than an extraordinarily powerful governor-general or commander-in-chief. And in a way that was characteristic of the traditional Russian concept of sovereign power, Potemkin had a personal concern for the well-being of his "subjects." It was not merely the concern which any good chief has for his subordinates, or a patron who knows that the loyalty of his clients depends on his interest in them. In fact he scorned the opinions of others and disregarded their sensibilities; his arrogance could be quite monumental, as indignantly noted by the French diplomats and émigrés who were used to the polite ways of Versailles, especially on the part of the monarch.[71] But Potemkin felt a sense of responsibility to the common people which is strongly reminiscent of the medieval idea of just kingship. He had almost none of this sense toward his officers and high officials. On the contrary, like the unrestrained and coarse Russian despots of the eighteenth century, he reputedly slapped officers and high officials, insulted them publicly by his words and his behavior, not to speak of taking advantage of their wives and daughters, if it suited his lust.[72] Toward the common folk, especially the soldiers, he was quite different. He considered himself their father and felt directly responsible for their well-being. Indeed, he strongly believed that the health, comfort, good cheer of the soldiers were his concern, in a human, as well as military, sense. By his orders the Russian sol-

70. "Vokrug Ochakova," p. 156; V. A. Bil'bassov, "Prints Nassau-Zigen v Rossii, 1786–1796," *Istoricheskie monografii,* IV (St. Petersburg, 1901), 523–592 passim; see also ZOOID, XXII (1900), 24.

71. A. G. Brikner, "Kniaz' G. A. Potemkin (po zapiskam grafa Lanzherona, khraniaschchimisia v Parizhskom arkhive)," *Istoricheskii Vestnik,* LXII, 1895, 822; *Mémoires ou souvenirs et anecdotes,* par M. le Comte de Ségur, II (Paris, 1826).

72. Brikner, "Kniaz' G. A. Potemkin," p. 824, and the more popular biographies of Potemkin, Soloveytchik's (see note 8) for example.

dier was freed (alas, for a time only) from the excruciating head-
dress and uniforms that Peter III had introduced in imitation of
Prussia. Potemkin had uniforms designed for comfort and to suit
the climate of Russia.[73] In his instructions to his subordinates he
warned that soldiers should be treated with leniency and trained
only for the sake of their military performance on the battlefield,
and not for show at parades.[74] Finally, the soldiers' health was an
object of his constant care, as witness his numerous instructions for
sanitary measures and the means he put at the disposal of hospitals
and quartermasters.[75]

In short, Potemkin's success—such as it was—in the huge and
complicated task of organizing and administering the vast territory
of South Russia was made possible by the combination of unusu-
ally great financial and political means at his disposal and of the
way he looked at the responsibilities of his position in human
terms. He was a sovereign in fact, if not in name, and he accepted
the traditional Russian notions of the responsibilities and burdens
of kingship.[76] His behavior illustrates the price he paid in psychological terms for this acceptance. Today we no doubt would diag-

73. "Mnenie kn. Potemkina ob obmundirovanii voisk (1783)," *Russkii
Arkhiv* (November 1888), pp. 364–367; *Bumagi Potemkina,* No. 38, p. 38;
Sbornik IRIO, XXVII, 238–239. The biographies of Adamczyk and Loviagin
cited in note 8 make this point forcefully and give illustrations.

74. "Vokrug Ochakova," p. 172; *Bumagi Potemkina,* No. 11, p. 8.

75. ZOOID, XI, 346–347, also Adamczyk, Chap. III. Folklore is, of course,
an unreliable source of historical information if it cannot be checked
against documents. But it may be worth mentioning that the popular or
soldiers' songs about Potemkin that have come down to the nineteenth
century show him in the posture of the fatherly military hero at the siege of
Ochakov and use the traditional epic form (*byliny*) to do so. Potemkin is
compared—as was the Kievan prince Vladimir—to the "beautiful sun."
P. A. Bezsonov (ed.), *Pesni sobrannye P. V. Kireevskim, izdannye ob-
shchestvom liubitelei rossiiskoi slovesnosti,* vyp. 9 (Moscow, 1872), pp. 309–
313; D. A. Rovinskii, *Russkie narodnye kartinki,* kn. II (St. Petersburg,
1881), 129–133 and IV, 411.

76. Cf. M. Cherniavsky, *Tsar and People: Studies in Russian Myths* (Yale
University Press, 1961); H. Fleischhacker, *Russland zwischen zwei Dyna-
stien: 1598–1613* (Wien, 1933); Studien zur osteuropäischen Geschichte,
N. F. I., especially "Voraussetzungen: Herrscher- und Gesellschaftsbegriff,"
pp. 15–39.

nose Potemkin as a neurotic individual, subject to periods of depression during which he could do nothing but loll on his couch, a prisoner of feelings of surfeit and anxiety.[77] Historians have explained this moodiness, Potemkin's frenzied activity and extravagant dissipation alternating with gloomy apathy by the extraordinary rapidity and ease with which he attained the heights of power and riches, by the fact—as he himself confessed—that he was too lucky.

Everyone agrees, and documentary evidence confirms it, that he was thoroughly "Russian"—in the sense of sharing his people's traditions, values, and even prejudices—individual. Living at the cosmopolitan court of Catherine II he seems barely to have been touched by the fashionable European culture of his day. He knew French, of course, he read and spoke it; but he did not live in its cultural realm as most courtiers did. At first sight, his intellectual interests were strange for a man of his position: mainly theology and religious questions in the traditional dogmatic framework of orthodoxy. There was little that he liked better than a good theological disputation, at which he was quite adept, citing freely and accurately the Eastern Church Fathers and their commentators.[78] We have mentioned that in his youth he had contemplated taking holy orders; he remained—amidst the skeptical court of Catherine II—a deeply believing individual, although his moral conduct was far from being above reproach, by even the most latitudinarian standards. His moodiness, therefore, may also be ascribed to a burning awareness of his great sinfulness. But we think it is also fair to argue that he genuinely believed that his vast power, by leading him to sin on a grand scale, also burdened him with guilt and conferred a particular responsibility. In the Russian tradition power is evil by definition, and should be accepted by no one but the God-anointed tsar, who shares thereby responsibility for his subjects'

77. See the suggestive portrait drawn by S. V. Eshevskii, "Ocherk tsarstvovaniia Elizavety Petrovny," *Sochineniia po russkoi istorii* (Moscow, 1900), p. 9.

78. Ségur, II, 287.

sins. The tsar's lot is to be pitied and his commands obeyed in a spirit of compassion and forgiveness. This is why the ruler is seen as a Christlike figure, for like Christ he has accepted the burden of power (or existence) to help men to the good life and guide them toward redemption.

But why should we recall this web of beliefs and attitudes when reflecting on the career of Potemkin? Why do such reflections not come to mind in the case of other influential and successful administrators or military commanders? One obvious answer is too simple-minded to be satisfactory: Potemkin was a "large personality"; he dominated wherever he was, in whatever he did. He had the outward appearance of the great role he played in fact; his mental equipment was outstanding: a quick and sharp mind, broad and realistic intelligence, excellent memory, a capacity for dreaming high dreams and bold adventures; he had, to an unusual degree, the ability to please, to make himself beloved and respected, as well as hated. But all of these qualities would have availed him little without Catherine II. In the final analysis, Potemkin became what he was because he was the favorite of the Empress.

But it was not only in the obvious and ordinary sense that he was a favorite. Catherine II kept a male harem and the list of her lovers—declared or secret, long-lasting or for a night—is impressively long. Potemkin, however, was alone in also becoming a political personality in his own right (the last favorite, Platon Zubov, also wielded political influence over the aged but still sensuous Catherine, but he never exercised even the shadow of the power Potemkin did). There is some evidence for the belief that Potemkin was Catherine's morganatic husband; but true or not, this is of little importance. What is significant is that Catherine accepted him as a counselor on equal terms with herself, trusted him completely to the end of his life, leaned on him. This is why she gave him full authority and such vast means to act in the way he did in South Russia. The letters of Catherine to Potemkin show that he enjoyed the highest degree of intimacy and affection, of genuine respect and trust, even after he had ceased to be her lover.[79] For fourteen years he was really her "husband" in the sense that he shared her responsibilities, plans, hopes, and work, whether he shared her bed or not. The contemporaries, the high-born and lowly commoners alike, understood or sensed this relationship (which neither Catherine nor Potemkin did much to hide).[80] He was, therefore, seen almost as a co-ruler and his ways only confirmed the public in this opinion. This situation lent to Potemkin's actions a force and authority that no one else in the empire could muster.

VI

Our description and analysis point to one obvious observation: the fundamental ambivalence of the style of Russian imperial policy in the eighteenth century, an ambivalence which the career of the main executor of this policy, Prince Potemkin, so well illustrates. This ambivalence may be expressed by the two sets of words: old and new goals, traditional and rational ways. As a matter of fact, the whole history of Russia in the eighteenth century may be described by this double antithesis. Indeed, it was truly a transitional period in the course of which the Muscovite past was jettisoned and the groundwork laid for a modern polity and culture. While the latter—in the form of literature, music, science—achieved a triumphant success in the nineteenth century,

79. For example, her addressing him as "Papa," Sbornik IRIO, XLII, 410; see also "Ekaterina i Potemkin (Podlinnaia ikh perepiska) 1782–1791," *Russkaia Starina*, XVI (1876), 33–58, 239–262, 441–478, 571–590; what Potemkin meant to her, Catherine made abundantly clear in her letters to Baron Melchior Grimm, Sbornik IRIO, XXIII. All of Potemkin's biographers cite her expression of despair on learning of Potemkin's death.

80. The official court poets of the day used for Potemkin neoclassical vocabulary identical to the images applied to the monarch since Peter the Great's time (Cherniavsky, Chap. 3). Some samples are to be found in S. A. Vengerov, *Russkaia poezia*, I (St. Petersburg, 1897), pp. 358–359, 388, 402–403, 790–791; Appendix, pp. 353, 354, 356. A similar observation may be made apropos Potemkin's monument in Nikolaev.

the former—i.e., political and public life—did not overcome the ambivalence of the eighteenth century. This ambivalent political heritage of the eighteenth century survived—albeit in somewhat changed forms—until the end of the imperial regime and has even bedevilled the Soviet rulers who overthrew it.

In the first place, there was an ambivalence in the goals pursued. The traditional goal involved the search for effective protection against the unruly inhabitants of the open steppe. That this defensive stance should eventually lead to Russia's taking the offensive and seek to expand its territory was not contrary to the pattern that may be discerned in the Muscovite past. This is how the khanates on the Volga had been subdued and how the Russians had pushed beyond the Ural Mountains. It explains why, to the mind of the Russians, Turkish domination over the northern shores of the Black Sea had to be broken, and why the Crimea could not be allowed to remain an independent Tatar state. The search for security along the border with the open steppe cannot be divorced from the spread of agricultural settlement. Ever since medieval times the Russian peasant had been pushing into uninhabited (or barely populated) territories in search of new land on which he hoped to obtain a better yield from his wasteful tillage and where he also could feel comfortably remote from the ever-lengthening arm of the state. In his classic work on the formation of the Russian empire B. Nolde has well shown how difficult it is to separate the state's conscious search for security and power from the elemental, unorganized advance of the peasant. The fact is that the two went together, dialectically determining one another.[81]

Such was also the pattern in South Russia, as we have tried to show on the preceding pages. Securing the borders of the empire, eliminating the most troublesome neighbors, and destroying the staging areas for raids went hand in hand with and were partly determined by the push for the agricultural settlement and development of the fertile steppe lands. The state, as we know, often

81. B. Nolde, I, especially Chaps. III and V.

took the initiative and provided the material means for the start. But there was also the elemental "organic" movement of Cossacks, the migration of various dissenting groups seeking to escape oppression by the state or the landlords. Last, there came the foreigners and Russian service nobles who, in pursuit of greater wealth, wanted to put into production the rich resources of the area. In so doing they followed tradition by introducing into the recently acquired territories the social, economic, and cultural patterns of the Russian core lands, more particularly by extending serfdom to the new regions.

However, there were also new goals which either had not been conceived of in the past or only dimly perceived as an accidental by-product of traditional aims. It might be easiest to characterize these new goals as the "modernization" of the empire, although the word "modernization" has by now acquired too many components of meaning derived from the experiences of our contemporary industrial society and has been laden with value judgments. Yet, unsatisfactory and imprecise as it is, the term correctly points to the dynamics of the situation we have examined. The government of Catherine II wished to activate Russia's economic life, to organize the exploitation of the empire's economic resources as rationally and effectively as possible. Furthermore, in good Petrine fashion, they believed that under Russian conditions this goal could be achieved only through the active leadership, participation, and rational control of the state. For this reason the new territories had to be assimilated to the administrative and social conditions of the core provinces and all local foci of authority and power subordinated to St. Petersburg. This meant working against the forces of social and cultural particularism and identity, against the free manifestation of individual and local autonomous creativity.

Such a pattern of goals and policies served to push hard the process of russification; its result was to dismiss as second-rate subjects all those who could not or would not comply. At the same time it undermined the very forces that would have made it possible to attain speedily and permanently the goal of economic prosperity and development. Local entrepreneurial energies were hamstrung and sacrificed to the needs (real or fancied) of the administration, the greed and the interests of the nobles and officials from Central Russia who had acquired estates there and who saw in the new territory and its people an object of exploitation only.[82] The long-range disastrous effects of such a policy on the heretofore tolerant attitude toward non-Russian nationalities and religions need not be spelled out here. But it was difficult for the central government to overcome this pattern as long as it also continued to drive for the Straits, to be involved in the eastern Mediterranean, and to pursue the conquest of the Caucasus. Indeed, the new acquisitions in the south would remain staging areas whose economic development was subordinated to military needs, and whose administration was kept out of regular civilian control.

Clearly such an ambivalence in aims had to be mirrored in the methods used in their pursuit. We have described the traditional methods of using the process of colonization for military purposes and of rewarding with land those most active in initiating and effective in leading this settlement drive. The expansion of the empire was prepared by undermining the neighboring polities in traditional and time-tested fashion: the most vital and valuable elements of the local populations were lured away into Russia and the native élites bribed into collaborating with and assimilating to the Russian ruling class. In this manner the Don Cossack Host was shaped into an obedient tool of the imperial government and the traditional élite of the Crimea neutralized politically. This had been the way in which Muscovy in the sixteenth century had incorporated the Volga khanates and gradually absorbed the Siberian vastness as well. The proven efficacy of these methods made them to be chosen again in the nineteenth century to bring about the reform of the Siberian administration and Russia's further expansion to the Amur and into the Caucasus.

Yet new methods were devised also; they are best described by the terms of "militarism" and "rationalization." The military es-

82. For instance ZOOID, XIII, 164.

tablishment set the pace and led in the assimilation of the new territories. Military commanders were also entrusted with the task of administrative organization. But unlike their sixteenth century predecessors, the military commanders of the eighteenth had a very positive notion of their task. They were not satisfied with leaving things alone as long as there was no unrest and the authority of the tsar was not questioned. On the contrary, they aimed at creating and introducing into the territories under their jurisdiction a new way of life and novel forms of social and economic organization. They aimed at imposing a pattern of rigid regulations, uniformity, and hierarchical subordination on everything. In administration they saw a counterpart of the military establishment. Hence their constant interference in the daily lives of those under their rule. In this respect their practices converged with the pattern of administrative centralization we have noted. The act on the provinces of 1775 was rapidly extended to the new regions, unprepared for it as they were. It meant imposing a cumbersome, confused, inefficient, and top-heavy bureaucratic machine on a sparsely populated and economically undeveloped region.

The character of the authority exercised by the main architect of the policy we have described, Prince Potemkin, evidences a similarly ambivalent pattern. In some ways he felt and acted as a traditional ruler was supposed to, shouldering the burden of power at the price of a depressing awareness of his own unhappiness and sinfulness. In this posture he earned the sympathy, attachment, and respect of the common man. In other ways he behaved as did an arrogant, capricious Russian nobleman of the eighteenth century on his estate. Entranced by a utopian scheme of general transformation, he gave no heed to the price that the people had to pay to bring it about; capriciously moody and inconsistent in his day-to-day decisions and interests, his energies were easily deflected in pursuit of his own glory and the satisfaction of his whims. He combined "rationality" and utopianism with a "romantic" urge to accomplish the impossible. He behaved almost like an old-fashioned patrimonial ruler, and at the same time he was the executive arm of a centralized, modern, bureaucratic state. All these paradoxes impart a particular flavor to Potemkin's political style and go a long way in explaining his unquestionable successes, as well as his failures.

Surely in every state and society, in every period, the new co-exists with much of the old, although in a state of dialectical tension. Eventually this tension is resolved as the traditional gives way and as the new adjusts to realities; a new pattern emerges.[83] But it is a striking feature of what we have chosen to call the Russian style of imperial policy in the eighteenth century, as exemplified by the activities of Potemkin, that there was no dialectical tension; that the opposition remained unresolved between the traditional and rational approach on the one hand, and between the old and the new goals on the other. The two facets of the style seemed to coexist without any one appreciably impinging on the other, or of being able to displace it completely. In other words, the Russian state pursued ambivalent goals with ambivalent methods and did not evolve a synthesis which would overcome the ambivalence. The results of its activities also bore the stamp of ambivalence and proved—in the final analysis—to be inadequate and unstable.

One explanation may be advanced for this state of affairs. Because the memory of the transformation wrought by Peter the Great weighed so heavily on their minds, the Russians of the eighteenth century remained overly conscious of the polarity between the old and the new, the native traditional and the borrowed Western "rationalistic" (in the eighteenth-century meaning of the term) ways.[84] Their acute awareness of this polarity para-

83. This scheme quite clearly does not apply to genuine revolutions—its absence is precisely what makes the revolution, turns men to violence, and exacts a heavy price for the new order that eventually emerges.

84. Of course, this condition can be largely accounted for by two related factors: the deep gulf that separated the élite from the common people (which, it is true, had begun to make itself felt in the second half of the seventeenth century, but which became truly unbridgeable in the reign of Peter the Great) and the prevalence of serfdom.

lyzed any efforts at overcoming it and at developing a satisfactory dynamic (i.e., pragmatically adaptable) pattern of political thought and behavior.

However that may be, the situation was paradoxical indeed. The pursuit of imperial expansion was crowned by glorious success: the empire's territory greatly expanded, in several directions Russia reached what may be called its "natural boundaries." The military power of the empire increased so that Russia could effectively play the role of a leading world power. The rational and active exploitation of the economic resources of the country was given strong impetus and reached a high level (comparatively speaking). In human terms, too, the policy seemed to be successful at first glance: new nations were annexed to the empire without much difficulty, their élites were absorbed into the mainstream of Russia's social and cultural life.

Yet this apparently successful result was vitiated at the core: it was incapable of organic life or development. The imperial polity that had been created proved capable neither of adjusting to novel situations nor of devising workable solutions to unforeseen problems. Indeed, the russification of the native élites only paved the way for a most painful emergence of the national question, it helped to spread the deep gulf between the common people and the educated classes to all the nationalities of the empire. Far from being undermined by the "rationalization" of the empire, the dreadful and harmful system of serfdom was temporarily strengthened and exported into the new territories. Lastly, uniform centralization and militarism froze the vital forces that were most needed to further progress and adaptability to the problems of genuine "modernization": local initiative and individual entrepreneurship, the energies and liberties for the development of new foci of power and authority capable of assisting in the creation of an increasingly varied and complex polity, of giving meaningful expression and support to the personalized authority of the autocratic tsar, and of providing workable substitutes for the rigid centralized bureaucracy.

Potemkin's career dramatically shows that in Russia authority derived from the personal and dynamic (charismatic in Max Weber's terminology) character of political power. It was in flagrant contradiction to the static bureaucratic framework that it had imposed on the country. When it became clear that personal authority was inadequate to the tasks set by modern imperial policy there was nothing that could complement or replace it effectively. Potemkin—like Peter the Great—had succeeded in using both traditional and rational methods in a policy that aimed at building a new empire which, by bringing to conclusion old political trends, would also initiate a modern dynamic social and economic development. But he had been able to do it not so much because of his great talent as by virtue of his special relationship to Catherine. It is this relationship that endowed his authority with the traditional personal character and made it acceptable to, and obeyed by large segments of the population. No one else in Russia could duplicate this combination later and thereby repeat his performance. Prince Grigorii Aleksandrovich Potemkin thus proved to have been not only Russia's greatest imperial statesman, but also the last.

ALEKSANDR A. KIZEVETTER

The Legislator in Her Debut

A SCHOLARLY HISTORY of the reign of Catherine II remains yet to be written. We have several extremely valuable monographs on specific questions of the period, but we have no comprehensive analytical survey of the entire period. In his *History of Russia from Earliest Times,* S. M. Solov'ev[1] covered only a little more than the first decade of Catherine's reign. Death cut

---

Aleksandr A. Kizevetter, "Pervoe Piatiletie pravleniia Ekateriny II," in *Istoricheskie siluety—Liudi i sobytiia* (Berlin: Parabola, 1931), pp. 29–54. Translated by Mary Mackler.

1. S. M. Solov'ev, *Istoriia Rossii s drevneishikh vremen,* 29 vols. (1851–1879), recent edition in 15 vols. (Moscow, 1959–1966).

short his monumental work just as he was preparing the volume which was to have ended with an account of the Pugachev rebellion. Brückner's *History of the Reign of Catherine II* [2] was inadequate even for the author's own time. Brückner had distributed his attention very unequally between Catherine's domestic and foreign policies, giving much more space to the latter. At present, his book is entirely obsolete in view of the monographs and the new archival materials that have been published since. Bil'bassov's opus, conceived so broadly and so many years in preparation, never reached the public and is shrouded in some sort of mystery. It was to have been published in twelve volumes and rumor had it that the whole manuscript had been completed. Yet only four volumes ever saw light: [3] the first and second, covering Catherine's life before she ascended the throne and the very first years of her reign, and the eleventh and twelfth, comprising the Russian and foreign bibliography on the period. The remaining volumes have disappeared without a trace, supposedly destroyed by their author. Whether that rumor is true, I cannot say, but, be that as it may, only small fragments of Bil'bassov's *History of Catherine II* have come down to us.

Because of the absence of an overall scholarly analysis of the period, certain strongly entrenched views on Catherine's policies, views that are by no means substantiated by critically checked data, continue to prevail both in writings on the subject and, even more, in the minds of the public. The following interpretation of the history of Catherine's reign has wide circulation to this day.

When Catherine ascended the throne she was under the influence of the fashionable ideas of the time, ideas she drew from eighteenth-century "enlightened" philosophical writings. Voltaire was her "spiritual father"; Montesquieu's *Esprit des lois* her political gospel. As a disciple of the French philosophes, she inscribed on her banner "Freedom" and "Equal rights for all," and

2. A. Brückner, *Katharina die Zweite,* 2 vols. (Berlin, 1883); Russian translation (St. Petersburg, 1885).

3. V. A. Bil'bassov, *Istoriia Ekateriny Vtoroi,* Vols. 1–2 (St. Petersburg, 1890–1891); German translation (Berlin, 1891–1893).

these slogans obligated her to effect basic changes in the entire political and social structure of Russia. Indeed Catherine set herself the following aims: (1) to provide a legal basis for the power of the Russian monarch, thereby putting an end to "despotism," and (2) to abolish serfdom, i.e., to alter radically the entire social structure of Russia on the basis of social equality. These were the aims that inspired her *Instruction* [*Nakaz*], a political credo in which she not only reiterated the basic ideas of Montesquieu's treatise, but actually reproduced long excerpts from it verbatim. These, too, were the aims of the reform measures she planned and carried out in the first five years of her rule. Then came an about-face in all her policies. Suddenly Catherine resolutely turned her back on the ideals of her youth and embarked on a policy in direct contradiction to these ideals. Freedom-loving dreams gave way to consistent absolutism; instead of abolishing serfdom, she extended and strengthened the social privileges of the serf-owning nobility, becoming "the nobility's Empress" in the full sense.

What caused this about-face? According to the prevailing interpretation, Catherine surrendered all her original ideological positions and betrayed the ideals of her youth under pressure from the nobility, to secure her power and to avert a clash with the dominant estate. The very first critics of her *Instruction* from among the high dignitaries[4] to whom she showed a draft, attacked her for the unabashed radicalism of her views. Panin said to her: "These are ideas that can break down walls." Others, too, regarded her treatise as an explosive bomb. And consequently she struck out much that had been in her first draft. Subsequently, Catherine was still more profoundly impressed—it is maintained—when she came into direct contact with the members of the commission she convoked in 1767 to draft a new code. What the noble members of that commission said and the instructions they had re-

4. "Dignitaries" refers here (and on p. 253) to the group of wealthy and high-ranking courtiers and officials (military and civil) that played a leading role in shaping the government's policies. While many members of this changing group were of old lineage, it also included numerous newcomers to Russia, to nobility, and to wealth.

ceived from their electors—the ruling class in Russia at that time
—revealed that they had no sympathy with her program of reform.
Political liberalism found no response among the nobility, and
any attempts even to restrict, not to speak of abolish, serfdom
aroused their strongest protests. Catherine realized that it would
not be safe for her to persist in her freedom-loving program.
After all, she had obtained the crown by means of a palace coup.
Her title to it was emphemeral, to say the least. There were influential groups among the high nobility who had not approved of
her seizure of power. In the first years of her reign Catherine
hardly felt secure. The steps to her throne were very shaky.
Plots against her rule were uncovered from time to time. Clearly,
it would not have been prudent in such circumstances to break
with the dominant estate. Catherine had no inclination whatsoever
to risk her position. Her greatest desire was to be Empress. Sensing
the danger, she unhesitatingly lowered the flag of her liberal
program, and after that throughout her reign, she followed in the
wake of the more influential circles of the nobility. She became
the Empress of the nobles and consolidated her autocratic monarchy through a firm alliance between the throne and the landed
and serf-owning nobility, passing on the burden of that alliance
entirely to the serfs, whose dependency on the gentry reached
its highest point during her reign.

Such is the frequently encountered interpretation of Catherine's
general course of action, echoes of which are found in scholarly
books and articles. According to this interpretation, Catherine's
ascent to the Russian throne was a sort of sudden jolt in the
natural evolution of political relationships in eighteenth-century
Russia. Brimming with the advanced ideas she had read about
in French books, convinced that all she had to do was to wave
her hand to bring about a complete change in the Russian state
structure along the lines of philosophical radicalism, Catherine
threw into confusion the prevailing political pattern with her
very first declarations and undertakings. Accordingly, the first
five years of her reign are viewed as a clash between her bold new

ideas and backward Russian reality; in this struggle, the latter finally won out, causing the Empress to set aside the dreams that had found expression in the *Instruction* and to surrender to Russian reality.

Is this interpretation in keeping with the facts? Did Catherine's encounter with the spokesmen for the Russian nobility in the Commission of 1767 really lead her to reverse her policies, a reverse that is often taken as the starting point for the overall characterization of her reign?

The answers to these questions must be sought in a careful study of Catherine's policies in precisely the first five years that preceded the convocation of the Commission of 1767, with a view to determining whether these policies did indeed contrast sharply with her subsequent legislation. I shall examine a number of the facts that shed light on these questions. The facts are all well-known, but they have not always been interpreted correctly, and that, in this writer's view, is the reason for the popularity of the above interpretation, an interpretation which is surely in need of considerable revision.

II

There is absolutely no doubt that throughout her reign Catherine looked to broad circles of the nobility for her support. And she did not, it should be noted right here, have to retract her original views to gain that support. The trappings of philosophical ideology with which those views were adorned did not render them in the least incompatible with the moods and aspirations of the majority of the nobility of that time. Catherine's first governmental actions and the contents of the *Instruction,* in which she set forth her credo, testify to this.

Let us take a look at both.

A few days after she ascended the throne, Catherine issued a so-called Comprehensive Manifesto (which was not included in the Complete Collection of Laws), in which she promised "to give the force of law to such government statutes as will enable the administration to operate by virtue of its authority and within its jurisdiction in such a manner as to ensure that in the future every institution has its limits and rules, by which means good order will be preserved in all things." This was a very cautious and general hint at replacing the arbitrariness of despotism (for which the same manifesto specially blamed Peter III) by lawful government procedures. The question arises as to exactly what kind of legal limitations of power Catherine had in mind, how far she was inclined to go at that time toward replacing despotism by legal forms of government.

An episode that took place in the very first months of her reign sheds light on this. The cautious Panin revealed his hand just a bit in a memorandum he wrote himself concerning the necessity of establishing an "Imperial State Council." In that memorandum, he pointed out that under the existing system of government in Russia, concern for the general welfare and preparation of new laws were concentrated "in the person of the sovereign alone." But, Panin wrote, "the sovereign can translate this concern for the welfare of the whole state into useful action" only if there is "a reasonable division of legislative power among a given small number of persons specially selected for that purpose." Otherwise state interests are bound to become a plaything of capricious favorites and "accidental persons," and whims and arbitrariness will dominate the state. To avoid such disorder, it was necessary, Panin believed, to establish a "supreme state organ of legislation," to be called an "Imperial Council." Panin proposed that this council be comprised of six persons (Catherine added in her own hand: "from six to eight"), of whom four would be the state secretaries in charge of internal affairs, foreign affairs, the army and the navy. Drafts of laws and all matters under the "personal charge of the autocrat" would be submitted to the council. The council would express its opinions on all these matters, and the sovereign would "by autocratic command announce the final decision." Every imperial order was to be countersigned by one of the state secretaries. Panin also drafted the manifesto which would establish such a council, stating that the purpose of the innovation was to ensure that in the future governments should not be guided "by the power of an individual, but by the authority of state institutions." [5]

Panin's plan aroused strong doubts in Catherine. There are indications that in August 1762 a decision was made to set up such a council, but by the end of the same month Catherine rejected the idea. In December the draft came up again. On December 28, Catherine signed both the act and manifesto establishing the council and even appointed all the members of the new body. But later her signature was nullified and the whole matter abandoned. We are not certain about the reasons for this decision, but we do know that Panin's draft was submitted to a number of dignitaries for preliminary opinions, and those opinions have come down to us. One—we do not know whose—stated that the author of the draft was "subtly" pushing toward a transition from a monarchical to an aristocratic system of government and that a "watchful eye" must be kept out for any repetitions of the attempt made in 1730 by *"verkhovniki"* [6] to restrict the autocracy. And Quartermaster General Vil'boa [Villebois] declared bluntly that in his opinion the implementation of Panin's plan would endanger the autocracy. Apparently, Panin foresaw the objections; he stressed in his memorandum that the plan was not motivated by any desire to "limit the autocracy." However, Catherine evidently believed Panin's opponents and the plan was doomed. It is not for nothing that Catherine pointed out in secret instructions to the procurator-general [of the Senate], A. Vyazemsky, that

5. The major portion of Panin's plan may be found in translation and editorial comment in M. Raeff, *Plans for Political Reform in Imperial Russia* (Englewood Cliffs, N.J., 1966), Chap. II.

6. In January–February 1730, upon the sudden death of Peter II, the members of the Supreme Privy Council (called *verkhovniki* or "top men") tried to impose restrictions (*konditsii*) on the autocratic power of Anna of Courland whom they had elevated to the throne. For the text of the conditions and brief discussion of the episode, cf. M. Raeff, *Plans for Political Reform*, Chap. I.

there were two parties among the high dignitaries: the first were honest, the second nurtured dangerous ideas and, she added: "There are some who think that if they have been in a [foreign] country for a long time, they are entitled to decide everything according to the policy of that beloved country of theirs."

Despite the existence of such plans, Catherine immediately took a strong stand in defense of unlimited autocracy; the facts prove that the "power of the person," against which Panin had cautioned and which manifested itself in an orgy of favoritism, prevailed throughout her reign.

While she had quickly drawn back from anything remotely resembling *political* reform, Catherine did effect some *administrative* changes in central and in local government during the first five years of her reign. The reforms concerning the organization of some of the central institutions (the principal one was the division of the Senate into departments) were devoid of any ideological content. They were purely technical, partial reorganizations of the administrative machinery and are of no interest for the purposes of this study. Of importance to this study are the measures and plans that concerned local government.

On April 21, 1764, an *Instruction* to Governors was issued. This document is of interest to us because it is based on the very same principles which received further development in the latter part of Catherine's reign. One might say without exaggeration that the above *Instruction* was actually a first step in the preparation of the future Statute on Provinces [*gubernia*] of 1775. Far from furnishing proof of a sharp turn in Catherine's policies, this document reveals that an unbroken thread connected both parts of Catherine's reign. According to the 1764 *Instruction* the governor was undoubtedly the embryonic form of the vicegerent of the 1775 Statute on Provinces. "In both instances the structure of the highest organ of power in local government was based on the principle of bureaucratic decentralization of administration. The governor in the 1764 *Instruction,* like the vicegerent in the 1775 Statute on Provinces, was called the "chief and guardian of the province [*gubernia*]." His responsibilities were all-inclusive, covering all aspects of local life. *All* local residents—those in service and those not in service—were subject to his authority. At the same time, like the vicegerent of 1775, the governor was completely independent of the central state institutions. He was not subordinate to the central colleges. In the original draft of the *Instruction,* he was subordinate only to the Empress. Catherine later added: "and to the Senate." Hence, the governor took orders from the Empress and the Senate.

This structure was based on the idea that the authorities must be brought closer to the local population, a crying need for which the members of the Commission of 1767 urgently pleaded. During the 1760's there was much talk in ruling circles about local government reform. Professor Yu. V. Got'e, who made a study of all the relevant drafts proposed in that period, came to some interesting conclusions. On the one hand, the plans anticipated the principles of the 1775 Statute on Provinces in many essential points; on the other hand, they were related to similar projects advanced back in Elizabeth's reign. In the archives Professor Got'e discovered a plan for the reorganization of local government, proposed in the 1760's, under Catherine, by Iakov Petrovich Shakhovskoi, who had been charged with drawing up the table of organization for local administrative bodies. This plan called for broad participation in local government by elected representatives of the nobility. In Got'e's view, Shakhovskoi's project was in direct relation to a plan, also discovered in the archives, suggested by P. I. Shuvalov, who proposed in one of his memoranda to Elizabeth that the state institutions in the provinces be combined with elected bodies in the districts [*uyezds*]. This is very similar to the combination that was actually put into effect by the 1775 Statute on Provinces. Hence, in matters pertaining to the reorganization of administration, there was no clash between Catherine's supposed radicalism and the supposed political backwardness of the members of the Commission of 1767. The deputies were not interested in political reform; they made all their judgments on the basis of the existing form of government. Nor was Catherine—in this period of her interest in the philosophers of the Enlightenment—an opponent

of autocracy. The episode with Panin's plan is sufficiently eloquent
testimony to this. Montesquieu's disciple firmly believed in the
necessity of autocracy in Russia. As for administrative reform,
even before the convocation of the Commission of 1767, Catherine
had already discussed, was preparing, and in some respects had
actually carried out the very plans which the deputies advocated.
Decentralization of administration, closer contact between the
administration and the local population, and the broad participation in local government of elected representatives of the local
nobility—all these principles were already on the agenda in ruling
circles during the first five years of Catherine's reign, and it was
not from philosophical tracts that Catherine derived her positive
attitude to these principles, but from plans proposed during the
reign of Elizabeth. Consequently, the prevailing notion that before
convocation of the Commission of 1767 Catherine ruled on the
heights of radicalism, risking a clash with . . . the class egoism
of the nobility, but then, in the end turned away from her ideals
for the sake of self-preservation evaporates into thin air. Catherine
may have plucked entire excerpts from Montesquieu's *Esprit des
lois* for her *Instruction,* but for practical action she turned to
Russian precedents from Elizabeth's reign. And, as we shall see
below, this did not result in as great an inner conflict as might
appear at first glance.

Therefore, regarding administrative reforms, there is no ground
for the contention that Catherine had to narrow the scope of her
original program or change her legislative policies under pressure
of opinions manifested in the Commission of 1767. The fact is that
Catherine's very first program never went beyond the aspirations
of the representatives of public opinion of the time.

III

The prevailing historical opinion also sees a turnabout in Catherine's social policies, coinciding with her confrontation with the
spokesmen for the nobility in 1767. According to that notion,

prior to the commission Catherine had dreams of equalizing the estates and abolishing serfdom, but on sensing the nobility's true feelings, she made a turnabout and became the "Empress of the nobility." Was it really so?

Soon after Catherine ascended the throne, she sent Panin the following note: "I forgot to tell you earlier today that there are many complaints among the nobles that their privileges have not been confirmed; this matter must not be forgotten and should be attended to at once."

Obviously, the nobles wanted the new Empress to confirm Peter III's Manifesto on the Freedom of the Nobility. Actually, Catherine went even further to meet their wishes. She set up a Commission on the Russian Nobility in February 1763, instructing it to revise Peter III's manifesto with a view to *extending* the privileges of the nobility. On March 18 of the same year the commission submitted a report to her. That report was doubtlessly the germ of the charter issued to the nobility in 1785. Hence, the charter—a most important legislative act of the latter part of Catherine's reign, second only to the Statute on the Provinces—was also conceived, in its general principles, prior to the convocation of the 1767 Commission, that is, at the time when Catherine was doctoring excerpts from the *Esprit des lois* for her *Instruction.*

The report of the Commission on the Russian Nobility proposed that a new law on the nobility incorporate a number of class privileges. The privileges it called for may be divided into three groups: (1) privileges that had already been granted to the nobility by Peter III's manifesto, namely, the right to serve or not to serve, to leave service at any time, and to enter into the service of foreign sovereigns, the only restriction being the obligation to return to Russia at the first summons; (2) privileges extending those granted under Peter III's manifesto and subsequently incorporated in Catherine's Charter to the Nobility of 1785, namely, freedom from corporal punishment, freedom from penalties not imposed by the courts, repeal of the confiscation of estates of the nobility, and complete freedom for landowners to dispose of their estates and all the forests and arable lands thereon; (3) finally, privileges not included in Peter III's manifesto and not granted by Catherine's subsequent legislation, namely, abolition of ennoblement through service ranks, granting nobles the right to settle in foreign countries permanently, with release from their oath of allegiance to the Russian crown and Russian citizenship on the condition that first they sell their estates and contribute one tenth of the sale price to the state treasury.

On October 11, 1763, Catherine ordered the Commission on the Nobility to draft laws on the basis of the proposals in their report. This work was discontinued after a while because of the decision to convoke a commission of deputies for the purpose of drafting a new code. This latter commission, as the reader will recall, drew up the Draft Plan on the Privileges of the Nobles, which served as the basis for the Charter of 1785.

From the above it is clear that there was no clash of any kind between the aspirations of the nobility and Catherine's original program. During the first five years of Catherine's reign, even before the 1767 Commission was convoked, Catherine took steps to broaden Peter III's manifesto and issued several edicts extending the privileges of the nobility. These were the decrees declaring that nobles would be discharged from service with officer's rank even if they had not risen to it, "so as to have an advantage over the non-nobles" (1762); on the right of landowners to consign their serfs to hard labor (1765); on the return to landowners of fugitive serfs who had been recruited for service in Holstein (1762); by the regulations of 1765 the nobles were granted exclusive rights to the distillation of alcohol. All this is very remote from egalitarian aspirations. Again, when in the early years of Catherine's reign many of the nobles' estates were swept by peasant uprisings, the Empress issued a manifesto (July 3, 1762) in which she declared: "We intend to keep the landowners' estates and possessions inviolate and to maintain the peasants in proper submission to them."

It cannot be denied that in those years Catherine did consider some sort of legislative intervention in the system of serf relationships and that she even made some attempts to call the attention of society to that matter. But let us examine the nature of her attempts. How far did they go? Can it be affirmed on the basis of these attempts that Catherine's ideas later changed direction sharply?

When she was still Grand Duchess, Catherine once scribbled the following lines on a scrap of paper: "It is against the Christian faith and against justice to make people slaves; people are born free." She had, she continued in the same note, discovered a very simple way to eliminate serfdom painlessly: every time an estate changed hands, the peasants living on it would be proclaimed free. In the course of a hundred years all estates would surely change owners and thus, in one hundred years, there would be nothing left of serfdom except the memory.

It is clear from the above note that even in the period of her greatest interest in emancipatory ideas, Catherine put off the abolition of serfdom for a whole century (a hundred years later it was indeed abolished, but not in the way Catherine hoped) and that she had no intention of abolishing it right away, during her own lifetime. There is another, very important, statement in the same note: the sudden abolition of serfdom, she wrote, would certainly not win the love of landowners, who were filled with stubbornness and prejudice. Not only did she write this prior to the convocation of the Commission of 1767, but she wrote it before the palace coup that gave her the crown. Consequently, Catherine never intended to abolish serfdom against the wishes of the landowning nobility.

Later Catherine raised the question in one form or another in her legislative proposals to the Baltic (Livonian) nobility in 1765 and in the subject she proposed for a competition under the auspices of the Free Economic Society in 1766, but all she suggested was some sort of regulation of the serf relations, control of the magnitude of serf duties, and granting serfs the right to own certain kinds of property. The topic she suggested to the Free Economic Society was: "Is it better for the peasant to own land or only movable property?" It is often contended that Catherine preferred the former to the latter. However, this contention is refuted by her remarks concerning Golitsyn's letters on the question of granting serfs the right to own land.

Hence, from the very beginning, Catherine's program on the peasant question was essentially one of legislative restriction of obligations. Of course, even this idea was opposed by the great majority of landowners, as is evident from the failure of Korob'in's proposals in the 1767 Commission. Nevertheless, the idea itself was not unprecedented. Ober Prokurator Maslov of the Senate had put it on the agenda during the reign of Anna.[7] In the very first years of her reign, Catherine received reports on the necessity of such restrictions from various persons. See, for example, reports by Ielagin, Piotr Panin (who wrote that the magnitude of the serfs' obligations "exceeds the limits of human endurance"), and others.

Finally, it must be pointed out that Catherine implemented a number of far-reaching measures even before the convocation of the already planned Commission on Codification of 1767. These measures, though they touched upon various aspects of the country's life, all came under a general social program, aimed at satisfying the interests of precisely the landowning nobility. Moreover, it is noteworthy that all of them were merely the development of undertakings begun under Elizabeth. I am referring to the nationwide land survey, the settling of foreign colonists on the vacant lands on European Russia's southern and southeastern outskirts, and the secularization of Church landed properties.

The idea of a general land survey had been suggested by Piotr Shuvalov in Elizabeth's reign and some modest attempts were made at the time to implement it, but without success. Catherine caught up the seemingly broken thread, improved its principles, and placed it on an all-Russian basis, beginning with 1765.

The first serious attempts to get foreign colonists to settle on

7. Anna Ioanovna, niece of Peter the Great, reigned 1730–1740. In her reign the Ober Prokurator was the head of the Senate.

the outskirts of European Russia were also made during Elizabeth's reign. This matter, too, Catherine developed, establishing a special department to take charge of it—the Office for Trusteeship of Foreigners—headed by her favorite, G. Orlov. A whole network of foreign colonies was established, principally in the Lower Volga region, though it was done with enormous difficulty and at great cost to the treasury.

Neither was secularization of Church lands Catherine's idea. The question had a long history, going back to the time of the Muscovite state. Decisive steps were taken in this direction during the reigns of Peter the Great and Anna. At first, the pious Elizabeth canceled everything that had been done in this respect under Anna, but toward the end of her reign she restored all of Anna's decrees. Actually, complete secularization had been decided on by Peter III. It merely remained for Catherine to implement it, which she did by 1764.

Thus, in all these major undertakings, Catherine was not by any means acting as a disciple of Voltaire and Montesquieu, transplanting the flowers of French liberal thought to Russian soil, but as a direct continuer of Elizabeth's and, in part, even of her own ridiculous husband's policies. Furthermore, none of these undertakings provided any reason for conflict with the nobility; quite the contrary. The nobles welcomed the land-surveying measure (this is expressed vividly in the memoirs of Bolotov), for it was in keeping with the basic interests of the landowning class. The indefiniteness of property boundaries was constantly giving rise to quarrels between neighbors, with adversaries often engaging in full-scale battles. Landowners would lead whole armies of field and house serfs against one another. Blood was shed in the combat. One can imagine that it was not very pleasant to live in constant fear of armed intervention by a restless neighbor. It was important to survey the land and set stable and permanent boundaries. Besides, the very survey offered landowners opportunities to add extensively to their property at the expense of uninhabited government land. This they did by clever interpretations of the numerous articles of the instructions for the survey and, in some instances, with the connivance of the surveyors. Bolotov's memoirs give a nearly literary portrayal of this. No wonder landowners, such as Bolotov, welcomed the surveying operation enthusiastically, singing praises to the *Tsaritsa* who had set the enterprise in motion.

How the colonization of the southeastern steppes by invited foreigners served the interests of the Russian landowners is not so obvious, but a careful study of the matter will bring this to light. The Russian peasants had always had a strong desire to move to the fertile south from the much less fertile central regions, and, in considering the matter, one naturally wonders why the government went to such a difficult and expensive effort at finding foreigners to colonize the unsettled steppe when the Russian peasants' desire could have been utilized for the purpose. The fact of the matter is that the Russian peasants were bound to the infertile central regions by *serfdom*. In striving to colonize the outskirts with foreigners, Catherine's government was protecting the interests of the serf-owning nobles, which required that a barrier be set up to prevent the peasants from finding refuge from serfdom in the inviting free south.

Finally, secularization was welcomed by the nobles with satisfaction and great expectations. The landowners had their eyes on the land that was being taken away from churches and monasteries and showered Catherine with appropriate projects. Prince Gagarin, the president of the College of Economy,[8] proposed that all the former monastery serfs be distributed among the nobles—100, 500, and 1,000 peasants to each. Governor Sievers made a similar suggestion. Desires of this kind are expressed in the instructions given to the deputies from the nobility in the Commission of 1767. True, disappointment was in store for them. As a rule, the estates secularized under Catherine were not distributed to private landowners

8. When the government took over lands and peasants of monasteries and dioceses it established a college, the College of Economy, for their administration. Peasants under the latter's jurisdiction were called "economy peasants."

but became the property of the state. However, there were exceptions to the rule, and even under Catherine there were instances of formerly Church peasants being turned over to private owners. Under Paul, the lands and peasants for the estates bestowed on the holders of Russian decorations[9] were taken from among the secularized lands. Besides, even without the above exceptions, the overall secularization was in the interests of the nobility just as were the overall boundary delineation and colonization by foreigners. Though Catherine did not usually turn secularized peasants into private serfs, the acquisition of large numbers of peasants on the secularized estates enabled her to continue giving more serfs from other categories of state property to private persons. It is well known that Catherine took considerable advantage of that opportunity all through her reign. The great landed wealth of those fortunates on whom fell her favor was based on gifts of that kind.

IV

Hence, if we glance at Catherine's acts of state during the first five years of her reign, we see that they were part of a series expressing a specific political program. The substance of that program might be formulated as one of unrestricted autocracy, deriving its support from the privileged land- and serf-owning nobility. Obviously, such a program did not require ascent to the heights of philosophical radicalism. It was a native Russian program, begun under Anna and carried out consistently under Elizabeth, with the majority of the nobles in full agreement with it. The reader will observe that we were able to establish continuity between the measures effected by Catherine's first administration and the precedents of Elizabeth's reign. The latter part of Catherine's reign was, as we have seen, marked by legislative acts that merely developed and completed undertakings of the first

9. Holders of some high decorations were awarded lands on either a temporary or hereditary basis. Under Paul I the main beneficiaries were the newly created knights of the Order of Malta whose commander Paul had become.

five years. Catherine did not need to descend from philosophical heights to low ground or to surrender to pressure from the nobles for the simple reason that her own original program did not conflict with the views of the nobility.

True, unlike her predecessors on the throne, Anna and Elizabeth, Catherine assiduously dressed herself in the finery of enlightened philosophy. However, this did not in the least hinder her from continuing the policies of these predecessors (who made no claim whatever to a reputation of crowned philosophers).

To be sure, there is another aspect which must be noted. I have already said above that there was no major conflict between Catherine's ideas of enlightened philosophy and her domestic program, which followed native precedents. It should be pointed out that Voltaire, that impassioned fighter for freedom of conscience whom young Catherine admired, was no radical on political and social issues either. Voltaire was the ideologue of enlightened absolutism, and it was not difficult for Catherine to reconcile her admiration for her "spiritual father" with her political program of an autocracy based on the nobility. With regard to Montesquieu's political ideas, however, the situation was more complicated. It should be kept in mind, though, that the claim— a legend started by Catherine herself—that her *Instruction* was practically a plagiarism of *Esprit des lois* is not true. A word-for-word comparison, made by F. V. Taranovsky, of the excerpts Catherine took from *Esprit des lois* with Montesquieu's text reveals that Catherine touched up the original text in a way hardly perceptible to the cursory eye to make it accord with her views. For example, in referring to the difference Montesquieu draws between a monarchy and despotism, Catherine inserted into the appropriate excerpt from *Esprit des lois* several words that gave Montesquieu's thought a different shade of meaning and enabled her to draw a sharp line between despotism and an autocratic monarchy, as well as between despotism and the legitimate monarchy Montesquieu had in mind.

Thus, the gulf that some scholars thought divided Catherine's first interest in the ideas of enlightened philosophy from her subsequent "soberly businesslike" policies is non-existent.

Concerning social principles, Catherine was very sympathetic to Montesquieu's idea on the importance of consolidating a privileged position for the nobility, but she refused to take notice of the fact that Montesquieu was referring to privileges of the nobility in a monarchy based on law so that the nobility might serve as a political buffer to protect the state from possible attempts at usurpation by the supreme authority. Instead, Catherine referred to the socio-economic privileges of the nobility as the bulwark of the monarchy's autocratic power. In other words, under the guise of plagiarism of Montesquieu, Catherine actually revised his doctrine to suit the program that the Russian gentry had proposed in 1730 to counter the power of the members of the Supreme Secret Council and which subsequently formed the basis of the social policy of the Russian imperial government in the eighteenth century.

Now the question of Catherine's attitude to serfdom remains. It was the prevailing notion for a long time that the paragraphs deleted from the original draft of the *Instruction* at the demand of Catherine's aristocratic critics contained statements on the need to abolish serfdom. However, when these deleted paragraphs were made public in the academic edition of the *Instruction,* put out under the editorship of Chechulin, it turned out that the abolition of serfdom had not been mentioned in the first draft. Catherine had gone no further than to propose the regulation of the serfs' obligations and recognition of their right to ownership of *movable property*. Her revisions of the original draft at the insistence of the high dignitaries considerably softened precisely those paragraphs, so that only hazy references to them appeared in the final version. The *Instruction* recognized "slavery" as a necessary institution and merely pointed out that misuse of slave-owning power should be prevented by law (Article 25). Catherine came straight out against legislative abolition of serfdom. Article 260 of the *Instruction* reads: "The law should not suddenly create a large number of freed [serfs]." As for averting the misuse of power by

the gentry, the *Instruction* merely proposed to establish trustee-
ships for landlords who tortured their peasants—a step already
legislated by Peter the Great. And instead of a specific recognition
of the serfs' right to own movable property, the final version of
the *Instruction* merely referred to it vaguely: "The laws may
determine *something beneficial* to the property of slaves" (Article
261). Finally, instead of writing into law specific regulations of
serf obligations and services, the final version of the *Instruction*
merely expressed the desire that the landowners be instructed "to
levy fees on the peasant with circumspection and subject him only
to those work duties that do not take him away from his house
and family."

The above—in this writer's view—calls for admission that the
widespread legend about a sharp turn in the course of Catherine's
policies and a sharp difference between the legislation in the latter
part of her reign and her original plan are not confirmed by the
historical data. It cannot be denied, of course, that Catherine's
legislation of the 1770's and 1780's was affected by her impressions
of current events, for example, the Pugachev revolt. But those
events did not cause a change in the general direction of her
legislative program. They merely hardened the attitudes that had
formed the basis of her policies from the very beginning of her
reign.

ALEKSANDR S. LAPPO-DANILEVSKII

The Serf Question in an Age of Enlightenment

THE POLITICAL COUP which brought Catherine II to the "All-Russian autocratic throne" ought to have affected, it would seem, not only high policy, but also the condition of the lower classes of society, for Catherine stated at the time of her accession that "natural law commanded her to work for the well-being of all people" and she had only "one aim—the happiness of all her subjects." She expressed an interest both in the historical destinies

Aleksandr S. Lappo-Danilevskii, "Ekaterina II i krest'ianskii vopros," in *Velikaia Reforma—Russkoe obshchestvo i krest'ianskii vopros v proshlom i nastoiashchem,* edited by A. K. Dzhivelegov, S. P. Mel'gunov, and V. I. Picheta (Moscow, 1911), I, 163–190. Translated by Mary Mackler.

of the Russian people and in their contemporary situation and could not ignore, therefore, the hard lot of the lowest classes of the population, whose vague expectations were manifested to some extent, in the peasant uprisings occurring in various parts of the country at the time.

As a matter of fact, the peasant question, that is, the question of attitudes toward serf bondage, of one man to another, acquired much greater significance during Catherine's reign. Efforts were made to establish criteria for its evaluation. By this time, too, the right to own serfs, a right enjoyed almost exclusively by the nobility, had ceased to be contingent on the rendering of compulsory service to the state, so serf bondage had more and more become an object of private civil relations. Aware of this, the Empress raised the peasant question herself and submitted it to Russian public opinion for discussion.

In posing the peasant question, Catherine II had to clarify for herself what aspects of it she wanted examined. She was not consistent in her views and legislative policy. While at the beginning of the public debate she showed some inclination to take into account, at least theoretically, general principles of justice and law in her legislative acts, she frequently allowed herself to be guided by political considerations that did not in the least contribute to the solution of the problem. In fact, she was increasingly influenced by other factors and ended up by surrendering to the reactionaries and removing the question of emancipation from the order of the day. She even contributed to the expansion of serfdom.

Before her accession to the throne, Catherine had expressed views on freedom and slavery based on abstract principles of religious ethics and natural law. Like Montesquieu, she had written in the spirit of the liberal ideas of her time, that all men are born equal and that "it is contrary to the Christian faith and to justice to make slaves of them."

Views of this kind had to bring Catherine to the idea of freedom for the peasants and of denial of the right of one man to own another virtually like "cattle." The serf, in her view, was as much a man as his master: "If a serf cannot be considered a person, then he cannot be considered a human being, in which event it must be admitted that he is a beast, and this would give us some reputation for humanity in the rest of the world. Everything that pertains to slaves follows from this God-pleasing precept and has been devised for and by cattle!" Hence, a serf is not only a human being, but he is a "person" as well: he is entitled to certain rights; "natural freedom" even of peasants should be restricted as little as possible. The author of the *Instruction* could have arrived at a (formally) similar conclusion on the basis of positivist jurisprudence, too. She wrote in the spirit of Montesquieu: "The equality of all citizens derives from their being subject to the same laws," and their freedom derives from each having the opportunity to do whatever he "ought to do." From this standpoint it was inevitable that the question of the lawfulness of serfdom arose. The obvious answer was emancipation of the privately owned peasants from "enslavement."

Yet Catherine could hardly have taken so radical a position for her time. She expressed herself much less resolutely in most of the articles of the *Instruction* and in the topics she suggested to the Free Economic Society for its competitions.

Apparently she had not yet given up the idea of "freedom" for the serfs when she was writing the draft of the *Instruction*. She had begun one of the articles with the words: "it can also be established that when one is free . . ." but she crossed this out and left only an article that said that the "laws may establish something of benefit to the slaves' personal property." And she never developed some of her ideas, such as those concerning the introduction of legal restrictions on enserfment and easier terms for gaining freedom. The articles prohibiting freed serfs from voluntarily re-enserfing themselves and setting a legal price for the purchase of freedom, the granting of freedom to the families of women who had been raped, and the fragment on the establishment of rural courts did not appear in the final text. The final text did express, however, Catherine's wishes that the enslavement of free persons be avoided, that peasants be free to marry, that their rights to property be protected, that the landlords be required by law to be circumspect in levying obligations, keeping in mind that the peasants should be required to leave their families as little as possible, and, finally, that "abuses of slavery" be prevented by law, that is, that landlords who tortured their peasants be punished.

The idea of the emancipation of the peasants did not disappear entirely from Catherine's presentation of the peasant question for discussion to the Free Economic Society, but it was expressed even more vaguely there and tied up with utilitarian political considerations. Disregarding the fact that "when a person's body is in another's power his goods are bound to be in that other's power, too," the society's patroness merely called special attention in a letter read to the Society on November 1, 1766, to the property rights of peasants. Realizing, no doubt, that "tilling the soil," which was of such importance to the state, could not prosper when the tiller "has nothing of his own" and that enslavement killed competition and was, therefore, damaging to the interests of the state, she suggested the following theme: "What constitutes the property of a tiller of the soil? Is it the land he cultivates, or is it movable goods? What rights might he enjoy to one or the other with benefit for the common good?" Thus, the Empress found it possible to discuss the right of the peasant to the land he tilled and to movable property without taking a stand on the question of his freedom or inquiring by what right a master owned a serf. And she hardly drew a clear line between "the common good" and the interests of the state, which could be interpreted in a much narrower sense.

This kind of approach to the peasant question could not have led to the realistic solution of the abolition of serfdom. At best, it paved the way for measures to mitigate the serfs' hard life. The fact of the matter is that Catherine II did not venture to dwell on the idea of even the gradual emancipation of the peasants—an idea that was, of course, closely bound up with the concept of peasant rights. Instead, she directed her main efforts to the limitation of serfdom. Actually, she subscribed to the theory which contended that the nobility had a natural role in a monarchy as an intermediate authority between the supreme authority and the people. Like the "best writer about laws" [Montesquieu], she believed that any violation of the prerogatives of the privileged sections of society (*les prérogatives des seigneurs, du clergé, de la noblesse et des villes*) would lead to the establishment of either a democratic or a despotic state. Since she regarded the nobles as the bulwark of the monarchy, and especially since, to a considerable extent, she owed the throne to them, she would hardly have ventured to abolish their right to own serfs. As a matter of fact, recognizing as she did the close link between the monarch and the nobles and between the nobles and the peasants, she readily allowed considerations of a utilitarian political nature to enter into the discussion of the peasant question. For example, she wrote in a letter to the procurator-general apropos the Senate's intention of enacting a harsh law against peasants who murdered their masters, that people who have no protection "in laws or anywhere else" easily become desperate for the slightest cause and that "in such cases" it is necessary "to act very cautiously" so as not to hasten "the already threatening disaster," for "the condition of the privately owned serfs is so critical that the only way to avoid [their revolt] is by calmness and by humane institutions"; "if we do not take steps to lessen the cruelty and alleviate the intolerable condition of the human race, they will do so themselves sooner or later, against our will." It was from this political, rather than juridical, standpoint, that the Empress concluded that it would be necessary to restrict serfdom, especially since the highest dignitaries, as well as her closest courtiers Panin, Golitsyn, Sivers, and others, also proposed the same kind of half-measures, at best.

And so, not wishing "all at once to make a large number of freed men through general legislation," Catherine gave up the idea of gradual emancipation and began to think exclusively along lines of the restriction of serfdom. She had already expressed herself in precisely this vein in her *Draft,* but at the same time had insisted that any improvements be made as "painlessly" as possible. Influenced by Montesquieu, she apparently did not approve of the linking of the "essential submission that bound the peasant inseparably to a given plot of land" to the "personal" [bond]. She proposed to the Commission on the Estates of the Realm that it find ways "to tie to the soil and establish on it the tillers themselves" in such a manner that "landlord and tiller" would profit equally and "certain painless and useful improvements would be produced in the lot of the lower order; also that the various kinds of abuses that oppress these useful members of society be eliminated."

Incidentally, Catherine II did take one step that brought about the actual emancipation of a considerable number of privately owned peasants: in the Manifesto of February 26, 1764, she proclaimed the nationwide secularization of ecclesiastical estates. The way for this confiscation by the treasury had been prepared by a series of earlier attempts by Russian governments. It was also part of the program Voltaire had proposed, so he had provided the Empress with the inspiration and rationale for carrying out what was essentially a fiscal and police measure. Though the secularization of the church estates, of course, improved the lot of nearly a million rural inhabitants who acquired the status of state peasants, it did not introduce anything really new into the serf relations that prevailed on the remaining privately owned estates.

Catherine hoped to affect these relations by other means—by placing restrictions on serfdom. Under the influence of the enlightened principles of her time, and also for political reasons, she tried to weaken serfdom and "set limits" on the power of the landed proprietors over their peasants.

Indeed, even before the publication of the *Instruction,* Catherine II tried to carry out her proposals aimed at lessening "domestic tyranny" those principles which later appeared in the final text. During her travels in the Baltic region, she noticed "the great oppression of the Livonian peasants" and suggested the specific rules restricting the landlords' power that were adopted by the Livonian Diet and published on April 12, 1765. However, these rules were only of local significance and even then did not have much effect on the Livonian peasants' conditions. Similarly, the question of restricting serfdom was also brought up in the Commission of 1767, but the ensuing discussion revealed the difficulties of "setting limits" on the landlords' power by legislation. Despite the "lament of the serfs," the deputies from various sections of the population at the meetings of the Commission of 1767, to which the privately owned peasants could not send representatives, tried to obtain the right to own serfs. A considerable majority of the nobles, among them persons with a certain amount of education, regarded serfdom as a more or less normal condition, in keeping with the monarchical system of government and "the character of the people," or else they did not think it possible to get along without it. They distrusted the idea of freedom for the peasants. They contended that it was dangerous to "instill a mental attitude of equality in the peasants" and that only when the lower class became educated would it be worthy of freedom; but if that ever happened, they did not know "where the land" for the peasants to own "would come from." Furthermore, they idealized their attitude toward the peasants, on the whole claiming, for example, that the peasants' condition was sufficiently secured by their owners' interest in maintaining their well-being. Finally, they considered the intervention of the state authority in their relations with the serfs an insulting violation of their privileges and damaging to the state's "prosperity and tranquillity."

From the attitudes revealed in the commission, the Empress could not help realizing how difficult it would be to implement her proposed limitations on serfdom. Meanwhile, the sessions of the Commission of 1767 were suspended because of the Turkish war, which temporarily diverted Catherine's attention from domestic reforms. Under these circumstances, Catherine once again altered her position on the peasant question: instead of setting limits on the landlords' power, she decided to narrow the sphere of the operation of serfdom. This might have been due, in part, to her desire to form a "third estate" (*tiers état*) and it was, of course, much easier to legislate. She tried to curtail the sources of enserfment, but she made no basic changes in the modes of its termination.

In her *Instruction,* Catherine II had already stated that "except in cases of extreme necessity to the state, such instances as would deprive people of their freedom should be avoided." She herself did not always observe this rule, as for example when she made gifts of inhabited estates, but she did try to practice it on many occasions.

The Empress paid special attention to one of the most dangerous modes of enserfment, namely the voluntary or involuntary adscription of persons during census-taking to owners who would assume responsibility for their punctuality in fulfilling their financial obligations. The government tried to undermine this mode of enserfment, primarily by increasing the kinds of cases that could be excluded from the earlier adscription rule. A plan for an Orphanage, approved by Her Majesty in 1763, provided that wards of both sexes, their offspring and descendants, were to remain free and under no circumstances be bound over or attached to any particular persons. Wards of the Orphanage were forbidden to marry serfs. The same rules applied, in part, to illegitimate children who were not raised in the Orphanage. As early as in 1767, the Senate, considering a proposal submitted by the office of the Ukrainian Slobodskaia *gubernia*[1] which called for the restoration of former procedures of adscribing children born out of wedlock to persons willing to raise them in their homes, ordered a "stay" of such procedures "until a general statute about it" was issued. In addition, by a decree of 1783, out-of-wedlock offspring of free mothers were to be registered in state villages, factories, or

1. Slobodskaia Ukraina, part of the Ukraine lying on the left bank of the Dnieper and reaching east to the Don River. Its main centers were Sumy, Kharkov, and Izium.

other enterprises on instructions from the local treasury office or at their own request, and a Statute on the Rural Population of treasury-owned estates, issued in 1787, declared that abandoned illegitimate children might be turned over to anyone who would have them, but only for a "specified number of years." At about the same time, an attempt was made to limit the adscription of orphaned minors, too. An instruction of 1765 to the governor of Slobodskaia Ukraine declared that young orphans without means of support may be turned over to "local residents" who wished to take them, but only until the age of twenty or, if taught a trade by their guardians, until the age of thirty. In 1775, another step was taken regarding orphans without means of support: they were placed under the care of the local welfare offices. The above-mentioned article from the 1787 Statute on the Rural Population also applied to young orphans who had no place to live. This meant that they were no longer permanently enserfed to those who raised them, but had to be freed after a certain time, a point that was clarified in a subsequent ukase.

Similar ordinances were issued concerning unassigned clergy. By 1766 "supernumerary" clerics left over after the 1754 census, as well as unassigned clergy who had been placed on the tax register in 1766, were removed from the tax registers; those who were fit for military service were to be drafted as well as assigned as orderlies, couriers, etc. In addition, special lists of the rest, those not fit for service, and "any number of females with them" were to be sent to the Senate. The decree on the 1769 census no longer required the adscription to landed proprietors of unassigned clergy who had not been drafted. After the Statute on Provinces (1775), these clergymen were readily accepted for clerical positions and, later still, as rural schoolteachers, and so forth. Thus, the adscription rule ceased to apply to the categories of illegitimate persons, minor orphans, and unassigned clergy. The general principle that freed persons were not to be enserfed, formulated quite a bit later, probably also limited serfdom.

As a matter of fact, Catherine II had formulated this rule,

though narrowly, as early as 1775 and had made it applicable to freedmen. In accordance with one of the unpublished articles of the *Instruction,* she had issued the Manifesto of March 17 [1775], permitting freedmen "to refrain from abscribing themselves to anyone" and to elect the status of townspeople (including the merchantry) or to a branch of the civil service. The same manifesto prohibited state offices from abscribing such persons "even if they sometimes make such a request." Catherine finally made this rule general in a personally signed ukase of October 20, 1783, ordering that it be applied to all "free persons of any nationality," "irrespective of origin or religion."

The majority of the above-mentioned rules were followed in the census of 1781–1782. The government wanted the census to be conducted "with the maximum benefit to the people" and instructed the Lower Land Courts, in the event of remissness or suspicion of concealment, to verify the district population rolls submitted to them. The lists drawn up by the lower courts were to be checked by the local Treasury offices, and in those *gubernias* where the Ordinance of 1775 had not yet gone into effect, by the *gubernia* chancery. Supervision of this kind ensured to some extent that the new rules would be applied to persons who were not subject to enserfment; such concern also may have facilitated the subsequent enactment of the laws of 1783–1787.[2]

At nearly the same time as she started to undermine adscription, Catherine II took steps to put an end to war captivity as a source of enserfment by ordering that prisoners of war, whatever their faith, be declared free men upon conversion to the "Orthodox religion," and be permitted to choose the kind of life they wished to live. Incidentally, the above-mentioned rule was given final and general formulation in a ukase the Empress signed on November 19, 1781.

Some other modes of enserfment were also restricted during

2. Reference is to the laws which extended the capitation and the secularization of Church lands to the Ukraine and the newly acquired southern territories.

Catherine's reign. True, the rule whereby the children of serfs were also serfs remained in force, but enserfment through marriage was restricted considerably.

For example, the old rule, "the son of a serf [woman] is a serf," no longer applied to male wards of the Orphanage even when, despite the ban, they married serf girls "through deception" (1763) or to male wards of the Academy of Arts and, probably, their descendants (1764). Persons who had been freed by their masters and given papers to that effect and who had then humbly asked to be eternally adscribed to other landowners, having married their serfs, but whose requests—by the time of the Manifesto of March 17, 1775—had not been acted upon and who had not been given official adscription papers, were deemed freedmen together with their wives (1780). It was also ordered (in 1781) that prisoners taken in Poland, but who remained in Russia, be freed together with their wives upon their conversion to the Orthodox faith "even if they had married someone's serf women or girls." In the above-mentioned instances, marriage to a serf woman not only did not enserf a free man, but freed the wife from serfdom. In some cases such emancipation was contingent on the payment of severance money to the landlord (laws of 1763 and 1780). It should be pointed out, however, that the reverse rule, "the daughter of a serf is a serf," the observance of which was demanded by some members of the 1767 Commission, was restricted only very slightly: it ceased to apply to girls raised in the Orphanage or the school for townspeople at the Resurrection Monastery. Unlike the girls from the Orphanage, girls from this school could, if they married a serf —at least, if they did so with the landlord's consent—make their husbands free.

Thus, we see that Empress Catherine II curtailed a little the modes of enserfment and of transfer to serf status, but she made hardly any changes at all in the modes of terminating serf status. Though she tended to decide "doubtful cases in favor of freedom," she nevertheless refrained from taking resolute measures, possibly because such action would have affected the interests of the nobility. Another reason may have been that serf owners were taking advantage of the right to set their people free, after ruining them, in order to avoid supporting them and paying taxes for them.

Termination of serf status depended on the owner's will, and this remained virtually unchanged. For example, payment of duties on the papers freeing a person were abolished, but the act of emancipation and the amount of redemption payments continued to depend on the owner.

The laws regulating termination of serf status also remained essentially unchanged. The government merely attempted to utilize some of them more fully. One of the more common modes of termination of serf status, namely conscription into the army (the quotas for which were a heavy burden on the population), continued to be quite important. Conscripted peasants and their wives were deemed "free from landlords"; regimental instructions issued to an infantry colonel in 1764 developed this rule further by extending it to "children born while their fathers were serving in the army." Such children were to be assigned "in accordance with the ukases concerning soldiers' children." Regimental instructions issued to a cavalry colonel in 1766 formulated the same rule more clearly: such children were to be "put in schools in accordance with the ukases."

In discussing attempts to widen the modes of the termination of the serf status, mention should be made of the ordinance granting freedom in cases of particularly serious transgressions by landlords. The ukase of 1763 on the submission of lists of recruits, while not an innovation, no longer carried restrictions on the granting of freedom to serfs who appeared in the local courts and proved that their masters had deliberately omitted them from the lists.

Wider use was made of the mode of termination of serf status by placing serfs at the government's disposal. The government often allowed serfs who had departed from "their estate" without leave or had run away from their masters to settle, on certain conditions, in the outlying regions of the country and be credited as recruits, etc.; and it sometimes transferred serfs to the status of townspeople by purchasing entire villages.

Clearly, Catherine II's efforts on behalf of the serfs were modest indeed. . . . Considering her views at the beginning of her reign, she might have been expected to concern herself more with finding ways and means for terminating the serf condition. Before her accession to the throne, she had dreamed that serfdom might be abolished by proclaiming the peasants of an estate free when that estate was sold to another landlord. And very much later, too, she drafted a law that would have granted freedom to all serfs born after 1785. . . .

The things Catherine did were of little significance. Apart from everything else, they did not work out very well.

Catherine narrowed the sphere of operation of serfdom, but she made no fundamental changes in the varied character of that system. In fact, despite the peasants' expectations, she strengthened the serf system and expanded it.

Actually, it was the real development of serf relationships, rather than their juridical development, that prevented the Empress from arranging all the conflicting elements into a harmonious system. For, while the privately owned peasant continued, in part, to be a subject of the law, he was also an object of the law.

The author of the *Instruction*, naturally, attached great importance to the "feeders of everybody," the "tillers of the soil," and was aware that their "enslavement" was harmful to the state. Consequently, she did not want to deprive them of all rights. Under earlier, not-yet-repealed laws, the peasant was still partially recognized as a subject of the law. For example, the law protected his life to a certain extent and recognized his right to be paid the same sum as a state peasant if he was dishonored or maimed. He could be a claimant, respondent, and witness in court (the last was restricted by army regulations). Concerning property rights, the law repealed an earlier ukase and allowed him to farm alcohol sales if a "reliable" landlord vouched for his punctuality in payment of dues. Frequently, however, whether the serf could take advantage of his rights depended entirely on the landlord's goodwill. Since the landowner's "subject" held "property not by law, but by custom," he could, with the landowner's permission, hold, use, and dispose of property and enter into transactions that were by no means always under the guaranty of the law. He could even buy serfs in his master's name and, to all intents and purposes, own them; he could even own an inhabited estate. He could, with his master's permission, register in the merchants' estate, and so forth. But in the above-mentioned and other activities, the privately owned peasant could always be made to feel the weight of the landlord's power, even when he benefited from the organization of a peasant commune or from the rare improvements the landlord might have made for the sake of "respectability" and the "prosperity" of the estate.

On the whole, while Catherine did very little to clarify the serfs' rights, she paid a great deal of attention to their obligations to the state, which consisted mainly of paying a head tax and serving in the army. But even when fulfilling their obligations as members of the state, the peasants continued to be dependent on their masters, who were charged with some of the responsibility for the payment of taxes and "punctual fulfillment" of other obligations.

Catherine II could, of course, point out that the privately owned peasants had certain rights under the law and certain tax obligations and that they came under the general jurisdiction with regard to criminal acts, murder, banditry, and flight. But she was unable to prevent the right to possess serfs from transforming state subjects into "subjects" of the landed proprietors in many respects and from closely approaching the right of private ownership.

Indeed, from her class-political standpoint, Catherine could not weaken the privileges of the nobility and, consequently, its "intermediary authority" between the "sovereign authority and the people." She herself kept reminding the nobles that their "nobility, distinction, and elevation, relative to the people derived solely from the essential need to keep it [the people] in order." However, by continuing to subordinate the peasants to the landlords, she changed their status more and more from that of citizens to that of "subjects" of the landed proprietors. The landowner was the "legislator, judge, and executor of his judgments, and, if he wished, plaintiff, against whom the respondent could not utter a word," while the peasant in his power was more often than not "dead as far as the law is concerned, except, perhaps, in criminal matters," although even in such matters, the peasant often slipped out from under the government's authority.

It was chiefly from this class-political standpoint, too, that Catherine II was prepared to strengthen those measures that ensured the peasants' "unquestioning obedience" to their landlords and to extend the masters' punitive powers over their peasants. Under a ukase of January 17, 1765, she permitted landlords to deport their "people" for "impertinence," that is, for other than colonization purposes, to hard labor "for as long a period as he wishes," and to take them back whenever they wished; the court "could not even ask him the reasons for the deportation or investigate the matter." Catherine also confirmed the landowner's right to send his house and field serfs to settle in Siberia while keeping them on his list of recruits and to conscript them whenever he wished to do so. In her Statute on Provinces, she also granted the landlords the right to have serfs jailed at their expense without giving a reason for such actions. She did, however, indicate in the case of Major-General Ettinger's widow[3] that "the judicial power should be protected against interference in it" by landowners in matters which (such as thievery and runaways) were not subject to domestic trial and punishment, and she expressed the desire that the Commission to Draft a New Code of Laws "include a provision for dealing with those who display cruelty against a per-

3. Elisabeth I. Ettinger had a serf flogged to death on suspicion of theft and planning the mass flight of fellow serfs. The Senate (Sept. 18, 1770, and Feb. 13, 1772) ruled that she had exceeded her domanial jurisdiction, and had her jailed for one month, fined, and her estate confiscated on grounds of incapacity. The Senate also suggested that pertinent clarificatory legislation be issued.

son." However, despite a statement issued by the College of Justice, pointing out that there was no precise law "concerning instances when serfs die soon after" beatings or harsh punishment, the Empress did not insist on her expressed wish being carried out and instead of obtaining the enactment of a law, merely instructed her vicegerent "to curb excesses, dissipation, extravagance, tyranny, and cruelty." At the same time, in the ukase of August 22, 1767, . . . she forbade peasants, on pain of stern punishment, to submit "impermissible petitions against their landlords, especially into her own hands," though she certainly knew of the torture and cruel punishments to which the peasants were sometimes subjected.

By means of the above-mentioned ukases, Catherine II did not so much directly limit the rights or increase the obligations of the privately owned peasants, as provide wider scope for the landlords' authority; as a result, the right to hold serfs, long related to slaveholding, came more and more to resemble a private property right.

True, such a concept of serfdom was never precisely formulated in law, and the Empress herself, it would seem, never expressed it. But it had evidently already received some recognition in her time, and it subsequently found its way into legislation. Foreign observers of the Russian social system, for example, said repeatedly that serfs, or "slaves," constitute the "private property of their masters, on whom they are completely dependent"; at the most, they pointed out that there was a certain vagueness in the concept of the object of that system: "judging from what they say, serfs are sometimes regarded as immovable property and sometimes as movable property"; from the latter standpoint, they belonged to their owners in the same way that farm implements and domestic animals were recognized as their property. This concept of serfdom was reflected in one of the very late ukases. Establishing the rules for claiming government and private debts from debtors personally or "from their estates," in a ukase of October 7, 1792, the Senate declared, among other things, that "enserfed, privately owned domestics and peasants are included, and must be included, as part of the estate," and that "in sales from one to another, deeds of purchase must be drawn up for serfs . . . as for all other immovable property."

It follows, therefore, that the law provided grounds for virtually equating serfs with the inventory of an estate. No doubt, the law already gave the landowner certain rights deriving from that concept of serf dependency even before the above ukase was issued. For example, the law recognized the landowner's right to dispose of his peasants, and Catherine II did almost nothing to weaken that right. On the contrary, she herself made gifts of money to her favorites so they might "purchase" peasants. During her reign it was possible to buy and sell serfs with or without land, buy whole families or individuals, transact sales on the estate or marketplace; contemporaries termed all this "veritable slavery." In her Charter to the Nobility, which widened the nobles' property rights in general, Catherine granted them the right "to purchase villages." She did not even risk the enactment of a general law on the right to sell serfs, though many of the deputies of the nobility were willing to restrict that right somewhat by prohibiting the breaking up of families. In a ukase written in her own hand concerning "confiscation proceedings" and "auctions," she merely ordered those involved "not to auction off people without land," which the Senate interpreted as meaning that "people who had no land (that is, landless peasants) were not to be auctioned"; she did not decree that they "were not to be sold at all." She also prohibited the sale of persons for conscription, but that ban merely resulted in the prohibition of formal sales of peasants for three months after the publication of the army recruiting ukase. As for the serf-owners' other rights, some of them were very harsh, such as the right to decide on marriages between serfs, or to transfer peasants to house service and to exploit their labor without restraint. Moreover, Catherine did not even restrict owners to these bounds. She hardly touched the landlords' rights and left the serfs' obligations to their "masters" entirely dependent on local custom or to the landlord's discretion.

With such broad, yet poorly defined rights, the landlord could do whatever he wished with his serf's person and property (except, perhaps, to inflict the death penalty); he owned him "like cattle" and did not permit him to dispose of what he had acquired. The only way the peasant could counter this was to run away or to conceal his possessions far from his master's eye. The Empress herself described this "order" in the following words: "except for imposing the death penalty, the landlord can do anything that enters his head on his estate."

Another source of the increase in the landlords' power over their peasants came from the masters' virtual freedom of obligations toward their serfs. True, "the evil Pugachev disease" prompted Catherine to remind the nobles that they did have responsibilities toward their peasants, but she did little to define these duties more specifically. Several times after 1762, though, she reaffirmed the old rule obligating the landlords to feed and support their peasants in times of famine and she tried to restrain the landlords from ruining and torturing their subjects on pain of [their estates] being placed under trusteeship, being "bridled" by the vicegerent, or having penalties imposed on them, but measures of this kind were ineffective and seldom put into practice.

Thus, while Catherine narrowed the concept of serfdom, she actually strengthened its substance. She had started out with such words as "freedom is the soul of all things," but she had arrived at legislation that virtually equated the peasant soul with "soulless objects." Since she did not protect the serfs' rights, she could not protect the serfs against abuses by the landlords; as a result, serfs were often completely deprived of "civic status" and sometimes driven to despair.

The author of the *Instruction* did not practice what she preached. Though she wrote that "instances of enslavement should be avoided," she not only did not reverse the process of the intensification of serfdom in Great Russia, but actually helped extend it to groups of the population who had not been serfs and to territories where serfdom had not yet been established.

For example, the law differentiated rather strictly between serfs and persons attached to privately owned factories. . . . The majority of the latter were classified as "possessional" peasants and enjoyed certain advantages as compared with ordinary serfs; and after the ukase of March 29, 1762, to this new category was also added: "persons freely hired for contracted payment," not purchased. Actually, they were often treated as serfs.

The serf system could not help affecting those peasants who were free from serf dependency under the law, especially the state peasants, whose numbers were greatly increased by the secularization of the Church lands and the inclusion among them of *odnodvortsy*[4] (1764) and some minor social group. True, the state peasants remained comparatively free. In one handwritten note, the Empress expressed the intention of "freeing all state, crown, and former Church-owned peasants as soon as regulations for them were drafted." However, their complete emancipation did not follow. On the contrary, they felt the full effects of the serf system. They were restricted by the treasury for fiscal reasons in the right to dispose of their land, and had to deal with crown officials who transferred the habits of serf-owners to persons whom they did not hold as serfs; they were a labor pool to be drawn on for the bestowal of gifts and for "adscription" to factories. State peasants who were attached to factories—which were later transferred to private ownership (this was especially true in the mining industry) —were transferred along with the factories, and they found themselves in harsh bondage to the owners. State peasants who lived on lands given away as gifts became the serfs of those to whom the land had been granted. In Catherine's reign, adscription of state peasants to private factories ceased and many private mining enterprises were returned to the treasury soon after the uprisings of peasants attached to Urals factories.

State peasants were not the only category of the population who were affected by the serf system. As a result of Catherine's ukases,

4. *Odnodvortsy*—see note 18 of "Voices of the Land and the Autocrat," p. 150.

serfdom was extended to new territories. For example, in 1775, the Byelorussian governor-general reported to the Senate that in the Byelorussian *gubernias* under his jurisdiction, "there are sales and other transactions involving serfs between persons who have the right to dispose of immovable property, in consequence of which serfs and peasants are moved to nearby and to remote *gubernias*." Since "the Byelorussian gentry did not usually sell peasants without land" (except runaway peasants from Russia), the governor-general suspected that the landowners in question were selling runaways from Russia under the guise of their own peasants. Pointing out that transactions of this kind could lead to other abuses and difficulties, he proposed to the Senate that the sale of peasants without land "for removal to Russia," be banned until the completion of the government-ordered census of runaways and the adoption of a statute on runaways and that until then such sales be permitted only "within these [Byelorussian] *gubernias*." The Senate drew a different conclusion from the Byelorussian governor-general's report. On the grounds that "under the proclamation on the annexation of Byelorussia, the inhabitants of those *gubernias* and the landed proprietors, whatever their origin or title, have been accepted as subjects of Her Imperial Majesty and are entitled to the same rights and privileges as are enjoyed by the Russian nobility," it did not consider it possible to deny them the right to sell serfs without land. Thus, the right to sell serfs without land was extended to the landed proprietors of the Byelorussian *gubernias,* which, naturally, intensified the Byelorussian peasants' bondage to them. Soon after this, the government did the same for the Ukrainian *gubernias*. For a long time, the Ukrainian landowners had been trying to turn their peasants into "their eternal subjects" and they had already succeeded in obtaining for themselves the well-known Charter of April 20, 1760, which they called "an order banning the movement of subjects from one landowner to another." The Russian government, accustomed to the ways of serfdom, immediately equated the Ukrainian *gubernias* to the Great Russian ones. Anyway, Catherine regarded preservation of

Ukrainian autonomy "a stupidity" and had no sympathy with peasant mobility. By the time of Rumyantsev's census [1765–1767], "the ordinary Ukrainian people," according to a contemporary, had already come to the conclusion "that the census would bring them nothing but serf bondage like that of the Great Russian peasants." It is probable that Catherine intended the well-known ukase of May 3, 1783, only to introduce the capitation tax in the Ukraine, rather than to establish full-scale serfdom there, but her order that every person residing in the Kiev, Chernigov, and Novgorod-Seversk vicegerencies "remain in their places and categories" naturally led to the establishment of a serf system there. The government itself recognized the Ukrainian peasants as tied to the owners of the land on which they lived and to whom they were adscribed during the fourth census. The sale of peasants separately from the land didn't gain full recognition under Catherine and was finally prohibited after her death by her successor.

Serfdom reached the south of Russia, too. Under the same 1783 ukase, the rural inhabitants of Slobodskaia Ukraine, who had lost the right of movement soon after the establishment in 1765 of the Commission for the Reformation of the Sloboskaya Regiments, were equated with the Ukrainian privately owned peasants, and a ukase published soon after Catherine's death, using almost the same words as the ukase of May 3, 1783, extended the ban on "unauthorized movement of the population from place to place" to the southern outlying regions. The ukase of December 12, 1796, extended serfdom to the Yekaterinoslav, Voznesensk, Caucasus *gubernias,* the Taurida region, the Don region, and the Taman [peninsula], "to establish for eternity each owners' property" and to hinder peasants from running away "from the interior *gubernias.*"

Considering how serfdom gained in strength and breadth during Catherine II's reign, the government could hardly have been expected to deal with the peasant question satisfactorily. Instead of embarking on reform, it suppressed the Pugachev rebellion and grew more and more reactionary in its policies toward the peasants. Nevertheless, Catherine never lost interest in the peasant question, not even in the last period of her reign. In 1781, for example, the Russian envoy in Vienna included among his dispatches [to St. Petersburg] Joseph II's manifestos emancipating the peasants and permitting them to purchase their land. These manifestos are not now among those reports. Instead, there is a note which says: "These enclosures were not returned from the Palace." And, judging from subsequent information, it was soon after this that the above-mentioned draft emancipating all children of serfs born after 1785 was written. One source, writing apparently several years after the publication of the Statute on the Provinces, refers to "Her Supreme Majesty's willingness" to "find a way to equate landowners and peasants and to put an end to the excessive tributes and work duties levied by some and to other violations arising therefrom." Apparently, Catherine had not ceased to think about the gradual emancipation of the serfs and the weakening of "domestic tyranny." But she was no longer so confident that this was possible. In 1777, in a frank conversation with one of her officials, she remarked, among other things, that the peasant question was very difficult: "it does not yield, no matter where you touch it." And apropos of Radishchev's exhortations to the landowners that they emancipate their peasants voluntarily, she exclaimed: "He is trying to persuade the landowners to emancipate their peasants! Why, no one will listen to him!" Having lost faith in the possibility of solving the peasant question either by legislation or by personal initiative, the author of the *Instruction* consoled herself with the thought that "no one in the whole world is better off than our peasants are under a good landlord." Hence, there was no reason for private persons to discuss their "lot." One foreigner wrote in the 1790's: "It was now impossible to mention the question of the injustice of the serf system without risking expulsion from the country (on instructions from the Empress herself)." And the sad fate of Radishchev, in whose works Catherine saw nothing but "dissension and corruption," testified that neither could a Russian discuss the question inside the empire without risking very harsh punishment.

To sum up, although Catherine II tried at the beginning of her reign to get the peasant question discussed and contributed greatly to arousing public interest in it, she did little to prepare its solution; she merely restricted the modes of enserfment and concerned herself little with the modes of termination of enserfment. She talked much about the harmful consequences of "enslavement," but she did not touch the heart of the serf system. She wished to improve the lot of the privately owned peasants, but she ended up by helping to strengthen the power of the landed proprietors and to extend serfdom. Throughout the long years of her reign the majority of the population remained enslaved by the privileged minority and waited in vain for acts that would basically alter the "unjust order," which was so damaging to the culture and the entire social and political system.

A. M. AMMANN, S.J.

Church Affairs

THE REIGN of Catherine II represents a time of tremendous development in areas other than political history. What Peter the Great had begun under the influence of German Protestant ways of thought developed fully under Catherine. Western culture and ideas now streamed into Russia almost unobstructed. They became popular also in the circles of wealthy burghers. In contrast to Peter's time, Western culture, which was now mainly taken from France, became familiar also to the native Russian

---

A. M. Ammann, S. J. *Abrisse der ostslawischen Kirchengeschichte* (Wien: Thomas Morus Presse im Verlag Herder, 1950), pp. 403–413. Translated by Brigitte McConnell.

people. There were not yet very many from among the rich gentry or bourgeoisie who assimilated such ways of thought on their own; for Russia's ties with the West were not yet close enough. "Western" views still had to be imposed on them from above. But the Empress, who was quite enthusiastic about them, saw to it that they found expression in legislation. Absolutism, that is the government's imperious concern for the people—and this also relates to questions of *Weltanschauung*—is a characteristic trait of Catherine's reign. This does not yet mean, however, that Catherine achieved her goal everywhere and in everything. Nonetheless, it was the enlightened rationalism to which Catherine paid homage, and nothing else that determined the deeds and regulations of the authorities everywhere. Therefore, if one does not want to consider this ratiocination, which was after all very shallow, as a phenomenon of Church history, one can separate . . . the political and cultural history of the country from its Church history. This is true without exception for the ethnically Russian lands.

It is a different matter, however, when we consider the Russian–Polish relations which were brought to a forced solution by the three Polish partitions during Catherine's reign. In these, Church questions played an important role.

In tracing the history of the Church in the original ethnic Russian areas one has to keep two lines of development in view. There are traditional questions which were solved by Catherine's intervention. In addition, however, there are several traits which are characteristic for Catherine's reign.

TRADITIONAL QUESTIONS

Above all the problems which her predecessors had left her to solve was the question of Church property. We know that Elizabeth, during her last years, wanted to take the administration of Church property away from the Church and transfer it to the Senate. However, her regulations to do this were not carried out during her lifetime. Her immediate successor, Catherine's unhappy husband Peter III (1762), had no time during his reign of only six months to undertake anything decisive. In spite of some undeniably efficient beginnings in other legislation, he was not fortunate in regard to the Church. He tightened the regulations of his predecessor in an arbitrary way and added various insulting decrees of his own. Thus in April 1762 a College of Economy was established by the Senate in the spirit of Elizabeth's regulations. It was to administer all persons and things belonging to the Church. In addition the Emperor quite unnecessarily wanted to induct the sons of priests into military service; he demanded that the priests dress like Protestant ministers and shave their beards, that only icons of the Saviour and the Mother of God be allowed in churches, etc. It is therefore not surprising that Catherine II was welcomed as joyfully at her accession by everyone as Elizabeth had been at hers. At the Troitso-Sergeevskaia Laura near Moscow, for example, she was triumphantly ushered in by the students of the seminary under the guidance of their rector Platon Levshin in a way which was obviously reminiscent of Christ's entry into Jerusalem. And yet how bitterly the Church was to be disappointed!

Only a few months after her accession she already sought the solution to the question of Church property. Her trusted agent in this matter was the archbishop of Novgorod, Dmitrii Sietschenov. She finally had Elizabeth's law on the registration of the properties of churches and monasteries carried out as well as the law on the census of all dwellers of monasteries. Only a single bishop resisted. This was, as was to be expected, Bishop Arsenii Maceievich of Rostov. She had him tried by a court of bishops which removed him from his office and sentenced him to confinement in a monastery (1763). As if she were still afraid of him, the Empress had him taken to the Reval fortress in 1767 where he was to disappear. He received a different name: Andreas Vral (the chatterbox). He died in this prison in 1794. That the bishops lent themselves to this game of their mistress shows how far they were already entangled in the toils of the state. In a speech to the bishops at that time, the Empress characterizes them as "people who are part of the administration and who are subject to the monarch's will as well as to the regulations of the Gospel." In contrast to what had happened in 1666 [1] there was no opposition to this. In May and June of 1763 the question of Church property was solved for good. A new inventory was made of monasteries and bishoprics which were classified into three groups; the administration of Church property was transferred to the state College of Economy. In 1765 church charities, too, were regulated by ukase of the Empress. These regulations applied for the time being only to the Old Russian countries. Catherine was, however, resolved to put an end to the autonomy of the Ukraine as well. Late in 1764 she therefore abolished the title of Hetman; [2] the last of them, Cyril Rasumovskii, resigned of his own accord. Ten years later (1775) the Russians conquered the last refuge of the free Cossacks, the so-called *sich,* which was situated below the rapids of the Dnieper. In 1781 the structure of the administration of the former Hetmanate was adapted to the Great Russian model and three governorships were established which were united in one general governorship. In the following years first the peasants of the Ukraine, who had hitherto been free, were subjected to Great Russian laws and thereby made serfs (1783), and finally all the properties of the Church and of the monasteries in the Ukraine were subordinated to the Russian College of Economy (1786). Thus the last remnant of an independent Ukraine ceased to exist; henceforth there was only one law for the whole of the Russian Empire, to which—with the exception of the East Slavs of Poland–Lithuania—all eastern Slavic nations and tribes were subjected.

Apart from the question of the administration of Church property her predecessor had left to the Empress also the task of

1. Refers to the decision of the Church Council in 1666 by which the Old Believers were condemned and turned over to the secular arm. The Church was allowed to keep the property it owned at the time.
2. Hetman—or Ataman—the traditional title of the elected chief of the Cossack military society.

reintegrating the *Raskol*[3] into the Russian national community. This split from the established Church had gradually proven itself so vital that it could not be disregarded any more. It certainly also would not have been in accordance with Catherine's way of thinking to persecute people solely for their religious convictions, for in the spirit of the Encyclopedists, she hated nothing as much as what those men called "fanaticism" and "hypocrisy." In December 1762 she therefore allowed the Raskolniks to practice their special rites without hindrance. She hoped thereby to perhaps be able to draw the *Popovtsy*,[4] from Starodub back to Russia. When this failed, however, she had their settlements invaded by the Russian military two years later (1764) and had about twenty thousand of these Old Believers deported to Siberia. Not even the abolition of the Raskol office in the course of the year of 1763 had managed to change the zealots' adherence to their old rites. In a written authoritative judgment on this whole question, which the Empress requested from the bishops, the *edinoverie* already emerges as a remedy for reconciling the conflict: the Church should recognize the old rites and be satisfied with a "harmony in belief"; the Old Believers, on their part, should quietly accept the episcopate of the state Church and Nikon's reforms and also confirm their "harmony in belief" with the Orthodox. For the time being, however, these guidelines were not effected. Yet circumstances helped Catherine. In 1771 there broke out in Moscow a devastating epidemic which had been brought in from Moldavia. The government could not gain control over it and gave a free hand to individual initiative. The Old Believers who lived in Moscow took advantage of this. The first ones to do so were the few "priestless"[5] who had lived in the

3. *Raskol*—or schism (Old Belief) refers to those (clergy and laity) who refused to accept the modernization of the ritual and the reform of church administration in the seventeenth century.

4. *Popovtsy*—Old Believers who refused the innovations of the official Church but accepted the priests (*popy*) consecrated by the official bishops.

5. "Priestless" were those Old Believers who refused to recognize the priests consecrated by the bishops of the official Church and who preferred to remain without priests and sacraments.

old capital since the seventeenth century. Under their leader Kovylin they founded a hospital for contagious diseases with a cemetery, the so-called Preobrazhenskii cemetery. A church hall, a home for youth and for the aged were attached to this. During the same year the Popovtsy of Vietka also founded a hospital with cemetery, church, and the corresponding charitable institutions, the so-called Rogozhskii cemetery. Their leader was Nikita Pavlov. Five years later the "priestless" of Pomorie and even the Filippovites followed suit.[6]

In Moscow the Popovtsy from Vietka were in a better position than most. Among the innumerable priests who were loitering about this town without a position, there were always some who were willing to enter service with the Popovtsy. These priests, however, had to accept strict supervision. They were also very much hindered in the execution of their priestly functions, for even though they were allowed to administer the sacraments—even the sacrament of marriage—they were not allowed to celebrate the liturgy; the reason for this was that no Antimensium[7] existed in Moscow that had been consecrated by a bishop who was recognized by the Old Believers. There was, after all, only one and it was in Vietka; from there all those which had been consecrated therefore had to be taken to Moscow. They were, however, handed out to the priests only as befitted the case. Usually the head layman of the parish guarded them. One can understand that these priests yearned for a bishop. The priests also were impeded by the fact that they had no myrrh consecrated by a "proper" bishop for the administering of some sacraments. When they then tried to overcome this embarrassment by "consecrating"

6. Pomorie—the region bordering on the White Sea in northeastern European Russia, a haven for Old Believers.
Ivan Filippov, leader of the priestless community of Vyg in the eighteenth century. Cf. R. O. Crummey, *The Old Believers and the World of Antichrist: The Vyg Community and the Russian State, 1694–1855* (University of Wisconsin, 1970).
7. Antimensium—an altar cover (frequently richly decorated) into which a relic was sewn and which could be used as a substitute for the altar.

some myrrh on their own authority, it caused new splits among the Old Believers. A church with priests, but without a bishop proved an intolerable hybrid in the long run. Thus the idea of *edinoverie* received new impetus. In a request to the civil governor of Moscow the Old Believers demanded as the price for their submission to the state Church the recognition of their old books and rites as well as a bishop of their own, who was to be subordinated to no other bishop of the state Church but responsible directly to the Holy Synod. The Metropolitan of Moscow, Platon Levshin, however, received these entreaties coolly.

In the meanwhile the enthusiastic sect of Khlysts[8] flourished undercover as in earlier times. There even appeared yet another variety of these often unnatural cults, the sect of the Skoptsy or self-mutilators.[9] Their founder was a simple peasant, Selivanov, who sometimes pretended to be God's son and sometimes Tsar Peter III. He was finally banished to Siberia.

At the same time two more rationalistic sects were heard of, the Molokans or "milk-drinkers" and the Dukhobors. They were mostly quiet people who in no way took part in public life.

While the Russian Church was rather preoccupied with all these divisions and splits in its midst it did not have to concern itself in any way for the heterodox who lived in Russia. Peter III had explicitly allowed all of them, Catholics, Lutherans, and Reformed, to own churches and cemeteries in the suburbs of Moscow. When Catherine II wanted to attract colonists from western Europe to Russia she also explicitly promised them freedom of religious practice, though any kind of proselytizing was forbidden to them everywhere, except among the Mohammedans. The government took this promise seriously. In 1765 the Apostolic Prefect of St. Petersburg with the consent of the government requested two priests from Rome for the Volga colonists. Thus everything would have been fine, had not the

8. Khlysts—or Flagellants, a sect of extreme Old Believers who believed in the mortification of the flesh through flagellation.

9. Skoptsy—sectarians who believed in the unredeemed evil of the flesh and therefore subjected their members to castration.

Catholics themselves caused the power-hungry Tsarina to interfere with the internal affairs of the Church. Actually there was an
eternal quarrel within the Petersburg parish between the clergymen and the parishioners as well as among the four "nations" of
which the parish was composed. This led to frequent appeals to
the Office of the Propaganda in Rome, but unfortunately also to
appeals to the Russian clerical and secular authorities. Finally (in
1766) Catherine appointed the Livonian Council as court of appeals for Catholics and at the same time asked this council to work
out a "Regulation" for the Catholic parishes. Thereby a fateful
course was taken which was to lead the Catholic Church into long,
oppressing dependence upon the state. The Regulation was issued
in 1769. It followed the model of the Russian vicarages of the state
Church and gave decisive voice to the laity in the choice of the
clergy and the administration of property. All this was to take
place under the supervision of the state; only at the very end was
the approval on behalf of "those who were concerned," that is, the
Roman Curia, to be obtained, too. This arrangement was made
binding by Catherine. It was now too late for objections.

Special Characteristics of Catherine's Reign

Apart from the traditional questions briefly touched upon above
—questions that were solved by Catherine's intervention—there
appear lines of development that are specific to the reign of this
empress. They manifest themselves above all in the area of clerical
and secular public education and in the spiritual development
mainly among the bourgeois classes. Only a few years after her accession to the throne Catherine asked a few trusted aides to draft a
reform of the clerical schools. Though this draft meant to keep
Latin as the language of instruction, as had been the custom
hitherto, it also tried to make instruction relevant to the urgent
social questions of that time. It envisaged treating theology the same
as any of the other university disciplines. This draft, however, never
came to anything.

Among the theologians of that time who had worked on the draft, Platon Levshin stood out above all. Catherine first made him the tutor of her son Paul, whose confidence the lively and intelligent man was able to win. He wrote a catechism for his protégé in the spirit of the new educational system. In 1770 he was appointed Bishop of Tver by the Empress, five years later Archbishop of Moscow, and in 1787 Metropolitan of Moscow. He shared the displeasure of the Empress with his protégé. He died only in 1812. He wrote a great deal, above all sermons, but also a history of the Church, which he only brought up to 1720, and four larger theological treatises. The latter were written entirely in the spirit of Theophan Prokopovich. Like Prokopovich he was very much dependent on the German Protestants. Above all he relied on the last "scholastic" among them, Johann Andreas Quenstedt (1617–1688), that is, on his main work *Theologia Didactico-polemico*. In his writings he used the Russian language. It also should be mentioned that in those decades the lectures of Prokopovich, which he had once delivered in Kiev, also appeared in print, partly in Leipzig, partly in Russia; they are, however, written in Latin, as was the custom during the author's lifetime. Thus Theophan's proclivity for Protestantism triumphed among Russian theologians, and it would retain its predominance for decades to come.

Clerical schools, however, formed merely an island, as it were, in the state. Repeatedly the theological "faculties" had been refused the right of domicile at the public universities, which meant that their teachers and students were denied participation in the intellectual life of the nation. The theological faculties were thereby degraded to class schools of the clerical estate. For the state theology was obviously superfluous. The state was content with a weak deism. This becomes quite clear when we look at the school statute which Catherine issued in 1786 on the Austrian pattern. From all schools that were intended for laity, Church and clergy remained entirely excluded. What changes had taken place in the relationship of Church and state since the times of Joseph of Volokolamsk! [10] The secularization of public life appeared complete. This does not mean that Catherine was not aware of the Church. On the contrary, she needed the Church; she controlled the bishops as well as their officials; they all had to obey her wishes, and only her wishes here on earth. But there were precise differences between her way and that of an Ivan the Terrible or even of a Peter the Great: for her, the unbelieving Encyclopedist, the Church had turned from a mediator of divine mysteries to a mere organ of administration for a special area of public life. The world was not viewed any more from above, from God, but from down below, from man, above whom at an endless, cool distance reigned a Supreme Being.

During those decades there lived in Russia—though he was more like a stranger among his contemporaries—a holy ascetic and preacher, Tikhon Zadonskii. He had been born in 1724 in a little village near Novgorod. Early he became a teacher in the seminary at the seat of his bishopric. He did not find satisfaction in this activity, however, and at the age of twenty-four he became a monk. After three years, in 1761, the government designated him auxiliary bishop of Novgorod; two years later he was entrusted with the diocese of Voronezh. He administered the office for only four years and in 1769 he retired to the Zadonskii monastery for good. There he died in 1783. He was canonized in 1861 by the Russian Church. He distinguished himself by a deeply religious mind, by his holy way of life, and by the indefatigable zeal of his soul. Already as a bishop he wrote much for the instruction of candidates to the priesthood, ministers, monks, and laymen. Most of all he had the Sunday sermon at heart. He energetically took upon him the task of establishing schools for his flock. In the Zadonskii monastery he lived as modestly as any of the lowly monks, performed regularly the manual chores necessary in such

10. Joseph of Volokolamsk, abbot of the Volokolamsk monastery in the early sixteenth century, advocated obedience to the secular power in return for the Church's right to keep its landholdings. He was instrumental in sealing the alliance between the Grand Duke of Moscow and the Church by terms of which the latter was subordinated to the interests of the former.

a community and besides wrote many short edifying treatises.
There are also reports of miracles which he is supposed to have
performed.

But Tikhon was only an isolated figure in Catherine's age. It
is therefore not surprising that during her reign the deistic views
of the Freemasons exercised an influence in Russia as never before.
Their main representative, N. I. Novikov, was at the same time
active as a publisher. Still more audacious than he—even to complete atheism—was A. N. Radishchev, mainly in his book *A Journey
from St. Petersburg to Moscow,* first printed in 1790. To be sure,
Catherine put an end to all this at the beginning of the nineties,
after the French Revolution broke out. The lodges were closed.
Novikov was imprisoned in the Shlisselburg; Radishchev was
first sentenced to death and then pardoned to exile in Siberia. But
from the changeover, initiated under Peter the Great, Catherine
went on to make a revolution. She had turned everything upside
down: she had put man in the highest place and she had made
man's relation to the Lord God into a special authoritarian department of government.

Postscript

THE READER of the preceding articles must be aware of the fact that whatever an author's conclusions with respect to Catherine II and her rule, he could not escape being impressed by the Empress' forceful personality. Not only did Catherine succeed in capturing and holding the throne for over thirty years, but also she put her own preferences, prejudices, attitudes, hopes, and accomplishments at the center of both the domestic and European stage. There can be no question that Catherine had a powerful influence in shaping events in her own lifetime; and in so doing she bequeathed to succeeding rulers a framework they had to take into account, whether they rejected it (as did her son Paul I)

301

or used it for their own designs (as did her grandsons Alexander I and Nicholas I). And so it is that our authors have to take a stand on Catherine II, whether they admire (Bil'bassov) or condemn her (Kizevetter). Even those scholars who deny a historically creative role to the single individual and firmly believe in the iron laws of "vast impersonal forces" cannot avoid ascertaining the nature and limits of Catherine's part in shaping Russian reality.

This preoccupation with the personality and role of Catherine II dates from her own lifetime. Her contemporaries saw in her the prime cause for whatever happened in her empire. They spoke of the "Age of Catherine"—as Voltaire had spoken of the *"Siècle de Louis XIV"*—and called her "great." True, much of this opinion was a result of Catherine's clever manipulation of public opinion, both foreign and native. Yet, even those who disbelieved Catherine's image of Russia and of herself acknowledged the positive impact of her personality and blamed evil conditions on the people's backwardness or the corruption of the court.[1] As for members of the "establishment," they naturally felt that military glory, diplomatic successes, and glittering court life, from which they derived direct benefits, outshone the darker sides of Russian life. Under the harsher and unsettled conditions of the nineteenth century, and in reaction to the narrowly repressive regime of Paul I (1796–1801) and to Alexander I's (1801–1825) preference for bureaucratic and militaristic solutions, the upper classes of Russian society came to view the reign of Catherine II as the "golden age of the nobility."

Another cause for the retrospective glorification of Catherine may be found in the fact that in her reign cultural and artistic life rapidly spread to the countryside. Retired noblemen socialized

1. The bibliography of contemporary opinions is found in V. Bil'bassov, *Katharina II. Kaiserin von Russland im Urtheile der Weltliteratur,* 2 vols. (Berlin, 1897). The bibliography first appeared in Russian; it has critical annotations, and lists all works on Catherine II published before 1896.

In the subsequent notes preference will be given to those works that are most recent, contain the best bibliographical data for further study and research, and are written in the more accessible languages.

with their neighbors, led a more sophisticated and intellectually more demanding existence on their estates, and patronized cultural activities in the provincial capitals, as well as in Moscow and St. Petersburg. This contributed to the creation of a truly national culture—literature, music, the arts, and scholarship were no longer imitative of the West; but a dynamic creativity of its own evolved. This development reached its glorious fulfillment in the 1830's, but its roots went back to the reign of Catherine II. Little wonder then that the educated Russian derived a sense of pride and dignity from his culture's coming of age, from its freeing itself from western European tutelage. Catherine's age seemed indeed a glorious one for Russia, and the Empress who had skillfully cast herself as its prime mover was given full credit for it.

All this goes a long way toward explaining why the Empress' rhetoric and public postures were taken at their face value by Russian educated society in the first half of the nineteenth century. In her own writings, Catherine not only used and popularized the vocabulary that was *de rigueur* for participation in civilization (*le monde policé*), but also gave expression to ideals and goals which were particularly attractive to members of an educated élite who had become conscious of their own dignity, worth, and accomplishments. The generation of educated service nobles that matured and actively participated in the reign of Catherine II was the first to be treated with respect; the personal dignity of the members of this nobility was publicly recognized and individual accomplishments were rewarded in a manner that was socially and psychologically flattering as well as materially advantageous. The heightened sense of moral consciousness and individual self-respect naturally enabled the most enlightened and perceptive members of this élite to see through Catherine's glittering façade and detect the ugly evils behind it. The corruption and immorality of so much of Russia's public life seemed most damnable and the necessity for a moral and spiritual reformation was sought. So amidst the chorus of praise and glorification of Catherine muffled and isolated voices of discontent and criticism were raised. Sometimes the critics advocated a return to traditional conceptions of morality and family life—this was the view taken by Prince M. M. Shcherbatov and the writer A. Sumarokov.[2] More frequently, Russian reality was condemned on the basis of notions derived from Western enlightenment; the position taken by Freemasons engaged in philanthropy, the work of friends and associates of Novikov, and the eloquent pleas of A. Radishchev are representative of this trend.[3] These critical opinions provided the basis for the interpretation of Catherine's reign that became dominant in the second half of the nineteenth century—that is, the contrast between the Empress' rhetoric and the empire's brutal and backward condition was devastatingly revealed.

Until the last quarter of the nineteenth century, the reign of Catherine II—except its foreign policy and military prowess—elicited little interest on the part of Russian historians. In view of the Russian intelligentsia's negative attitude toward the Russian state, military and diplomatic successes made little impression on the élite and had no place in its intellectual development. That is why the studies of Catherine's foreign and military affairs had little part in shaping public attitudes on the reign or in orienting historiography. The study and writing of history in Russia received great impetus in the 1870's under the influence of the new philosophies of history—Positivism and Marxism—as well as the publication of source materials. The printing in the 1830's of the monumental "Complete Collection of Russian Laws," which to this day is an essential mine for any serious study of Russia in the eighteenth century, was an exception to the rigid policy of deny-

2. M. M. Shcherbatov, *On the Corruption of Morals in Russia,* ed. A. Lentin (New York: Cambridge University Press, 1969). Sumarokov's publicistic works are to be found in editions of his collected works; they have not been translated.

3. On Radishchev the best study is Allen McConnell, *A Russian Philosophe: Alexander Radishchev, 1749–1802* (The Hague, 1964). There are no studies in Western languages on Novikov or the Freemasons. For general discussion, see Marc Raeff, *Origins of the Russian Intelligentsia: The Eighteenth-Century Nobility* (New York: Harcourt Brace Jovanovich, Inc., 1966), Chap. 3.

ing scholars access to official documents. Later, during the decade of reforms—the 1860's—the state archives were opened up. The Imperial Russian Historical Society was established in 1866 (and it was followed by many local societies) and it made available in its *Sbornik* (*Collection*) the bulk of Catherine II's papers, which had been preserved in the archives of the Council of State; these included her correspondence with the leading Western intellectual luminaries and many dispatches and letters from foreign diplomats. The Society also published a sizable portion of the instructions given to the deputies to the Commission on Codification of 1767 and of the minutes of its debates.[4] Many of the articles included in this volume are based on these invaluable and indispensable source publications.

The publication of Catherine's papers shed much needed light on the concrete conditions in the country and on the reactions and opinions of various groups of the population. It was at last possible to follow the arduous work of drafting and elaborating major legislative acts, and to pinpoint the changes the Empress made after consulting her advisers and officials. And the appearance of official sources encouraged the publication of the memoirs, diaries, and correspondence of Catherine's contemporaries. Later, under the sponsorship of the Academy of Sciences, literary historians undertook a complete critical edition of Catherine's own writings, as well as of the works of her contemporaries.[5] Finally, the Revolution of 1905 led to a relaxation of censorship and in its wake the suppressed works of Radishchev and Novikov, as well as the records of their trial, were opened for study.[6]

The availability of this documentation allowed historians of

4. Imperatorskoe Russkoe Istoricheskoe Obshchestvo, Sbornik, Vols. 1–148 (St. Petersburg, 1867–1916). Materials on Catherine's reign fill approximately twenty-five volumes. The publication of the sources on the Commission of 1767 was interrupted by the Revolution of 1917 and not resumed.

5. Imperatritsa Ekaterina II, *Sochineniia, na osnovanii podlinnykh rukopisei i s ob'iasnitel'nymi primechaniiami A. N. Pypina*, Vols. 1–5, 7–12 (St. Petersburg, 1901–1907). The edition was not completed.

6. V. Bogoliubov, *N. I. Novikov i ego vremia* (Moscow, 1916). On Radishchev, see McConnell, *A Russian Philosophe*.

the positivist school to follow their inclination in tracing origins in and influences from more advanced societies and cultures on the seemingly backward Russia of the eighteenth century. They found support in the natural French desire to trace the impact of French ideas and letters on Europe *au siècle des lumières*. A number of studies traced and illustrated Catherine's connections with the leading philosophes and demonstrated her debt to Western political ideas, especially in her *Instruction* (*Nakaz*) to the Commission of 1767.[7] The major intellectual source, whose influence Catherine openly acknowledged as we have seen, was French Enlightenment literature. Of course, court life, too, was fashioned by the examples of Versailles and Trianon. But this situation raised an important question: how far did this French influence go? Was it limited only to Catherine and the courtiers around her? How about the remainder of the educated élite? That the country at large was not much affected by it seems clear from the memoirs and descriptions of contemporary observers.[8] And how genuine and effective was French enlightened ideology (even if one could define it clearly) in the formation of Catherine's policies?

As the rhetoric of Catherine II became better known, and it had to be taken seriously into account on the basis of the sources made available, it became clear that her claims were a far cry from the reality she found on her accession and from the condition of Russia at her death. The rhetoric, taken at its face value, was contrasted with the true socio-economic conditions that stood revealed by the instructions and debates of the Commission of 1767. The growing awareness of Russia's agricultural difficulties and agrarian unrest, which culminated in the revolution of 1905, as well as the ideological debate between Marxists and Populists concerning the nature and fate of peasant institutions, served to move the history

7. Maurice Tourneux, *Diderot et Catherine II* (Paris, 1899). Louis Réau, *Correspondance de Falconet avec Catherine II 1767–1778* (Paris, 1921).
8. The best known—satirical—sources for this are the comedies of Denis I. Fonvizin (*The Brigadier, The Minor*) and the journalism of Novikov. There are many editions of these; unfortunately only Fonvizin's comedies have been translated.

of the peasantry and the origins and nature of serfdom into the forefront of scholarly preoccupations.[9] The most imposing monument to this concern was the classic monograph of V. Semevskii, which is still the most valuable source on agrarian conditions.[10] On the basis of the new evidence, the claims of Catherine and the norms set forth in her *Instruction* were compared and contrasted. Historians learned that Russian serfdom had fettered the majority of the peasantry and had left them defenseless against the cruel abuse and exploitation of their masters. Could Catherine be anything but hypocritical, therefore, since her liberal-sounding rhetoric did not stem the deterioration in the condition of the serfs? If proof were needed, did not the Pugachev rebellion and the fate of the Ukrainian peasantry provide it readily and dramatically? The hypocrisy could not be explained away by the plea of ignorance since both the liberal and conservative contemporary publicists had pointed to the condition of the peasant as the most serious problem of the regime.

The critical orientation of late nineteenth-century historiography on Catherine II fitted in well with the two major political preferences of the Russian intelligentsia in the decades preceding the revolution: "radical liberalism," finding its practical expression in the Constitutional Democratic—Cadet—Party on the one hand, and Marxism, in its several varieties, on the other. Both of these orientations shared a basic populist sympathy for the peasantry, hence their common condemnation of any regime that had not led

9. For this ideological debate one can now read: Richard Kindersley, *The First Russian Revisionists: A Study of "Legal Marxism" in Russia* (Oxford, 1962). Arthur P. Mendel, *Dilemmas of Progress in Tsarist Russia: Legal Marxism and Legal Populism* (Harvard University Press, 1961). Andrzej Walicki, *The Controversy over Capitalism: Studies in the Social Philosophy of the Russian Populists* (Oxford, 1969).

10. V. I. Semevskii, *Krest'iane v tsarstvovanie Ekateriny II*, 2 vols. (St. Petersburg, 1881, 1901). Also his *Krest'ianskii vopros v Rossii v XVIII i pervoi polovine XIX veka*, 2 vols. (St. Petersburg, 1888). Useful comments on populist historiography can be found in Michael B. Petrovich, "V. I. Semevskii (1848–1916): Russian Social Historian," in John S. Curtiss, ed., *Essays in Russian and Soviet History in Honor of Geroid Tanquary Robinson* (New York, 1963).

to outright emancipation of all serfs.[11] Obviously, on these terms,
the performance of Catherine II was found to be wanting. The
liberals who took the ideas and even the rhetoric of the Enlightenment seriously were incensed by Catherine's failure to act on her
sonorous and pious promises. Liberal historians (e.g., Kizevetter)
strongly denounced Catherine and her rule for glossing over the
continuing brutalization of serfs by their masters and for avoiding
any limitation on the autocratic power of the ruler. A careful
textual analysis of the *Instruction* and a comparison with its foreign sources, especially Montesquieu's *Esprit des lois,* showed that
Catherine had deliberately misinterpreted and adapted her literary
sources in the spirit of enlightened bureaucratic absolutism.[12]

Instead of taking such a "discovery" as a point of departure
for a reevaluation of Catherine's political ideas, aims, and methods,
historians of the liberal school used it as further illustration of her
hypocrisy. The liberal scholars obviously put great value on freedom of expression and on individual security. Approving Catherine's efforts at protecting literature, fostering journalism, and
spreading education, the liberals could not fail to be shocked by
the closing of Novikov's journals and publishing house, the persecution of Freemasons, and the harsh sentence given to Radishchev. Nourishing a deep-seated distrust and hatred of state
power, the liberal intellectuals were unimpressed by Catherine's
successes—such as they were—in foreign affairs and showed little
interest in and understanding for the institutional and legal necessities of government. The liberals' intellectual prejudices not only
excluded important areas of eighteenth-century public life from
the scholar's purview (military and diplomatic history, for example,
are almost virgin territory in modern Russian academic historio-

11. Of course, orthodox Marxism was hardly sympathetic to the peasantry
as a class. But Russian revolutionaries, even Marxist ones, could not fail
to have sympathy for peasants as the overwhelming majority of the exploited and oppressed Russian population.

12. F. Taranovskii, "Politicheskaia doktrina v Nakaze imperatritsy Ekateriny II," *Sbornik statei po istorii prava, posveshchennye Vladimirskomu-
Budanovu* (Kiev, 1904), pp. 44–86.

graphy)[13] but also imparted a naïve viewpoint and lack of understanding for the structure of power to which Catherine II had to adjust her actions. Her performance was judged by the standards of late nineteenth-century liberal ideology which believed in a noninterventionist state and the free interaction of cultural, economic, and social factors.

As for the Marxists, both before and after 1917, they did not believe in the active historical role of the individual and they were skeptical of the value of institutional aspects of government. Marxist scholars focused their attention on the economic exploitation of the peasantry and the inadequate development of trade and industry. They dogmatically concluded that all of Catherine's public acts were deliberate propaganda to hide the true fact of her acting only in the interest of the serf-owning nobility (whose puppet she was alleged to have been) in the class struggle between peasants and their masters. To the extent that they paid any attention to it, Marxist historians had only scorn for Catherine's enlightened rhetoric and contempt for the cultural and artistic life of the upper classes. In Stalin's time, more particularly during World War II, this negative stance was mildly qualified with respect to the diplomatic and military successes of the Empress, and her expansionist policy was praised from a Great Russian chauvinist standpoint.[14]

13. From Albert Sorel, *La Question d'Orient au XVIIIe s. Les origines de la Triple Alliance* (Paris, 1878) to Isabel de Madariaga, *Britain, Russia, and the Armed Neutrality of 1780: Sir James Harris's Mission to St. Petersburg During the American Revolution* (Yale University Press, 1962) and Herbert H. Kaplan, *The First Partition of Poland* (New York, 1962), diplomatic affairs have been studied by Western scholars on the basis of foreign archives. Military history had, of course, been carried on in military academies and general staff schools. Its practitioners have, however, concentrated exclusively on the technical aspects. For an introductory guide to this literature, cf. L. G. Beskrovnyi, *Ocherki voennoi istoriografii Rossii* (Moscow, 1962).

14. V. P. Potemkin, ed., *Istoriia Diplomatii,* 3 vols. (Moscow, 1941–1945), and what amounts to a second edition, supervised by A. Gromyko, 3 vols. (Moscow, 1962–1965). Since World War II there have appeared valuable collections of documents and less valuable popular biographies of such

Marxist and Soviet historians have studied and published a
great deal on important facets of Russian life in the second half
of the eighteenth century. Naturally, they have concentrated on
problems of class conflict and economic development: peasant
revolts, most particularly the Pugachev rebellion (their interpretation of the movement in terms of class struggle and as a consequence of increasing feudal oppression, however, is rather simple-
minded),[15] the economy of serfdom,[16] the development of trade
and industry,[17] and the spread of oppositionist ideologies among
the lower strata of educated society.[18] Inasmuch as Soviet historians
think in terms of social laws that regulate "vast impersonal
forces" of class struggle and economic production, they rarely
focus their attention on Catherine's regime, on the activities of her
government, but tend to study broad topics over the span of the
entire century. Their contribution to a profile of Catherine II is,
therefore, understandably, meager.[19]

With the qualified exception of diplomatic history, foreign
scholarship has not substantially contributed to the illumination

military heroes as Rumiantsev, Suvorov, Seniavin, and Kutuzov. Also E.
Druzhinina, *Kiuchuk-Kainardzhiiskii mir 1774 goda* (Moscow, 1955), one
of the rare serious diplomatic studies.

15. V. Mavrodin, *Krest'ianskaia voina v Rossii v 1773-1775 godakh:
Vosstanie Pugacheva* (Leningrad, 1961-1966), 2 vols., a third volume is
to follow. See also the review article by John T. Alexander in *Canadian
Slavic Studies*, Fall 1970.

16. N. L. Rubinshtein, *Sel'skoe khoziaistvo Rossii vo vtoroi polovine
XVIII v.: Istoriko-ekonomicheskii ocherk* (Moscow, 1957). M. T. Beliav-
skii, *Krest'ianskii vopros v Rossii nakanune vosstaniia E. I. Pugacheva:
Formirovanie antikrepostnicheskoi mysli* (Moscow, 1965).

17. P. G. Liubomirov, *Ocherki po istorii russkoi promyshlennosti* (Moscow, 1947). I. Kulisher, *Istoriia russkoi torgovli do deviatnadtsatogo veka
vkliuchitel'no* (St. Petersburg, 1923). Cf. also B. B. Kafengauz, *Istoriia
khoziaistva Demidovykh v XVIII-XIX vv.*, I (Moscow-Leningrad, 1949).

18. I. Ia. Shchipanov, ed., *Izbrannye proizvedeniia russkikh myslitelei
vtoroi poloviny XVIII veka*, 2 vols. (Moscow, 1952). M. M. Shtrange,
Demokraticheskaia intelligentsiia Rossii v XVIII veka (Moscow, 1965). Cf.
also *Istoriia Filosofii v SSSR*, Vols. 1 and 2 (Moscow, 1968).

19. For example, *Absoliutizm v Rossii (XVII-XVIII vv.). Sbornik statei
k semidesiatiletiiu so dnia rozhdeniia . . . B. B. Kafengauza* (Moscow,
1964).

of the reign of Catherine II. The picture is beginning to change a little as Soviet archives become more accessible to foreigners. Until now the Western literature on Catherine II has fallen into two main categories: contemporary descriptions by travelers, residents, and pamphleteers (both pro and con) and biographical treatments focusing on the private life of the Empress—her amours —and the sensational events of her reign.[20] From a scholarly point of view they are of dubious worth, and the nonspecialist is best advised to turn to Russian literary classics or contemporary travelogues if he wants to learn what Russia was like in the second half of the eighteenth century.[21]

Where does this leave us in our search for knowledge and understanding of the reign of Catherine II and our endeavor to estimate the Empress' own contribution to Russian history? As the selections in this volume indicate, the reign was extremely important—and not only because of its length; it can be considered, truly, to have been seminal. Nevertheless, many questions remain open and it might be useful to review the most significant "problem areas" and to indicate in what way most recent scholarship contributes to their clarification.

The broad and complex field of political institutions needs extensive and intensive study. The selections in this volume only allude to the many administrative reforms carried out by Catherine's government. The major acts—for example, the Statute on Provinces, the Charters to the Nobility and to the Towns—have been the object of formal textual analysis, essentially descriptive and aimed at tracing literal antecedents to specific paragraphs and

20. In addition to the titles mentioned in the Preface, see, for instance, George Soloveytchik, *Potemkin: Soldier, Statesman, Lover, and Consort of Catherine of Russia* (New York, 1947).

21. For example the handy anthology, Harold B. Segel, ed., *The Literature of Eighteenth-Century Russia*, 2 vols. (New York, 1967), and the selections in Peter Putnam, ed., *Seven Britons in Imperial Russia, 1698–1812* (Princeton University Press, 1952). For further references to travelogues available in English, Peter A. Crowther, *A Bibliography of Works in English on Early Russian History to 1800* (Oxford, 1969).

phrases.[22] But these antiquated studies revealed neither the institutional origins of the legislation nor the dynamic import the laws had on contemporary political structural patterns. More specifically, the older scholars ignored the fact that every institution develops a dynamic pattern of its own, and that to discover its impact one has to study the institution in its structural and functional aspects. But once embarked on such an approach one quickly realizes that an essential aspect of institutional changes in the reign of Catherine II derives from the nature and makeup of the personnel in government offices and from their relationship with the nobility and court factions. An ancillary problem is the survival of traditional family solidarities and hierarchies and the effectiveness with which they are displaced by the impersonal system of Peter the Great's Table of Ranks.[23]

This line of investigation brings us to the crucial question of the character and function of the autocrat: was Catherine a mere tool of the ruling class (whatever that might be) or a creative and dynamic force in her own right? and what was the function of her authority in the fabric of Russian polity? [24] The answers to

22. A. A. Kizevetter, *Gorodovoe polozhenie Ekateriny II 1785 g. Opyt istoricheskogo kommentariia* (Moscow, 1909). Vladimir Grigor'ev, *Reforma mestnogo upravleniia pri Ekateriny II* (*Uchrezhdenie o guberniiakh 7 noiabria 1775 g.*) (St. Petersburg, 1910). S. A. Korf, *Dvorianstvo i ego soslovnoe upravlenie za stoletie 1762–1855 godov* (St. Petersburg, 1906).

23. Useful remarks on this little studied issue may be found in: Hans J. Torke, "Das russische Beamtentum in der ersten Hälfte des 19. Jahrhunderts," *Forschungen zur osteuropäischen Geschichte,* XIII (Berlin, 1967). A. Romanovich-Slavatinskii, *Dvorianstvo v Rossii ot nachala XVIII veka do otmeny krepostnogo prava,* 2d ed. (Kiev, 1912). Marc Raeff, "The Domestic Policies of Peter III and His Overthrow," *American Historical Review,* LXXV-5 (June 1970), 1289–1310. N. L. Rubinshtein, "Ulozhennaia komissiia 1754–1766 gg. i ee proekt novogo ulozheniia 'O sostoianii poddanykh voobshche,' " *Istoricheskie Zapiski,* XXXVIII (1951), 208–252. See also the suggestive remarks in the introduction and last section of S. B. Veselovskii, *Issledovaniia po istorii klassa sluzhilykh zemlevladel'tsev* (Moscow, 1969).

24. Michael Cherniavsky, *Tsar and People: Studies in Russian Myths* (Yale University Press, 1961). Marc Raeff, "Pugachev's Rebellion," in Robert Forster and Jack P. Greene, eds., *Preconditions of Revolution in Early Modern Europe* (Baltimore: The Johns Hopkins Press, 1970), pp. 161–202.

some of these questions can be given only after much ground-breaking statistical work has been done: identifying, describing, classifying the members of the government, of the service class, and of the economic and cultural leadership of the empire. So far ideology has blocked the work of Soviet scholars and Western historians have been hampered by practical obstacles in the analysis of the great mass of records preserved in the archives of Catherine's local and central institutions.[25] But the first steps have been taken to describe how some administrative reforms were initiated, drafted, and implemented; how some institutions actually worked, and the role played by court factions in bringing about changes in the administration and in policy. A number of American doctoral dissertations have broken new ground along these lines and have put the institutional history of late eighteenth-century Russia on a modern track.[26] These studies also throw some incidental light on the character of Catherine's power and her method of government.

New questions are also being asked about the economic history of Catherine's Russia. Scholars, especially in the West, are not only interested in the overall picture of Russian industry and in the obligations (in money and kind) imposed on the peasantry. They want to know how economic decisions were reached and

25. Although they do not focus on the reign of Catherine specifically, the following two articles are preludes to the statistical study of the Russian officials: Walter M. Pintner, "The Social Characteristics of the Early Nineteenth-Century Russian Bureaucracy," *Slavic Review*, XXIX-3 (September 1970), 429–443; and S. M. Troitskii, "Materialy perepisi chinovnikov v 1754–1756 gg. kak istochnik po sotsial'no-politicheskoi i kul'turnoi istorii Rossii v XVIII v.," *Arkheograficheskii ezhegodnik za 1967 god* (Moscow, 1969), 132–148.

26. Completed dissertations may be found listed periodically in the *Slavic Review*. For those completed before 1959, cf. Jesse J. Dossick, *Doctoral Research on Russia and the Soviet Union* (New York, 1960). The Fall 1970 issue of *Canadian Slavic Studies* carries a number of articles that give the main conclusions of some recent dissertations on the reign of Catherine II. See also the now published John T. Alexander, *Autocratic Politics in a National Crisis: The Imperial Russian Government and Pugachev's Revolt, 1773–1775* (Bloomington: Indiana University Press, 1969).

what accounts for the slow rate of change and low level of Russian agricultural production. In searching for answers historians have come to realize that as much depends on the social, psychological, and intellectual context in which economic decisions are taken as on the quantity and quality of resources and the political framework. Professor A. Kahan has identified the social and cultural pressures on the noble land- and serf-owner, and Professor R. W. Augustine has tried to characterize the landlords' conceptions of their economic interests and priorities.[27] It appears that eighteenth-century noble landowners did not think in "modern," that is, efficiency and production-oriented terms. Rather, their economic behavior was governed, in K. Polanyi's terminology, by a traditional, pre-market system of values. In this context it is easy to understand why Catherine had so much difficulty in launching the modernization and improvement of Russian agriculture. These patterns of thought explain more than the limits of Russia's capital resources. In one study which examines the reasons for the failure of progressive landlords and economists, Professor Confino discovered that one of the major roadblocks in the path of agricultural modernization lay in the pattern of social and cultural organization in the village.[28] In his most recent and truly pioneering work, he has described the tight and complicated web of social relationships and agricultural techniques that governed the Russian village community, in particular the three-field system of tillage and the custom of equal inheritance.[29]

27. Arcadius Kahan, "The Costs of 'Westernization' in Russia: The Gentry and the Economy in the Eighteenth Century," *Slavic Review*, XXV-1 (March 1966), 40-66. Wilson R. Augustine, "Notes Toward a Portrait of the Eighteenth-Century Nobility," *Canadian Slavic Studies* (Fall 1970), and his unpublished dissertation, Columbia University, New York, 1969.

28. The efforts made in the direction of modernization by the Imperial Free Economic Society (founded in 1765) have been marvelously described and analyzed by Michael Confino in his work, *Domaines et seigneurs en Russie vers la fin du XVIIIe siècle* (Paris, 1963).

29. Michael Confino, *Systèmes agraires et progrès agricole—L'assolement triennal en Russie aux XVIIIe-XIXe siècles—Etude d'économie et de sociologie rurales* (Paris-La Haye, 1969).

Studies of Russia's industrial development have broken no new ground; the positive comparison between the levels of Russian industrial production and those of France was made by E. Tarle over half a century ago.[30] True, more factual data have been gathered on some industries by Soviet historians, but no original conclusions have been made as yet on their basis.[31] The impact of Russian expansion and of the settlement of the southern steppe lands still needs to be investigated, as it had serious consequences for the serf economy in the nineteenth century.[32]

The achievements of Catherine and of her contemporaries in the realm of culture have held the attention of past scholars, as the articles in this book show. In recent years literary scholars have continued to evince interest in the problem of Western influences, mainly French, on Russian ideas and writing in the second half of the eighteenth century.[33] We now have many new factual details on the personal contacts between Catherine II and the philosophes, Diderot and Voltaire in particular, as well as additional information on the sources and international contacts of Russian writers with the progressive *littérateurs* of the West.[34] But at least two facets of Russian culture in Catherine's time need more exploration, and happily the first steps have been taken in this direction.

30. E. Tarle, "Byla li ekaterininskaia Rossiia ekonomicheski otstaloi stranoi?" in *Zapad i Rossiia* (Petrograd, 1918), pp. 122–149.

31. E.g., N. Pavlenko, *Istoriia metallurgii v Rossii XVIII v.* (Moscow, 1962). Cf. the useful remarks in Part I of William B. Blackwell, *The Beginnings of Russian Industrialization, 1800–1860* (Princeton: Princeton University Press, 1968).

32. The first steps in this direction have been taken by Hans Halm, *Gründung und erstes Jahrzehnt von Festung und Stadt Cherson* (Wiesbaden, 1961). E. Druzhinina, *Severnoe prichernomor'e v 1775–1800 gg.* (Moscow, 1959).

33. From the vast and ever growing bibliography on eighteenth-century Russian literature, let us only mention the irregular serial *XVIII vek* published by the Institute of Russian Literature of the Academy of Sciences of the USSR and a recent collection of articles, *Epokha prosveshcheniia— Iz istorii mezhdunarodnykh sviazei russkoi literatury* (Leningrad, 1967).

34. Diderot, *Mémoires pour Catherine II*, ed. Pierre Vernière (Paris, 1966).

Of primary importance is the question of the dissemination of Western culture to the lower classes or, in other terms, the "westernization" (however defined) of Russian national life. Here the Soviet scholars have done important research and have provided us with a wealth of information on the arts and crafts of the period, as well as on the contributions of artisans and artists from the people (usually serfs) to the artistic and cultural milieu of the noble élite.[35] Whether the increasing creative participation of artists from the people introduced traditional and folk elements into the "higher" manifestations of culture in Russia remains an open question. Much work unencumbered by ideological or emotional *parti pris* will be necessary to provide even an approximative answer.

A second concern of scholars is whether the excessive emphasis on French influence on Russian cultural life in the second half of the eighteenth century has not distorted our perspective. French domination of court life and belles lettres is indisputable. But it hardly seems to hold true for the intellectual and scientific activities that took place within the framework of the Academy of Sciences, the University of Moscow, and a growing number of special schools. Russian critical and social ideas and the revival of religious thought at the end of the eighteenth century cannot be understood on the basis of French Enlightenment notions alone. The studies carried on under the aegis of Professor E. Winter in East Germany have convincingly shown the seminal role played by German ideas and intellectuals in eighteenth-century Russia.[36] In matters of law, and of social and economic policies, the teach-

35. Most useful material is contained in biographies and encyclopedia entries for major Russian artists. But also see T. V. Alekseeva, ed., *Russkoe iskusstvo XVIII veka—Materialy i issledovaniia* (Moscow, 1968). N. Kovalenskaia, *Russkii klassitsizm* (Moscow, 1964). Iu. V. Keldysh, *Russkaia muzyka XVIII veka* (Moscow, 1965). T. Livanova, *Russkaia muzykal'naia kul'tura XVIII v ee sviaziakh s literaturoi, teatrom i bytom*, 2 vols. (Moscow, 1953).

36. A full bibliography of these studies is to be found in Marc Raeff, "Les Slaves, les Allemands et les 'lumières,'" *Etudes Canadiennes Slaves*, I-4 (1967), 521–551.

ings and examples of German cameralism and *Polizeiordnung* (police ordinances) were decisive and direct. In the realm of scholarship, science, and philosophy the dominant influence proved to be the body of ideas popularized in eighteenth-century Germany under the heading of *Aufklärung* (i.e., Enlightenment). They had their metaphysical and epistemological roots in the natural law doctrines and the rationalist systems of Pufendorff, Christian Wolff, and Leibniz, rather than in the inductive empiricism of Locke and Newton. These influences gave a particular bent to the Russian reception of the French and English radical enlightenment and prepared the ground for the dominant role played by German philosophy in Russian thought and literature throughout the nineteenth century. The *Weltanschauung* and social ideals of the Russian intelligentsia cannot be understood unless the German sources of eighteenth-century Russian culture are taken into account.[37] Naturally, developments in Russia proper also played a prime role; the most important of these was the psychological impact and ideological consequences of the Pugachev rebellion. The revolt helped to change the educated élite's image of and attitudes toward the peasant serf and the popular elements of the national tradition.[38] This change in social perception selectively determined the pattern of emotional and intellectual affinities and permanently conditioned the development of Russian culture and thought to our own day.[39]

Catherine's extension of the empire's borders runs as an impor-

37. Some remarks can be found in Hans Rogger, *National Consciousness in Eighteenth-Century Russia* (Cambridge: Harvard University Press, 1960), and in Marc Raeff, *Origins of the Russian Intelligentsia,* Chap. 3. Cf. also Marc Raeff, "Eighteenth-Century Thought in Russian Culture," in John Garrard, ed., *The Eighteenth Century in Russia,* forthcoming.

38. Jean-Louis Van Regemorter "Deux images idéales de la paysannerie russe à la fin du XVIIIe siècle," *Cahiers du monde russe et soviétique,* IX–1 (1968), 5–19, and concluding remarks in Marc Raeff, "Pugachev's Rebellion," *loc. cit.*

39. Bypassing the enormous and rather unsatisfactory literature on the "Russian soul," etc., let us call attention to the stimulating article by Robert MacMaster, in his "In the Russian Manner: Thought as Incipient Action," *Harvard Slavic Studies,* IV (1957), 281–300.

tant theme on the pages of the present volume, yet neither the
pre-revolutionary nor the Soviet historians have paid much attention to the problems involved in shaping a multinational polity
and in devising an institutional framework for it—problems which
began to engage the government's serious attention in the reign
of Catherine II and determined the background of the nationality
problem in Russia at the end of the nineteenth and in the early
twentieth centuries (and perhaps even in Soviet times).[40] Not
only did her policy affect the history of the many non-Russian
nationalities in the empire, but it was closely bound up with the
economic and social development of Russia proper, the expansion
of its own population, and the ideological and political conceptions
of the Russian élite and imperial government. Because the basic
administrative local structures were set up in her reign, her government's outlook and methods of incorporation of non-Russian
societies provide much of the needed background for an understanding of the later difficulties over the nationalities.[41] Here again we
are faced with the failure of Russian historiography to come to
grips with the institutional and political conceptions of Catherine
and her advisers.

Another important problem requiring study is the ramification
of the unchallenged power of the autocrat, the absolute ruler who
was the state and actively participated in the most vital sectors of the
nation's life. The direct impact was immense, but there were other
consequences. Social forces remained amorphous and this condition led to political and institutional weaknesses. Yet, Russia was
changing, and was developing in the direction of economic and

40. For a beginning, one may consult Boris Nolde, *La formation de
l'empire russe*, 2 vols. (Paris 1952–1953). Georg von Rauch, *Russland:
Staatliche Einheit und nationale Vielfalt* (München, 1953). Ia. Zutis,
Ostzeiskii vopros v XVIII veke (Riga, 1946). Marc Raeff, "Patterns of Russian Imperial Policy Towards the Nationalities," *The Nationality Problem
in the Soviet Union*, Edward Allworth, ed., forthcoming.

41. For a case study, Alan Fisher, "Enlightened Despotism and Islam
under Catherine II," *Slavic Review*, XXVII-4 (December 1968), 542–553
and the concluding chapters of Alan Fisher, *The Russian Annexation of
the Crimea, 1772–1783* (New York: Cambridge University Press, 1970).

cultural "modernization" or "westernization," to use somewhat imprecise but sufficiently connotative terms. What was the role of the state in this process? By what political and social means and to what purpose did the state play this role? These are not new questions, to be sure. They were implicit in Karl Marx's historical analyses and in their modern form they were asked by Max Weber in the beginning of the present century. Recently the question was again raised in Soviet historical journals apropos of the role of the tsarist government in Russia's economic (i.e., industrial) development in the 1890's. The debate was cut short when it threatened the major assumptions of official dogma. But the fact that it did occur is significant enough; it shows that when historians study institutional and socio-economic developments on their own terms they have to deal with the complexities of the factors which determine power, authority, and select goals. The simple identification of power, will, and interest proves inadequate, and the statement that the state merely expresses the interests (and will) of the ruling class does not suffice. Involved in the problem is the nexus of factors (psychological, intellectual, religious, social, etc.) that determine the wills, conception of self-interest, and acts of the classes and groups that make up a given polity. In the West the problem was easy to tackle (if not easy to solve) since the interests and policies of one major class—the bourgeoisie—were readily documented. But in Russia a number of conditions dating back to the sixteenth century, such as early centralization, prevented the emergence of dynamic and goal-directed autonomous groups or corporations. The "successful" rulers of modern Russia, Peter the Great, Catherine II, and the reform-minded emperors of the nineteenth century, seem to have recognized the necessity of such groups or classes if Russia was to hold her own among the European powers.

Reflecting on this situation, the German historian, Dietrich Geyer, suggests in two insightful and stimulating essays, that the autocratic state, more specifically the government of Catherine II, fostered the emergence of active and creative autonomous groupings by means of administrative, economic, and political meas-ures.[42] Geyer argues that the main object of the great acts of 1775 and 1785, as well as a series of lesser measures, was to help in the formation of an active, socially and economically secure middle class on the one hand, and on the other, to channel the creative energies of the traditional estates, in the first place the nobility and to some extent the state peasantry, into economic and cultural endeavors. It was Catherine's hope, Professor Geyer argues, that once the state guaranteed their security of person and property, the members of these groupings would not only enhance the ma-terial prosperity of the empire (and the power of the state), but improve the condition of the people and stimulate a more sophis-ticated and rewarding cultural life for all. Still further, the ab-sorption in these manifold activities by such groups, Geyer ex-plains, undermines the traditional exclusive concentration and dependence on a single activity, decreases the uncompromising suspiciousness and conflict between the various strata of the pop-ulation, and encourages the formation of a harmonious pluralistic society. In the fashion of true enlightened absolutism, Catherine II did not believe that such an evolution need undermine the autocracy. On the contrary, the autocratic state and its officials would be needed even more than ever to guarantee peace and security, harmonize the various interests, and reward and guide all subjects in the pursuit of common progress.

This hypothesis—whether ultimately validated or not—offers a most fruitful line of inquiry: the historian should turn to a thorough examination and dynamic interpretation of the social,

42. Dietrich Geyer, "Staatsausbau und Sozialverfassung—Probleme des russischen Absolutismus am Ende des 18. Jahrhunderts," *Cahiers du monde russe et soviétique*, VII-3 (1966), 366–377, and "Gesellschaft als staatliche Veranstaltung (Bemerkungen zur Sozialgeschichte der russischen Staats-verwaltung im 18. Jahrh.)," *Jahrbücher für Geschichte Osteuropas*, XIV-1 (March 1966), 21–50. Geyer's ideas have been applied to a study of Paul I's ideas and actions by Claus Scharf, "Staatsauffassung und Regieroungspro-gramm eines aufgeklärten Selbstherrschers—Die Instruktion des Gross-fürsten Paul von 1788," in E. Schulin, ed., *Gedenkschrift Martin Göhring—Studien zur europäischen Geschichte* (Wiesbaden, 1968), pp. 91–106.

economic, and administrative institutions in Catherine's Russia and attempt to discover and define the purposes and method of her legislation. Such an inquiry leaves room for an assessment of the relative role of the individual, that is, the fascinating personality of Catherine II, and of "those vast impersonal forces"—for example, social groups, economic factors, national traditions, etc. Specifically, we will be able to see more clearly the factors that fostered innovation and creativity (as well as those which hampered them) and implanted conceptions of rationality and modernity, traits which Catherine II herself exemplified by her political genius and intellectual energy.

When such a history is written Catherine II's reign will appear to have set the pattern of Russia's development in the nineteenth century. Her rule will then be viewed as the "hinge period" between Europe's dramatic and violent intrusion into Russia under Peter the Great and Russia's participation, *à part entière,* in the political and cultural destinies of the West in the nineteenth and twentieth centuries.

Suggestions for Additional Reading

THE FOOTNOTES to some articles and to the Postscript provide the student with essential guidelines for further research and study of Catherine's reign. Below are listed the most accessible and readable works in English that illuminate the background to some of the issues discussed in the present Profile.

The handiest bibliographical guide is Peter A. Crowther, *A Bibliography of Works in English on Early Russian History to 1800* (Oxford: Basil Blackwell, 1969).

A charming sketch of life in eighteenth-century Russia is provided by Miriam Kochan, *Life in Russia under Catherine the Great* (London and New York, 1969), in European Life Series,

Peter Quennell, ed. For a general analytical synthesis of Russian history in the eighteenth and early nineteenth century, Marc Raeff, *Imperial Russia 1682–1825: The Coming of Age of Modern Russia* (New York, 1970), Vol. IV in the Borzoi History of Russia, under the general editorship of Michael Cherniavsky. It has a substantial bibliographical essay to guide the student's researches further.

Educational and scientific developments are summarized by Alexander Vucinich, *Science in Russian Culture: A History to 1860* (Stanford University Press, 1963). Intellectual and ideological matters are ably presented by Hans Rogger, *National Consciousness in Eighteenth-Century Russia* (Cambridge: Harvard University Press, 1960). Among the better general histories of Russian literature we may mention Dmitri S. Mirsky, *A History of Russian Literature* (New York, 1955). The somewhat popularized but scholarly biography of A. Radishchev by David M. Lang, *The First Russian Radical* (London, 1959) offers colorful detail to supplement the intellectual biography by Allen McConnell, *A Russian Philosophe* (The Hague, 1964).

On the Commission of 1767 and its socio-political aspects one finds useful information in Paul Dukes, *Catherine the Great and the Russian Nobility* (Cambridge University Press, 1967).

Religious aspects are revealed by the writings of St. Tychon and St. Seraphim in George P. Fedotov, *A Treasury of Russian Spirituality* (New York, 1948)—the introduction is very stimulating; philosophical trends are described and discussed briefly in Vasilii Zenkovsky, *A History of Russian Philosophy,* 2 vols. (London and New York, 1953); and samples of social and political thought are given in Chaps. 3 (Shcherbatov), 4 (Novikov), 5 (Fonvizin), 6 (Karamzin) of Marc Raeff, *Russian Intellectual History: An Anthology* (New York, 1966). Brief discussions of a variety of social, institutional, and intellectual trends can be found in Marc Raeff's essay, *Origins of the Russian Intelligentsia* (New York, 1966), referred to earlier.

A useful summary of Catherine's reign in terms of political history can be found in Chap. 19, Vol. VI of the *Cambridge Modern*

History (Cambridge University Press, 1909), written by Otto Hoetzsch. For the all-European context one should read the brilliantly intelligent, perceptive, analytical synthesis of Leonard Krieger, *Kings and Philosophers, 1689–1789* (New York, 1970), Vol. 3 in the Norton History of Modern Europe, under the general editorship of Felix Gilbert.

Contributors

A. M. AMMANN, S. J., is professor of Eastern Church History at the Pontifical Oriental Institute (Pontifirio Istituto Orientale) in Rome.

SERGEI V. BAKRUSHIN, 1882–1950, was a graduate and a professor of the University of Moscow, a member of the Academy of Sciences, and a specialist in medieval and Siberian social and political history.

Vasilii A. Bil'bassov, 1838–1904, worked most of his life on a monumental biography of Catherine II. Allegedly the whole work was completed in twelve volumes, but only the first two appeared —in 1890, with a German translation in 1891–1893. The other volumes were not published and the manuscript has disappeared. In addition, in two volumes, Bil'bassov brought out the most comprehensive bibliography on Catherine II up to 1896 and four volumes of studies written in preparation for his *magnum opus*. It is from the latter that the present selection is drawn. Bil'bassov was a conservative and a nationalist who admired Catherine's reign rather uncritically.

Grigorii A. Gukovskii, 1902–1950, was a prominent historian of literature associated with the Institute of Russian Literature of the Academy of Sciences of the USSR. He was purged during the Zhdanov period (ca. 1948) and died in exile. The present article is a chapter in the most comprehensive history of Russian literature available, and the particular volume from which it was taken appeared before the tight ideological constrictions of Stalin's last years.

Aleksandr A. Kizevetter, 1866–1933, was a graduate of the University of Moscow and a specialist in the history of the municipal organization of Russian towns in the eighteenth century. He actively participated in the liberal movement in the late nineteenth and early twentieth centuries and became associated with the Constitutional Democratic (Cadet) Party. Forced to emigrate after the Revolution of 1917, he spent the last decade of his life teaching at the Russian university which had been established by émigrés in Prague. He was one of the best representatives of the "liberal" tradition in Russian historiography. He excelled as a writer of historical essays in which he could bring out the political-moral implications of past events. The articles reproduced here are drawn from a collection that brought together essays and biographical sketches written before 1917 and in the first years of his exile.

ALEKSANDR S. LAPPO-DANILEVSKII, 1863–1919, a graduate and professor of the University of St. Petersburg, was a member of the Academy of Sciences and best known for his research in the social history of pre-Petrine Russia. He was a positivist who came under the influence of "populism" (*narodnichestvo*). The present article was written for a five-volume work—*The Great Reform*—published in 1911 to commemorate the fiftieth anniversary of the Emancipation of the serfs.

IVAN K. LUPPOL, 1896–1943, was a specialist in the philosophy of the French Enlightenment; he also wrote on the Russian radical élite of the late eighteenth and early nineteenth centuries. He fell victim to the Stalinist purges. The selection presented is from his biography of Diderot, which appeared also in French translation in the 1930's.

ALLEN MCCONNELL, born in 1923, was educated at Brown and Columbia Universities. He taught political science at Brown and is now professor of Russian history at Queens College, New York. The recipient of grants from the Social Science Research Council and the American Philosophical Society, he has written many scholarly articles and is the author of the most useful study of Alexander Radishchev, entitled *A Russian Philosophe: Alexander Radishchev, 1749–1802* (1964).

PAVEL N. MILIUKOV, 1859–1943, was a student of V. Kliuchevskii at the University of Moscow, and gave up a promising academic career to enter politics. He became the leader of the Cadet Party and after 1917 he went into exile to Paris where he published a Russian language daily and monthly review. His important historical work consists of a seminal monograph on the economic policy of Peter the Great, which he submitted as his magisterial dissertation, and a survey of Russian cultural and social history based on courses he taught at the beginning of his career. During his exile he revised and expanded this synthesis of the Russian historical process and published it in four volumes in Paris, 1930–

1937. The two selections in this volume are drawn from this version. Miliukov was a positivist and believed that every society follows a similar evolution once it has acquired the basic elements of economic and institutional organization. From this conviction emerged his belief that there are no radical breaks in a nation's development.

SERGEI D. SKAZKIN, born 1890, is a member of the Academy of Sciences and a specialist in the "feudal" period of Russian history. The three-volume *History of Diplomacy,* from which we take our selection, was the first general diplomatic history to be published in the Soviet Union. It appeared on the eve of World War II and reflected the Soviet nationalism and Great Russian patriotism that Stalin had come to stress in the second half of his rule.

MARC RAEFF received his Ph.D. from Harvard University in 1950. Since 1961 he has taught at Columbia University, where he has been Professor of History since 1965. His main research interests lie in the intellectual and institutional history of Imperial Russia during the eighteenth and early nineteenth centuries. He has published the results of his research in learned journals in the United States and abroad. His major books are: *M. M. Speransky: Statesman of Imperial Russia, Siberia and the Reforms of 1822, Origins of the Russian Intelligentsia: The Eighteenth-Century Nobility,* and *Imperial Russia, 1682–1825: The Coming of Age of Modern Russia.*

AÏDA DIPACE DONALD holds degrees from Barnard and Columbia and a Ph.D. from the University of Rochester. A former member of the History Department at Columbia, Mrs. Donald has been a Fulbright Fellow at Oxford and the recipient of an A.A.U.W. fellowship. She has published *John F. Kennedy and the New Frontier* and *Diary of Charles Francis Adams.*